Data,
A
Love
Story

Data,
A
Love
Story

How I Gamed

Online Dating to

Meet My Match

Amy Webb

Dutton

DUTTON

Published by the Penguin Group

Penguin Group (USA) Inc., 375 Hudson Street, New York, New York 10014, USA
Penguin Group (Canada), 90 Eglinton Avenue East, Suite 700, Toronto, Ontario M4P 2Y3, Canada
(a division of Pearson Penguin Canada Inc.) • Penguin Books Ltd, 80 Strand, London WC2R 0RL,
England • Penguin Ireland, 25 St Stephen's Green, Dublin 2, Ireland (a division of Penguin Books
Ltd) • Penguin Group (Australia), 707 Collins Street, Melbourne, Victoria 3008, Australia (a
division of Pearson Australia Group Pty Ltd) • Penguin Books India Pvt Ltd, 11 Community Centre,
Panchsheel Park, New Delhi–110 017, India • Penguin Group (NZ), 67 Apollo Drive, Rosedale,
Auckland 0632, New Zealand (a division of Pearson New Zealand Ltd) • Penguin Books, Rosebank
Office Park, 181 Jan Smuts Avenue, Parktown North 2193, South Africa • Penguin China,
B7 Jiaming Center, 27 East Third Ring Road North, Chaoyang District, Beijing 100020, China

Penguin Books Ltd, Registered Offices: 80 Strand, London WC2R 0RL, England

Published by Dutton, a member of Penguin Group (USA) Inc.

First printing, February 2013
10   9   8   7   6   5   4   3   2   1

 REGISTERED TRADEMARK—MARCA REGISTRADA

LIBRARY OF CONGRESS CATALOGING-IN-PUBLICATION DATA
Webb, Amy, 1974-
Data, a love story : how I gamed online dating to meet my match / Amy Webb.
p. cm.
Includes bibliographical references.
ISBN 978-0-525-95380-7 (hard cover)
1. Online dating.   2. Dating (Social customs)   3. Webb, Amy.   I. Title.
HQ801.82.W43 2013
306.730285—dc23
2012029016

Printed in the United States of America
Designed by Nancy Resnick

While the author has made every effort to provide accurate telephone numbers, Internet addresses,
and other contact information at the time of publication, neither the publisher nor the author as-
sumes any responsibility for errors or for changes that occur after publication. Further, the publisher
does not have any control over and does not assume any responsibility for author or third-party
websites or their content.

Penguin is committed to publishing works of quality and integrity.
In that spirit, we are proud to offer this book to our readers;
however, the story, the experiences, and the words
are the author's alone.

For Brian,
who continues to score a perfect 1,500.

And for Bella,
who would have given him 100 points extra.

Contents

Introduction

This isn't a typical introduction.
Start here first!

I want to tell you from the outset that my story has a happy ending. I eventually met the man of my dreams, and we had a storybook wedding. We started a family, bought a great house, and are in the process of living happily ever after. But the events that led up to my finding him and settling down were sometimes harrowing, were often depressing, and at one point involved me taking a trip with a color-coded set of spreadsheets to see a therapist.

I'm getting ahead of the story, though.

For many years, I dated the wrong men, and though we were initially happy, all of my relationships came to a pretty terrible end. In between, I patiently agreed to be set up. I went to bars and clubs, trying to appear nonchalant and relaxed, as if that would attract the perfect man. I quickly found that "least expecting it" was not a reasonable path to true love. After a particularly bad date one night, which culminated in my drinking a whole bottle of wine and scribbling a bunch of formulas and theories down on notebook paper like a crazed mad scientist, I realized that we've all been going about finding our matches the wrong way. Whether we're dating in the real world or online, we're relying too much now on hope and happenstance. And these days, algorithms, too. We don't allow ourselves to think about what we really want in a partner, and then we don't sell ourselves in order to get it.

The problem, you see, doesn't have to do with a lack of good people left to date.

The problem is us. It's you and me. Our friends, our families. Hell, I'm even going to place blame on all the dating and relationship books on our physical and virtual shelves. Men aren't some strange foreign planet women must explore and conquer. And not all women are emotionally intelligent or have mysterious hormones coursing through them. We're complex beings. If you want true love and a long-lasting marriage, you need to start by figuring out what makes you happy.

When you turn this page, you're going to join me in the middle of a storybook romance that ended in heartbreak. Then you'll follow me on all the terrible dates that followed. You'll be there on the night that I smoked too many cigarettes, drank too much wine, and made a very long list of requirements for all future dates. And for what inevitably came next: making a decision to game the system, using math, data, and loopholes. You'll learn, as I did, which keywords, types of photos, and other qualities make for a successful online dating profile. And once you've found the right person for you, what it is you should do next: how soon to make contact, how to keep scoring your own list, and how to approach those critical first few dates.

You will probably laugh at me—maybe out loud, while you're reading this in bed or commuting on a train. You will most definitely shake your head. "What in the hell was this woman thinking?" you'll wonder. In fact, you'll say that a lot in Chapters 6 and 7. Your cheeks will grow hot a few times. It's okay—my sister was deeply embarrassed for me too.

But don't worry. All of my initial missteps and eventual dating experiments were worth the effort. Like I said, this is a story with a happy ending.

1 | Missed Connections

He quoted me to me.

Hilary pierced the heaviest of my cardboard boxes with a pair of opened scissors, trying to penetrate the layers of tape I'd used to secure everything. "You pack like Dad," she said. "This thing is hermetically sealed. What do you have in here?"

"Books," I mumbled, standing between two suitcases in the living room of what was now my new home. It was a small one-bedroom rowhouse apartment near the Philadelphia Museum of Art. From the window, I had a gorgeous view of the river and trees below, which provided a good alternative to what was behind me: a dusty old futon in place of the plush couch I'd been sitting on for the past year, mismatched chairs next to my parents' old dining room table, and a kitchen with a two-burner stove, an oven that had no visible temperature settings, and a refrigerator that only came up to my armpit.

Still, I was relieved to be in this crappy old apartment, unpacking boxes with my sister. It was the best space available on such short notice. I'd never imagined that I'd find myself in this situation.

A year and a half earlier, I'd left Tokyo International Airport en route to Chicago to see my family. It was my second stint living in

Japan; I was working for *Newsweek* magazine covering pop culture and tech trends. I was twenty-eight and exploiting every opportunity that crossed my path. Did I want to jet over to Korea for the week to cover the World Cup soccer finals? Sure! Would I mind traveling to northern China to report on factory workers? I'm there! Could I meet up with Japan's biggest pop star and interview him about his music? You bet!

I had an amazing job and was meeting fabulously interesting people. I naïvely assumed that it was only a matter of time before I met another foreign correspondent, someone who was brilliant, handsome, and well traveled. We'd get married, have two smart, culturally savvy, multilingual children, and move to a new country every five years. By the time our kids were ready for Harvard, we'd have a small warehouse full of antiques and cultural artifacts we'd been collecting from all over the world, some of which we'd move into our Parisian pied-à-terre. We'd bring the rest back to Manhattan and move into a modest town house on the Upper West Side.

But as the years wore on, I discovered that most of the American journalists I knew were either already married or were mostly interested in short flings with Japanese women. I had plenty of men to date, just no long-term prospects. I was growing lonely and increasingly skeptical of my ability to land a great husband while living overseas, so I'd made a tough decision to move back to the States. I'd planned to move back gradually, shuttling my things from Tokyo to my parents' home in Chicago over the next few months as I figured out what to do next.

It was a stressful trip. My travel agent had, once again, not considered the size of my layover airport. This time it was Seattle, and thirty-five minutes wasn't nearly enough time to get through immigration and over to my departure gate. I'd missed my connection.

I arrived at the desk slightly out of breath and stood at the back of a long line. I was in my usual travel ensemble: a comfy old pair of dark-wash jeans, a white T-shirt, a gray hoodie, and a black leather jacket. I always wore a pair of diamond studs my parents had given me for my bat mitzvah and a banged-up but reliable Seiko wristwatch that I could easily set to new time zones. Especially on long plane trips, I kept my extremely thick, curly brown hair in a loose ponytail to prevent frizz, though that never seemed to work. I didn't bother with makeup or contacts, but I did keep a tube of Vaseline in my pocket. My lips always chapped while I was up in the air.

The agent was entirely too chatty with the man she was helping, talking about Seattle coffee, then baseball. I watched him pull his wallet out of his back pocket and expected him to present his credit card and pay so that she could move on to the next person in line. Instead, he opened it to a collection of photos and pointed to a young boy. "Well, isn't he precious!" she cooed.

"Are you fucking kidding me?" I said under my breath. I let out a long sigh, then "Kore ga Nihon de okoru koto wa nai," in Japanese. *This isn't the way things are done in Japan!*

That caught the attention of the guy standing in front of me. He turned around slightly—I could see he was holding a book written in Japanese. He had a high-tech mobile phone in his other hand, which he'd been fiddling with since I got there. He wore rimless glasses, black jeans, and black shoes and looked like a really fashionable, athletic computer hacker. My eyes drifted down to his ring finger . . . it was bare. It was possible that he was one of those Japanese men who purposely don't wear wedding rings while they travel, but this guy seemed different.

He pressed one of the buttons on his phone and it lit up to display the time.

"Shit!" I said, this time in English. The flight I was trying to make was boarding in ten minutes.

"Sumimasen kedo," I said, touching his arm. "Would it be possible for me to go in front of you? I'm trying to catch a plane," I said in the politest Japanese I could muster.

He was starting to make a call as he turned around to look at me.

"Actually," he said in perfect English, "I think we were both on the same flight from Tokyo. We missed the connection."

I couldn't believe it—I'd just made the mistake that always drove me nuts in Japan. People there assumed I didn't speak their language, so they insisted on trying to communicate in broken English. My face grew hot, an indication that my usual blotchy red patches would soon be arriving all over my neck. I was a terrible liar and even worse when it came to hiding embarrassment. My skin always betrayed me.

"Here," he said. "Follow me." He walked up to the desk and motioned for me to stand next to him. "Excuse me," he said to the agent. "We're trying to get on that next flight out. We need your help." He smiled the entire time, and his deep voice was transfixing. The agent actually smiled back at him—the opposite reaction I'd gotten from every single airline industry professional, ever—and asked for our tickets. The next flight was now sold out, but she could get us seats on the very last flight out of the night.

"I can't seat you together, though. Is that okay?" she asked, tapping away on her keyboard. I looked down, trying to hide my smile. Actually, I thought we'd look nice as a couple.

Tickets in hand, he asked if I wanted to take a walk outside with him. "Do you smoke?" he asked.

I'd never been a regular smoker. While I had an occasional cigarette in college, I did everything I could to avoid them in Asia. Everyone smoked—even inside buildings—and tobacco was cheap. I was actively trying *not* to smoke in Japan so I didn't become a smoker for real. But this guy seemed interesting, and he was so good-looking. I wanted to talk to him more, so I followed him outside to the approved smoking area. He pulled a pack of Camel Lights out of his pocket, gave me one, and held out a light. It was the first cigarette I'd had in several months. I inhaled deeply and immediately felt my head spin.

"So I'm Henry," he said, exhaling. His mother was Japanese and his father was American, but he'd lived his entire life in the Midwest. He always thought he'd be a journalist, but circumstances conspired otherwise. He spent some time as a professional golfer and some more time working in restaurants. He eventually decided on law school but moved to northern Japan for two years to teach English first.

It was an eerily familiar story. I'd originally planned on becoming a lawyer. I wanted to be a litigator, then solicitor general, a position that would have me arguing cases before the Supreme Court. Then, in my senior year of college, it came time to take the LSAT, the exam to get into law school. For reasons I still can't explain, it was the first and only time in my life I didn't prepare for something. I went in and took the test cold. I did surprisingly well, given my situation, but I wasn't going to get into a decent school with those scores. So I decided not to go at all. Without another plan in place, one of my professors suggested that I move to northern Japan for a year or two while I figured out my next steps. I liked learning languages, and this seemed like a grand opportunity for adventure. Through his connections, I'd serve as a foreigner-of-all-trades, teaching some English, helping out with cultural events, and spending time with a small, remote community.

"While I was there, I started freelancing," I told Henry. "That grew into a full-time job. I wanted to get better at what I was doing, so I took some time off to go to grad school for journalism at Columbia University. Then I moved back to Tokyo for *Newsweek.* I became a journalist sort of by accident."

"What kind of writing do you do?" he asked, lighting another cigarette.

"Mostly culture and technology trends around Asia," I said, taking the pack from his hand. "Do you mind if I have another?"

Nodding, he held out his lighter for me again. "I just read this incredible story about how Japanese teenagers are all having unprotected sex with their close friends," he said. "Apparently they say that they're not in danger of getting an STD as long as they only sleep with other kids in their circle. There was this line . . . ," he said, searching his memory. "Girls now share boyfriends like they'd share chips. Everyone's hand is in the bag."

"Wait," I said, as the blotches fired up again on my neck. "I wrote that!"

"Really?" he said.

"You just quoted me to me!" I said back, immediately regretting using a line from *When Harry Met Sally*. I took a nervous drag on my cigarette.

"No!" he said. "First, I love that movie. . . ." Then he reached into his bag and pulled out a copy of *Newsweek*. I watched him flip to a page with DANGEROUS LIAISONS: JAPAN'S CASUAL "SEX FRIENDS" RISK MORE THAN BROKEN HEARTS written at the top in bold typeface. He pointed to the byline. "You're Amy Webb?"

Henry went on about how much he'd enjoyed my story as we finished our cigarettes, and I asked him what else he liked to read as we walked back to the gate. We read the same magazines—*Popular Science, The New Yorker, The Atlantic, Wired*—and liked the same authors: Robert Heinlein, William Gibson, Nick Hornby.

Ultimately, our conversation turned to why I was traveling home. I explained my gradual move back to the States and was surprised to hear him commiserate. Henry had experienced similar problems. The Japanese women he'd met were only interested in a prototypical blond-haired, blue-eyed American, not someone who looked Asian. Up where he lived, there weren't many alternatives. "It can be incredibly lonely," he said. He'd had a few long-term relationships in the U.S., women who had eventually broken up with him but with whom he'd stayed very close friends. It wasn't like that in Japan.

As we waited in line to board the plane, Henry rifled through his bag and found a copy of *Job: A Comedy of Justice*. It was the next Heinlein book I'd been meaning to read. He pulled out a pen and scribbled something in the back.

"Here," he said, handing me the book and pen. "You can have

this—I just finished it. Put your email on the last page. Maybe we can get together the next time you're in Japan." As I tore out the page to give back to him, I noticed that he'd already written down his name, phone number, and email.

I took my seat near the front of the plane, and he continued to the rear, well past the emergency-exit row. I opened the book and stared at the first sentence and then quickly flipped to the last page, wanting to look at Henry's handwriting again. We had a four-hour flight back to Chicago. I tried to contain my excitement, but I couldn't help myself from indulging. Maybe he wanted to be some kind of international lawyer? Maybe he also wanted to move from country to country and have fabulously intelligent children, just like I did?

By the time we landed at O'Hare, it was close to midnight and the airport was nearly deserted. A janitor was pushing around a heavy cart, emptying a trash bin, while a security guard rested with his back against the wall, watching late-night CNN on the overhead monitors. As I neared baggage claim, I saw my parents sitting on a bench, chatting with another couple. Then I heard Henry's voice behind me. "Are those your parents talking to mine?"

In the car, my mom told me that Henry's family lived about three hours north of us. They'd been talking to his father and stepmother for a few hours, while they waited. "Apparently his mother is Japanese and moved back to Tokyo," she said. "He's going to law school in the fall, but did you know he wanted to be a journalist? Incredible!" she said as my dad took the south exit toward home.

Three weeks later, I was back in Tokyo packing up my apartment. Henry and I made plans for me to spend the weekend with him. It was an uncharacteristically spontaneous move on my part. Though I barely knew him, I never questioned whether I should take a train into a remote village and stay at his place. We had a great time. We visited a traditional Japanese *onsen,* bathing together in giant outdoor hot springs. He made me dinner, letting me watch him work in the kitchen.

That first night, he invited me into his bed, and we didn't leave again until late afternoon the following day.

The next month, he visited me in the States. We ordered pizza one night and sat on the couch, drinking wine and reminiscing about the corn, mayonnaise, shrimp, and other bizarre toppings offered by Pizza Hut in Japan. He started fiddling with the pizza box and tugging at the label as I got up to use the bathroom. When I came back, he was on his knees looking up at me, holding something between his fingers. I could still see "Amy Webb" written across the paper label that he'd fashioned into a ring.

"Amy . . . ," he started to say.

"I . . . I can't," I stammered. "We can't. You're joking, right?"

"I'm not joking," he said, grinning at me. "I want to marry you. Let's elope. Let's just go!"

The sensible part of me knew that I couldn't get engaged after dating someone for a few months, no matter how charming and romantic he was. I wasn't ready to get married yet. And I didn't want this to be my engagement story. I was a meticulous planner, someone who enjoyed the act of creating spreadsheets and making timetables that tracked activities down to the second. I took extreme pleasure in collecting and color-coding data, and especially in checking items off my lists. Getting in a car with Henry's pizza-box ring and driving until we found someone to marry us was exactly the opposite of the wedding day I'd imagined. I knew Henry would feel rejected, but I wasn't ready to marry him yet.

At the end of the summer, Henry started law school in Philadelphia and asked me to move in with him. It was never a city on my radar. If I was going to move back to the States permanently, I thought I'd settle down in New York City or in Chicago, where my family lived.

I'd also started to sense that maybe Henry and I weren't 100 percent compatible. For one thing, he was a pack-a-day smoker and was now totally uninterested in any sort of physical activity. He liked spending long hours in pubs, drinking with friends. I hated loud, smoky bars and would much rather that we spend time alone as a couple, touring a new museum or art gallery. When I looked around at my friends in relationships, though, none of them seemed to be totally and completely well matched. Henry and I had such a great story. It seemed like destiny had somehow brought us together, and that was enough reason for me to say yes to Philly.

I took the first job I could find, at a local weekly newspaper. I was happy to be employed but miserable every single day at work. Occasionally I got to do some investigative stories, but I was mainly stuck writing articles about mundane city hall meetings that no one read. Adding salt to my ego's wounds, I wasn't even at the biggest weekly paper. We were a very consistent number two.

Adjusting to my new life in Philly was difficult, and I grew somewhat depressed. I'd been bouncing around cities, experiencing something exotic and new on a near-daily basis, but I was now just another American reporter shackled to a row house that didn't feel like home. Henry, on the other hand, was in his element. Law school was an exhilarating challenge. He was surrounded by like-minded, smart people who, in that first fall semester, all felt like they were comrades fighting together in the same war.

On the weekends, I tried to cajole Henry into touring the city. There was the art museum, farmers' markets, and an artists' colony nearby. We could take a long walk along the river, drink coffee, and chat away a Sunday like we did that first weekend together in Japan. He was never interested, instead preferring to sleep in past noon on the weekends and stay out late drinking at the local bar with his new law school friends.

There were other minor irritations too. Though our taste in music was strikingly similar, Henry seemed to control what songs played on our stereo. For me, that unfortunately meant a constant stream of the few Broadway show tunes I didn't like. *Les Misérables* and *Cats* were on a nonstop loop in our house. *Les Mis* I didn't mind as much, but *Cats* was so derivative and repetitive—I was starting to hate it because that sound track was now part of Henry's evening ritual. He'd run a bath, turn it on, and chain-smoke in the bathtub. I soon wished I had no memory of "Memories."

One weekend, Henry told me his best friend from home was coming to visit. Since he was an only child, this guy was the closest thing he had to a brother. I hadn't met him yet, so I wanted to make a good impression. Wanting to stock the refrigerator in advance, I asked what he liked to eat and drink. I also asked what time he was arriving and how long he planned to stay.

"Why are you asking so many questions?" Henry would say over and over. "I have no idea when he's getting here. He's driving from Chicago."

"But . . . a day even? I'm sure he has a target?" I asked. I never got an answer. As Henry grew impatient and inexplicably angry with me, I tried to understand why scheduling didn't matter at all to him. The whole thing seemed totally insane. If my sister was coming to visit me, even by horseback, I'd want an idea of when to expect her so I could be at the door, ready to give her a hug. I'd make sure to have soy milk ready so she could make a latte when she woke up the next morning.

Before long, Henry and I were fighting regularly. I'd talk to my sister and mom on the phone almost every day, in part to vent and in part seeking advice. I also turned to the only friend I'd made at work, a plucky British journalist named Juliet. She was brilliant and under-utilized but always in a great mood. She and her filmmaker boyfriend, Ben, had met in college and had decided to settle in Philadelphia. They seemed to have this fabulously exciting life, always eating at new restaurants and attending midnight movie premieres and making friends everywhere they went. The more time I spent with Henry, the more I daydreamed about being a third companion in their amazing partnership.

Juliet and I had a daily ritual. At eleven A.M., we'd walk up the street to a coffee shop. I'd order a black coffee and would confide in her my latest struggle with Henry as she overflowed her breakfast tea with honey and entirely too much milk. "This is probably just a phase," she'd say. "You're stressed at work and he's stressed at school. Someday you'll get married and we'll all toast that missed connection at the airport. You two are lovely together!"

I kept hoping that Juliet was right. I was less and less happy in our relationship, but I wanted to believe that we were just transitioning to our new life together in the States. Eventually, things would bounce back to where they'd been.

That winter, Henry said we should get a Christmas tree. Neither of us was religious, but I'd grown up in a very Jewish household. While I didn't believe in God now, I strongly identified with my heritage and culture. I'd endured harassment as a kid and in college because I was Jewish, and choosing to erect a tree with tinsel and lights felt like acquiescing to all those hateful people. I also knew that my mom would be deeply disappointed in me. But I thought that picking out a tree and decorating it would bring Henry and me closer together. The tree itself wouldn't matter, I reasoned.

A few days before Christmas we had another big fight. We hadn't had sex in several weeks, and I was hoping that we could talk through whatever the problem was. But instead of talking, he stormed out and said he wouldn't be back. The writing wasn't on the wall for me; it was twinkling in red, blue, and green. I sat alone in the dark, staring at the tree. *This isn't who I am*, I thought. *I'm not me in this relationship.*

If we broke up, where would I go? I'd lived in Philadelphia for only six months. I didn't know that many people, and while I was miserable with Henry, at least I had someone to come home to each night. I'd uprooted my life to be with him, and the thought of having to start over again made me nauseated. My fear and insecurity about having to rejoin the dating pool trumped how alone and angry Henry made me feel.

We struggled through the winter and early spring, living together but barely speaking. One sunny afternoon, I asked Henry to sit outside with me.

"Can we talk about what's happening with us?" I asked.

"Sure," he said, avoiding my eyes.

I told him that I didn't feel like we were communicating very well. It seemed that we'd grown apart, and the more I tried to talk to him about things, the worse it got.

"Just over a year ago you asked me to marry you, remember?" I asked. "I want to feel like that again."

Henry didn't say much, but he did offer me a cigarette, just as he had when we first met. I lit the end and inhaled. "I do love you," he said. The "do" sounded to me like ellipses leading to something I didn't want to hear, and it made my stomach knot.

"Maybe we should take a short break," I said, trying to manipulate the conversation. I'd been holding out hope that we could somehow regain those feelings we'd had at the beginning. That passionate infatuation was so intense and visceral that the thought of losing those feelings, and Henry, was too much to bear. Still, I reasoned that if I offered this nuclear option, it would jolt him into talking about whatever it was he was feeling.

"Because if—"

"I think that's a good idea," Henry interrupted, finally looking at me directly. "Let's spend a few months apart and see where we stand. Take the weekend to move your things out. I'll help you find an apartment."

I blinked hard a few times and put out my cigarette. Something was wrong—I probably didn't hear him right. This wasn't making sense. This is the opposite of what's supposed to happen. Are we breaking up? I suddenly noticed that my cheeks were not flushed, but instead very wet. My upper lip tasted salty.

Henry wrapped his arms around me and held me close to him. "I do love you," he said as I sobbed into his shirt.

Hilary flew in the next day, ready for her sisterly duties, to help me pack up my things and move out. Though she was three years younger, she had leapfrogged ahead of me in many ways. She was so confident and secure, and she was so well put together. She always had the right outfit for the occasion, accessorized with a perfect, gleaming smile. Hilary was exactly what I needed when I was falling apart.

Henry and I made a list of who would take what: I'd get the bedroom set; he'd keep the couch and living room furniture. We decided that it would be best if he left me alone in the house while I boxed up my half of our relationship.

Hilary wanted to take a midday break and have lunch in the Italian Market, a Philadelphia neighborhood lined with outdoor cafés, gelato shops, and cheesemongers. We'd just finished eating hoagies and were walking back toward my car, takeaway espressos in hand, when I heard Hilary gasp.

"No fucking way!" she yelled. "Hey, asshole!" she called out.

I looked around, slightly embarrassed about the scene she was now causing.

"Henry!" she shouted.

I hadn't realized that the man in the couple walking just ten feet in front of us was actually Henry, arm in arm with a short brunette. I recognized her immediately. She was another law student, one who'd been in our house several times. In fact, I used to tease Henry about how much she flirted with him. Stupid, blind Amy. How did I not see this coming?

I remember hearing Hilary continue to shout as I slid my keys into the lock of my car door. The seat felt unusually warm. I looked in the rearview mirror to find Hilary standing in the middle of the street, hands on her hips, ripping Henry to shreds.

He didn't love me, I knew now. Henry told me he had never broken up with a girlfriend before—instead, he engineered a way for her to end it each time so he wouldn't have to feel guilty. I was just the next in what I suddenly realized had been a string of confused, gullible women.

I felt my heart pounding so hard it hurt my chest. My tongue went numb. Was it sliding down the back of my throat? I couldn't breathe. I was moving my boxes out of our house that weekend; was that law student moving hers in?

Then everything went black.

Now here I was, standing with Hilary in my crappy new apartment, staring at a bunch of cardboard. I was thirty and no longer building toward marriage and a family. I was stuck in a city I'd never intended to call home with a ratty old futon and the pillow-top mattress Henry and I had spent one happy afternoon picking out.

"Why did you have to use so much tape?" Hilary asked again. "Never mind. I know why."

2 | Single in the City

Learning how to date—
and to hate dating—again.

S everal weeks after my breakup with Henry, some of the staff at my office staged a mutiny. Without much warning, my editor got fired along with all of the news team. They spared Juliet but not me.

While I was looking for another job, I decided to start consulting. With my background in technology and journalism, I was able to track trends and forecast how the media landscape was going to change. I started with one small client, but within a month I'd signed half a dozen companies wanting me to advise them. Knowing it was a huge risk, I put my job search on hold and set up a home office in my kitchen so I could focus on building my new company full-time. I loved nothing more than to work on a monumental challenge. The concentration and endurance it required empowered and excited me.

There was one small problem: Besides a police officer and his sister who lived in the apartment above me, I didn't see anyone else most days of the week. I still went out with friends, but it was impossible to meet any potential dates. There were no coworkers who could introduce me to their brothers or old college roommates. I was thirty, and while I wasn't against going out to clubs on the weekends, standing in line while a group of twenty-one-year-olds in front of me got carded didn't help my self-esteem.

Some of my friends had been trying to set me up on blind dates, but they never worked out. Either we had nothing in common or there was just no chemistry. I'd also been meeting up with Juliet's friends at local bars. They were stylish, artsy, and smart, and I always lost my confidence around them. When I did meet a man who was my age, attractive, and steadily employed, he was unfortunately already married.

Instead, I found myself working until midnight or later and then staying up to watch old episodes of *Sex and the City,* to live vicariously through Miranda. She was smart, driven, and career focused, and she still managed to eventually find a husband. I felt ashamed admitting this to my professional friends living outside of Philly, who were either already happily married or seemed to not care about whether they'd ever start a family. Surely I wasn't the only thirtysomething woman struggling to figure out how to simultaneously chase a career and a long-term relationship?

Meantime, one of my friends from home was newly pregnant, and another that I'd known in Japan had just given birth to her second child. On weekly calls with my grandmother, I was bombarded with unsolicited details about four of my cousins' wedding plans.

Then there were the fix ups. What is it about happily coupled people wanting to fix up everyone else around them? One cousin insisted that I go out with a friend of hers. She told me he was a lawyer representing celebrities, and he asked me to meet him at an Asian restaurant for an early dinner. He showed up a half hour late, fake European kissed me on each cheek, and then sat down at our table with two BlackBerries flanking his water glass. He would start by asking me a question, like, "So what was it like living in Japan?" Just as I'd begin to answer, he'd interrupt with a bigger, better story. "You know, I once spent a day with a Japanese tea *sen-SEI* master," he'd say, mangling the word for "teacher."

He'd drone on for five minutes, then abruptly say, "But you don't want to hear all about that. Now back to you!"

I told him that originally, I'd planned on going to law school. "Do you watch the show?" he interrupted, asking if I watched one of his clients' shows. I started to explain that I'd never really watched it, but it was such an indelible part of our pop culture that—

"And wait . . . just hold that thought . . . ," he said, typing something into his BlackBerry. "You little prick!" he shouted, either laughing or grumbling into the screen, I couldn't tell which. "Okay, okay, sorry about that," he said. "Now back to you. So you watch the show?"

Less than ten minutes later he took a phone call and said there was an emergency at work. "This has been fun!" he said, shoving his arms into his jacket. He threw several twenty-dollar bills on the table without looking at the check and made for the door. "Let's set something up in a few weeks."

Without a bustling social life in Philly, I was traveling back to Chicago to see my parents most weekends. Hilary, who'd moved to Greensboro, North Carolina, was also traveling back home often. My mom hadn't been feeling well—she was tired all the time, and she'd recently gained a lot of weight. Our family doctor blamed it on a sudden acute case of type 2 diabetes and told her to watch what she was eating. That diagnosis didn't quite jibe with the fact that her skin seemed to be yellowing, and she didn't have terrible eating habits to begin with. But she took his advice and focused on getting healthy.

Still, she had enough energy to find me dates. Often, on a Friday before I'd leave for the airport, my mom would call and ask me to bring home something nice to wear to dinner.

"Do you remember Charlie from high school?" she'd ask. "He was in some of your classes?"

"No, why?" I'd say.

"We ran into him at the grocery store. Would you believe he's still single? You're going out with him tomorrow night."

I did remember Charlie, of course. He was a star football player in high school. Not too bright, but athletic and popular. I was invisible to him then, so why in the hell would he want to date me now? Because, as it turned out, he'd gotten divorced at twenty-three and his ex-wife had custody of their two sons. Charlie was now a chubby cliché, living in his old bedroom, his '89 Camaro parked in his parents' driveway in the same spot it was fifteen years ago.

And then there was Chaz, the manager of a diner where I'd wait-ressed midnights one summer between high school and college. I'd just walked out of the airport and toward my dad's car when Hilary bolted toward me for a hug. "Don't be mad, but Mom and Dad are forcing you to go out with that sleazy manager from Silver Moon," she whispered. "We have to meet him in an hour. I'll go with you."

I didn't bother dressing up. My kinky, frizzy brown hair was mostly back in a ponytail, and I'd swiped some mascara on so that behind my tortoiseshell glasses, I looked slightly more awake than I felt. I had on the same faded jeans and gray hoodie sweatshirt I'd been wearing since leaving Philadelphia—it was an outfit Hilary would never, ever be seen wearing in public. Though it was technically my date, and we were only dining at Applebee's, Hilary had a full face of makeup and had flat-ironed her otherwise curly dark blond hair. She was wearing a chic blue V-neck sweater to match her bright blue eyes, and dark-wash jeans with a freshly pressed crease on each leg.

When we were together, strangers assumed that Hilary was the jet-setting older sister and that I was the opera singer still trying to make it professionally. It was the opposite, of course. Hilary had been audi-tioning and taking smaller roles, singing in regional companies, while she continued to train and wait for her big break. She spoke five lan-guages well enough to charm everyone around her, and it meant she was constantly being afforded unthinkable offers. Like the Italian fam-ily she met at a restaurant once who invited her to stay at their estate in Florence. They threw a big summer party every year and wanted Hilary to sing for their guests. They gave her a round-trip ticket to Italy, set her up in a villa, and took her shopping for a week.

We looked more like distant cousins—one from a well-groomed family, and one from the wrong side of the tracks—than sisters.

Chaz was already waiting for me at Applebee's. He hadn't expected Hilary, but I was grateful she was there. He was already on his second Long Island Iced Tea and well on his way to a DWI.

"I'm going to use the bathroom," I said without even sitting down. "Just get me a water."

I found out later that while I was gone, Chaz had peppered Hilary with a whole bunch of questions. Why wasn't I married? Was I moving back to Chicago permanently? Was I seeing anyone?

When I got back to our table, Hilary stood up, grabbed my elbow, and led me toward the door. "He just asked whether or not he was getting laid tonight," she said.

"With who?" I asked.

"Who do you think?" she said, rolling her eyes. "Come on, let's go." We stormed out of the restaurant without bothering to say good-bye.

I continued to marvel at all of the dates my mom and cousins forced on me. In theory, these were the people who knew me the best. They should have known that I could never, ever be happy in a relationship with an ambitionless, horny, third-shift diner manager. Or an obnoxious, self-important lawyer. The harder they tried, the more bizarre the date. There was the produce guy at our grocery store. The Starbucks barista who wanted to become a chef. The sweet, bumbling postal worker who, for some reason, didn't own a phone.

These dates provided some needed comedic relief for my mother, who was now feeling—and looking—much worse. She decided to get a second opinion, this time at Northwestern University in Chicago. They ran a full battery of tests and gave us a different diagnosis—neuroendocrine cancer—than the one from her internist. While we waited in the exam room, they were making an emergency appointment for my mom with a team of researchers at MD Anderson, a hospital campus in Texas specializing in unusual cancers.

The doctor tried to share her prognosis with us, but my parents refused to hear it. "We'll just take this one step at a time," my dad said. The burden of learning exactly how sick she was, and what that meant for our family, instead fell to me and me alone.

"Don't make plans for the spring," her doctor told me. It was already late August.

Knowing what was ahead for us, I started getting my mother's affairs in order, straightening out her insurance, researching her pension and retirement plans, making sure her finances were secure so that my dad could continue without her.

Doing long division by hand, repetitively entering data into spreadsheets, and making financial projections weren't necessary tasks, especially since most of it could be handled with a basic computer program. But these activities were the only ways I could escape what was happening to us. I was no longer sleeping, so I resorted to sorting data and making elaborate graphs that I knew no one needed. I'd done the same thing as a little kid every time insomnia struck, which was several days a week. I'd lie awake in bed, doing math sets to calm my anxiety. I'd stare at my digital clock, counting the line segments that made up each of the numbers; 10:58 P.M. had twenty segments. What time of day produced a prime number? What was the square root of 9:26 A.M.?

I took a strange comfort in those numbers. Numbers were black-and-white; they were clean data. Data that didn't cause me to question why now, *why us*? Math made sense to me. I could use it to solve some of my parents' worries. It wasn't some untreatable disease for which there was no ribbon or lapel pin.

My mother's illness didn't stop her from working, and it certainly didn't alter her drive. She had been a fourth-grade teacher for more than thirty years and had gone back to school more than once to take additional classes. Though it wasn't required, she'd accumulated most of the necessary credits for a PhD. She'd taken on the newly minted teachers from a nearby teaching program and mentored all of the graduates using a curriculum she developed with the university. She designed after-school and summer enrichment programs. In the early 1980s, after irate parents complained to her school's principal that their kid had gotten someone else as a homeroom teacher, a special list was established, allowing the parents of incoming kindergarteners to reserve a spot in her classroom four years later.

My dad supported her numerous ideas and schemes, which seemed to be taking more and more time. He was patient and supportive and sometimes thrown into a family dynamic that was culturally very different from what he'd known. Education was more important than anything else in my mother's very large Jewish family. My father was raised in a devoutly Christian setting, where other things took precedence. Although he had graduated high school two years early—he had a savant-like ability to read an enormous amount and to retain everything, almost word for word—education wasn't a focus in his family. He hadn't been encouraged to go to college and instead had joined the retail ranks, managing several stores. Still, he helped launch some of my mom's projects and was often asked to mentor students.

With every new class in the fall, it seemed like my mom took on a new set of kids who needed her. School systems use standardized tests to determine which kids need academic help, but few measure emotional development. One year, she had a student who tested fine but was failing most of his subjects. He didn't have any friends—the kids in class interacted with him only to tease him. My mom suspected he had Asperger's syndrome, a form of autism. The student's parents denied there was anything wrong, so my mom became his best friend. She coached him every day and arranged for a school therapist to work with him. My mom stuck with him through middle and high school. When he got his acceptance letter to law school, my mom was the first person he called.

Hilary and I were on the receiving end of her drive to succeed too. My mom pushed us to work harder and be smarter than we could push ourselves. She didn't care if we got the best grade or if we won a particular competition, as long as we'd worked ourselves to exhaustion. All of our achievements were quantified and recorded. Hilary and I each had giant binders, with certificates, citations, and letters documenting our accomplishments. We were in every music contest offered. We were senate pages. We were in after-school leadership programs. We took classes in languages, art, and even sewing. Doing each activity meant learning something new. She wanted us to develop cognitive skills, learn time management, and be ready for whatever life threw at us. By the time I graduated high school, I didn't have a one-page résumé. I had a hundred-page book.

She was my inspiration in so many ways. Like her, I loved to work. It kept my mind focused in the present, not on the uncertainty of what lay ahead.

My mom's cancer scared me. But watching my father clean up the shower floor so she'd never have to see the clumps of her black hair in the drain forced me into near paralysis. My dad never left her side. He loved her completely.

What if I never find someone to love me like that?

When Henry got down on his knee and popped the question using a cardboard pizza-box ring, it wasn't the first time I'd been offered marriage. Years earlier, I'd nearly made a lifetime commitment to my college boyfriend, Allen. We'd met during a summer music clinic—it was an intensive week of master classes and rehearsal. I was practicing clarinet performance and he was working as a mentor. Allen was twenty-four and in his second year of a master's program studying to be an orchestra conductor. I was eighteen and an incoming freshman at the same school of music that fall. We spent the week flirting madly and continued calling each other and writing letters until I started classes. We fell for each other quickly, and we were inseparable that first semester.

By the spring, Allen wanted confirmation that we were both heading into a long-term commitment. He wanted to know when I'd be ready to talk seriously about marriage, and he reminded me that there was no rule saying I had to wait until graduating from college before walking down the aisle. We drove out to the East Coast to meet his parents. When we got back, my parents visited the campus to meet him. Everyone got along. He was very smart and extremely driven and had a bright career ahead of him. Everything seemed to be exactly as it should, except for one small issue: I was no longer attracted to him.

I trusted Allen's advice and admired his worldliness. I just couldn't muster the same romantic feelings I'd had for him that summer we'd met. For many people, that first year of college is as much about taking classes as it is about finding and exploring a new independence. I was living on my own on a huge campus full of people. Yet I'd felt increasingly tied down with Allen, and without an outlet to experiment.

One of the most important things Allen taught me was how to be open and completely honest in a relationship. That's why when I realized my feelings for him had changed, I thought I should be candid with him and ask for his opinion.

We'd had a lovely evening out—he'd taken me to a great sushi place in town and we spent the whole time talking about whether I should stay in the school of music or instead work on a political science and economics degree. I'd wanted to rehearse for major roles as a lawyer in a courtroom, not become principal clarinetist for some orchestra somewhere. When we got back to his apartment, we relaxed on his bed. He was stroking my hair when I changed the subject.

"I have another problem I need your help with," I started.

"What's that?" he said, smiling back at me.

"I'm having some feelings that I don't know what to do with. You know that I love you and that I really count on your advice," I said, looking into his eyes. "The problem is that I can't really stand kissing you. It's like . . . it's like I'm kissing my brother or something. I like to cuddle with you, I just really don't want to have sex with you. Have you ever felt that way before with someone you were dating?"

"What?" he shouted, his smile now gone.

"It's just that . . . that . . . ," I stammered.

"You're so fucking immature," he fired back and walked toward the door.

"But I thought we could talk about this," I said, naïvely thinking that we would dissect our feelings and analyze the problem as we had my political science major, or what went wrong with the lasagna we'd made last weekend.

"Here's your coat," he said, shooing me out of his apartment. "We're done."

As soon as I got home, I called my mom crying. "I don't know why he broke up with me," I sobbed. "What did I do wrong? He said he loved me . . ."

"Oh, honey," she said. "I'm so sorry." The sound of her voice—melodic, warm, knowing—always enveloped and comforted me, no matter the situation. "Every relationship goes through a rough patch, but if you've been feeling this way for a long time, it's a good thing you told him. You'll probably look back years from now and realize he wasn't the right one for you."

Once again, she was right. Allen and I may have shared lots of similar interests and values, but he was much further along in life than I was. I still wanted to date around and hook up with random guys I'd met at frat parties. He wanted marriage and to start a family. In fact, just weeks after we broke up, he started dating the woman who would become his wife only two years later.

Allen and Henry weren't good matches for me. Allen was a great teacher and mentor, and I looked up to him. As much as I may have admired his intellect and talent, it should have been obvious to me that manufacturing sexual attraction in short spurts wouldn't sustain a long-term relationship. I'd originally thought that Henry and I were a perfect match not because of how we met, but because his mother and half of his family were Japanese. I'd mistakenly thought that our shared experience in Japan was important enough to build a marriage on, and that we'd spend our lives traveling the world with our culturally diverse, sophisticated family.

Watching my father care for my mom now, I yearned for someone who would support me like that regardless of the situation. But even my parents occasionally experienced rough patches.

Though they'd been married for more than three decades, their wildly different family backgrounds surfaced during arguments. I knew that the tensions they felt had less to do with their thirty years of marriage and more to do with the thirty years of values and experiences they'd developed individually before meeting each other.

How was I supposed to find someone who fully understood me? Who saw the world through the same sort of lens I did? Who shared my hopes, dreams, and ambitions?

3 | Signing On

You are a: woman seeking man.

J ust try it for a month," my mom said on speakerphone from the front seat of the car. Hilary was driving her to chemo, to keep her company while she received treatment. I was back in Philadelphia, sitting in my crappy kitchen. It had been months since my breakup with Henry, and the room was now doubling as my fledgling company's office. The kitchen table, covered in file folders and my seventeen-inch MacBook laptop, served as my desk.

"The sites aren't full of creepy weirdos anymore," Hilary chimed in from behind the wheel. "I know a ton of people who met each other online."

"You should try JDate," my mom continued over the loud clicking of a turn signal in the background. "You'll try it for a month and see what happens."

"Fine," I said. "I'll make you a deal. I'll sign up for JDate if you stop setting me up with every random person who crosses your path."

"Yeah, Mom," Hilary said. "Chaz from Silver Moon? What were you thinking?"

On a certain level, online dating made perfect sense to me. Dating sites use data: We enter facts about ourselves, and then others can search for and evaluate our profiles. Online dating would be like shopping for shoes online at Zappos: I'd like a professional who has a great sense of humor. Size: six feet tall and two hundred pounds. I was tired of being set up—clearly none of my friends or relatives had any sense of whom I'd find attractive—and I felt too old to play club and bar roulette every weekend. I wasn't interested in dating around anymore. I wanted a husband.

I decided to start with JDate and Match.com, and then later on I'd join eHarmony. Each site advertised something unique. JDate's advantage for me was obvious: It's full of Jews looking for other Jews to marry. Match.com was the largest dating site, which meant that it would have the biggest pool of men. eHarmony promised "true love" using its matching formula and "29 Levels of Compatibility." If I cast a wide enough net, it was statistically probable that I'd find the right person, I reasoned.

Still, sitting at my kitchen table/desk, I started my nightly ritual of creating the next day's schedule. I'd read Nick Hornby's book *About a Boy* and loved how the main character, who was independently wealthy and had nothing to keep his day occupied, divided his day into thirty-minute units in order to pass the time. Now that I was working for myself, the system seemed like a brilliant way to keep me organized. Except that I used twenty-minute units so that I could push myself to squeeze more into each day.

I blocked two units after lunch to create my JDate profile. *Forty minutes should be ample time*, I thought. I'd very quickly sign on, then I would be able to spend the rest of my allotted units searching other profiles. That afternoon I had a client meeting, which meant that I couldn't accidentally waste the rest of the day trolling through the site. If I had leftover time, I'd begin my Match.com profile.

After lunch the next day, which was a very quick trip across the street for a sandwich, I returned to my kitchen table/desk and set a timer for one unit—twenty minutes—on my computer. I displayed it in the upper-right corner of my screen and hit the Play button on iTunes. It was still rotating through a Japanese music mix I'd listened to years ago.

I opened Firefox, my Internet browser of choice, and typed in JDate's web address: http://www.jdate.com. There, on the home page, was a happy couple cuddling. With their dark hair and olive skin, they could have been my cousins—they were attractive, normal-looking people. Next to the couple was JDate's first question for me:

You are a:
Woman seeking man

Regrettably, "Woman seeking man who's not a lying asshole" wasn't an option.

Where do you live?

JDate wanted a zip code. I'm not planning on living in Philadelphia indefinitely . . . should I use the zip code where I hope to live next? I'd like to live in DC or New York City, but if I met someone in one of those places, I'd have to drive two hours each way. That wasn't practical. I could enter a prestige neighborhood in Philadelphia instead, which would let me restrict the dating pool only to men who were successful enough to afford a house in one of the ritzy parts of town. Then it suddenly occurred to me that maybe I shouldn't enter my real information at all. What if I met someone who turned out to be nuts and he used my zip code to figure out where I live?

"This is ridiculous," I said aloud and typed in an honest "19130."

What type of relationship are you looking for?

On the screen, there were more choices than I'd anticipated, and I could select as many as I wanted: date, friend, marriage, long-term relationship, marriage and children, activity partner. Whatever I answered would show up as part of my profile, and it would be factored into JDate's matching system. Obviously, I wanted to get married. But I didn't want to scare off potential dates. I could choose long-term relationship, but at that point, why not just pick marriage?

I looked up at the corner of my screen. I'd already wasted half of my first unit of time second-guessing myself about how to answer. I clicked on all of the choices and moved on to the next set of questions.

> *Your drinking habits:*
> On occasion
>
> *Do you keep kosher?*
> No
>
> *What are your smoking habits?*

"Smoking only when stressed-out" wasn't an option. I wanted to quit, and I certainly didn't want to be in another relationship where we had to constantly go outside, even in the winter, to light up. If I dated a nonsmoker, then maybe I'd be one too.

> *What are your smoking habits?*
> Nonsmoker
>
> *Your education level:*
> Master's degree
>
> *What do you do?*

Rather than a box where I could write an explanation of my consulting company, there was a drop-down menu. I scrolled through Communications, Health Care, Child Rearing, Manufacturing, Warehousing, and Graphic Arts but didn't see anything that came close to describing what I do. And why was "Warehousing" a choice? What did that even mean?

Then I heard a faint buzzer start to sound. It was my timer—I'd already blown through my first unit.

I clicked on "Other" and went on to the next screen.

Next, JDate wanted me to select my religion from another drop-down menu, and suddenly the religion I was raised in looked incredibly complicated and unfamiliar: Reform, Conservative, Orthodox, Modern Orthodox, Traditional, Conservadox, Reconstructionist, Willing to convert, Other. "Culturally Jewish but not practicing" was the last choice and the one that seemed closest to being what I called "Jew…ish."

I continued answering questions and entering personal information. Then JDate wanted a username. Should I try to be clever? I could use JungianAnimus or MooresLaw, but those might sound pretentious. Only a philosophy nut would get my inside joke about how women and men communicate, and a nontechie might think I was a lawyer named Moore. I noticed that iTunes was now playing an old Japanese favorite about the night sky and unrequited love, which seemed ominous, but my creativity was waning. I typed in the "night sky" part of the title, *yozora,* and clicked the maroon Finish button, which took me to a payment screen, where I opted for a three-month plan at seventy dollars. *This better not take longer than that*, I thought, entering my credit card information.

I clicked on the Process Order button and was suddenly taken to another screen asking me to describe myself in more detail. I looked again at my timer and saw that I was now halfway through my second unit. I actually did have to leave for a client meeting. Why was this taking so long? I just want to see the available men on JDate!

I put my cursor in the blank window and thought about what to write.

I'm recently out of a serious relationship . . .

I tapped the Delete button over and over until all the text had been erased. Common sense—and every romantic comedy I'd ever seen—said that I'm not supposed to talk about previous relationships.

> I'm looking for a smart, funny professional who's interested in travel . . .

Great, I thought. *Now it looks like I'm advertising for a male escort.*

Behind the JDate window, I noticed a folder labeled "Amy" on my desktop. I clicked into it and opened my résumé. At the top was a really great summary section, which I'd been tweaking and perfecting during the past few weeks. I'll just copy and paste that section, change "Amy Webb" to "Yozora," and . . .

About Me:

Yozora is an award-winning journalist, speaker, and future thinker, adapting current and emerging technologies for use in communications. She has spent twelve years working with digital media and now advises various start-ups, retailers, government agencies, and media organizations as well as our clients all over the world.

There were so many other fields to complete. What were my favorite books? Best places I've visited? What I like to do for fun? I scrolled down to the "specialties" area of my résumé, copied all of the bullet points, and, skipping all the other sections, pasted them into the "Things I could never live without":

—Future of technology
—Emerging platforms
—Content management systems
—Monetization
—Fluency in Japanese

—Conversational ability in Mandarin
—Fluency in HTML, CSS, JavaScript, and other web languages

Next, JDate wanted a photo of me to finish my profile. I opened iPhoto and started sorting through old photos. There was the picture of me finishing the first and only 5K I've ever attempted. It was a frigid night in Chicago on New Year's Eve, and I'd agreed to accompany a friend who was an actual athlete. Just after the starting gun went off, a group running next to me stopped to open a bottle of champagne. I was going at such a slow pace that they'd managed to toast the evening, drink a full glass, and still pass me only a third of the way into the race. I did finish—at the end, it was me, an elderly woman, and two guys who'd stumbled out of a nearby bar plastered and were now screaming the *Chariots of Fire* theme song.

There were other photo possibilities, like the picture of me at Columbia standing next to the *Alma Mater* statue. I was wearing a suit and looked professional, possibly even important. There was a photo of me wearing a sea blue *yukata,* a lightweight kimono used in the summer. I was visiting a friend's relatives on Japan's northern coast and for the hell of it we decided to dress up and do karaoke.

As I scrolled through the photos, they seemed to get worse. There was the one from my last speaking gig. I was onstage at a huge journalism-technology conference, and apparently, the photo had been taken while I was mid-*th* sound. I didn't look great, but with the wide angle you could see a packed crowd of people laughing and enjoying themselves. There was another of me on a Segway—I looked geeky and hi-tech, but I was squeezing my legs so hard I looked constipated. There were too many to choose from, so I uploaded the three least-bad photos and continued through JDate's questions.

Height and weight:

There were two little windows staring at me, daring me to answer. I figured I should at least be honest about my height. At five foot six, I was a little taller than average, and that would be difficult to hide in person. Weight, on the other hand . . . everyone carries weight differently. I could be honest and say I'm a non-chunky but not-skinny 160 pounds, but to a guy I may sound like an ogre. I could lie and say 120, but I'm obviously not a size 2. I clicked on the opt-out choice "Will tell you later," and then on the maroon Finish button just as my alarm buzzed. I was out of time.

I felt frustrated and rushed but satisfied that I'd cast myself out into the dating pool. Once I finished with meetings and work for the day, I'd create a similar profile on Match.com and would start searching for my husband.

That night, I brought my MacBook and a cup of coffee outside to my patio. The previous tenant had left a green plastic table and chair for me along with an ashtray. It was a tiny space overlooking a neighbor's backyard, which was dotted with rusty old toys. The play-set swing was now coiled around the top, immobilized by years of weather and neglect.

I plugged my laptop into an outlet just inside the door and lit a citronella candle to ward off bugs. There, hidden beneath the table, was a pack of Marlboro Lights that I'd stashed away for emergencies. While there was nothing necessarily wrong—it was a gorgeous summer evening—it was a perfect time to settle in and enjoy just one cigarette along with my coffee. I lit up, inhaled, and signed on to JDate.

Now that I was a full-fledged member, the site looked different. Instead of a happy couple and some marketing talk about how perfect they were together, I was presented with twenty different smiling men, all ostensibly ready to date me.

I clicked first on JSB324. He was twenty-nine, had brown curly hair, and was six foot three. His gallery included a photo of him in front of the pyramids in Egypt. In another, he was sitting between his grand-father and someone who looked like a twin brother, and they were all wearing matching black ZAYDE IS 80 T-shirts. He wasn't the kind of handsome that would stop me on the street, but the more I looked at him, the more he grew on me. He had a boyish grin and bright eyes.

I scrolled down to read his profile. JSB324 listed "Teacher" for pro-fession, but he seemed more like a summer camp counselor. "I like warm weather, comedy, playing the guitar, and capture the flag," it read.

On the screen, JDate gave me a number of options to let JSB324 know I was interested. I could click on a button to "flirt" with him, and the system would open a window with a dozen automated pickup lines, like, "How is it you haven't been snatched up yet?" and "I'd better call FedEx; you're the total package." I could also click on a Secret Admirer button, which would alert JDate that I liked him. JDate would then work on my behalf to see if he felt the same way.

I clicked on "Favorite" and marked his profile for later viewing.

AdMan2 seemed promising. His main profile photo was of him standing outside in the snow on what must have been a skiing trip. He was extremely good-looking: dark eyes, strong nose, straight white teeth. The next photo was of him on the beach playing volleyball. His About Me section read, "I'm a well-adjusted energetic guy who enjoys being active. I love my work, traveling, and trying new things. I'm look-ing for someone who's independent."

"Favorited" and "Admired"!

I thought about sending him a message. Below the buttons, there was an area where I could type and send AdMan2 an email through JDate's system. It would be easy enough for me to send something like "Hey, AdMan2. I used to ski in northern Japan . . . ," but I'd been told never to make the first move. Men don't like to be chased, I was cautioned. If I sent him a message first, I might come off as seeming too aggressive.

Better to take a passive approach and rely on the Secret Admirer button, I figured.

I went back to the main page to see who else was listed. There were tabs allowing me to sort by most active, newest, and closest geographically, and at the bottom of the screen little arrows indicated that there were sixty-eight more pages of profiles for me to browse. I decided to skip a few pages ahead and clicked on page 7.

Suddenly, the men didn't look so great. There was MickeyMan, whose main photo showed him sitting next to a giant Mickey Mouse. The username should have been a clear warning, but I decided to click through his gallery anyway. Every single photo was taken at Disney World. There was MickeyMan wearing jean shorts and a blue shirt, his arms wrapped around a Mickey Mouse character in a wizard costume. There was MickeyMan again, in the same jean shorts but a different shirt, posing with Mickey Mouse in a red velvet cloak. In his About Me, he wrote, "If someone has a question about Disney history, quotes, or movies, I'm the one to ask. I can quote every line from every Disney movie. I'm also a Star Wars expert, and I've surprised a few people at work with how much I know about the series (even people who claim to know more than I do)."

The next profile was for XAY7YS6. He was Asian, and while that didn't preclude him from being Jewish, it was statistically improbable that we had the same upbringing. There were a staggering number of photos in his gallery. One showed him posing with a leather Wolverine glove, with the claws sticking out. In the next photo, he was wearing black sunglasses that wrapped around his head and was pointing a mobile phone directly at the camera. In the next photo, he was wearing a suit, the same sunglasses and had his arm outstretched, this time holding an opaque martini glass. In the About Me section, he wrote "X-Traordinary Asian Male For XXX-Quisite Jewish Lady. I want to fall in love with a hacker, go on a spy mission, and evade a marriage proposal all within a 24 hour period."

There was no button for "awesomely horrific."

I went back to the home screen and determined that JDate must be somehow ranking profiles based on popularity, which would make sense. Dating sites need to showcase enough viable possibilities right away so that newcomers will be willing to buy new memberships.

I also noticed that I could monitor my profile's metrics. I could see who had clicked on my profile and with what frequency. There were options to track who'd sent me flirts, instant messages, or emails and even who'd Favorited me. I realized that JSB324, AdMan2, Mickey-Man, and XAY7YS6 all knew that I was looking at them tonight. I'd unwittingly done the digital equivalent of a drive-by.

I went back to the home screen and considered more profiles, this time being more selective about where I was clicking. I tried Agent120. He was classically attractive: thick brown hair, green eyes, tan. I could clearly see his face in all his photos, and he showed enough of his chest to reveal that he was in very good shape. He was dressed in button-down shirts and black slacks and looked professional, but also like he was ready to have a great time. None of the photos seemed staged. It was as if someone happened to catch him just after he'd heard a fantastic story.

In his profile area, he'd said that he's culturally Jewish, only drinks socially, and is a nonsmoker. In the About Me section, he wrote, "I take measured risks, in love and in life. To me, nothing is more devastating than a missed opportunity. Work is extremely important, and I'm driven by success. I'm looking for someone who is independent, hard-working, and has a fulfilling professional life. I try to maintain a healthy lifestyle, but I'm not a gym rat. I'm not looking for a cardio queen who can't function without her daily spinning class. I want a partner, someone who can counsel me on what I'm doing and who's willing to take advice from me when needed. A risk everyone should take: 80s night at karaoke. You'll find me first to the stage."

Finally. "Favorited"! "Admired"!!

I could see myself going out with Agent120, and now that I'd clicked his Favorite button, he'd know I'd accept an invitation to go out. He'd understand if I had to spend the weekend at work, and he didn't want a supermodel athlete. Plus, I love karaoke!

I moused over to the email box, desperately wanting to send him a message. Though I felt a nagging sense that I shouldn't, I started to type:

Hi there . . .

"Fuck," I sighed. What do I write? This is what I hated about dating in the real world. There's never a good way to break the ice. I'm smart, I'm funny, and if we could just pick up about ten minutes into a conversation, everything would be fine. I wished JDate had a button that I could press to skip the small talk and fast forward to the middle of what I knew would be a great first conversation.

Hey there. If you're free on Thursday night, I'll give you a careless whisper and then . . .

Fuck . . . Fuck! Fuck!! Why can't I do this? He's either not going to remember the George Michael song or he'll think I'm telling some lame joke.

Hey there. Want to give me a call? 867-5309 . . .

With my luck he'll misunderstand the Tommy Tutone reference and actually try calling.

AGENT120: Hi . . .

Just then, a notification window popped up. Agent120 had sent me an instant message while I was mumbling obscenities to myself. He was online, looking at my profile as I looked at his.

AGENT120: Hello? Anyone there?

I stared back at my screen. I wasn't prepared to suddenly chat with him. What should I write back?

YOZORA: So you do karaoke?

AGENT120: With every breath I take. :-)

I typed back, hoping and praying he'd make no mention of show tunes.

YOZORA: Clever.

AGENT120: I'm Glen.

We continued chatting back and forth. It turned out that he'd never been to Japan, but he'd always wanted to visit. We had the same eighties music tastes—Brit pop, not hair bands—and he challenged me to a karaoke battle. We agreed to meet the next day at a nearby bar, Flynn's Tavern, which had Karaoke Thursdays.

I signed off of JDate and sent an email to Hilary, Juliet, and my mom telling them I'd taken the plunge and was getting ready for my first online date. Moments after I hit Send, my phone rang. I barely had the chance to say hello after picking up.

"You can't go out with this guy tomorrow night," Hilary said.

"Are you ever not on your BlackBerry?" I asked. "I sent that message like forty-five seconds ago . . ."

"You should make him wait at least a few days," she continued.

"But tomorrow night is karaoke," I started.

"Making someone endure your voice is more like an after-marriage kind of thing for you," she said. "Not a first-date thing . . ."

"I'll be fine," I said. "It's karaoke. You're not supposed to sound good. Besides, I'm sure he can't sing either," I said.

"What are you going to wear?" Hilary asked. "Never mind, I already know. Black pants and some kind of black shirt, I assume."

I knew Hilary was right and that I needed to update my wardrobe. For years, my standard work uniform had been black slacks, a button-down shirt of some kind, a blazer, and heels. Aside from that, I owned one pair of jeans and several old, threadbare pairs of yoga pants. Anytime I wasn't at work, I wore jeans and a hooded sweatshirt. I didn't have time to shop before tomorrow, so black pants and shirt it would be.

"Maybe just let him sing," she said. "Pretend like you can't find anything good in the book. Call me after."

I saw Juliet the next day, and she congratulated me on my first JDate connection. "I wonder if he's an actual agent of some kind?" she asked, referencing Agent120. "Maybe Ben knows him? He must work in one of the film agencies. He sounds lovely!" she said.

If Hilary was an honest critic, Juliet was my biggest unconditional supporter. Wanting me to get over Henry, she was always suggesting that I date lots of people. Online dating hadn't yet taken off in the UK, and it was rare to date multiple people at once. Instead, you'd court one person and hope it worked out. Juliet wanted me to take the opposite approach.

I'd wrapped up my afternoon meetings and walked down to Flynn's, eager but nervous. What if I'd just had beginner's luck and this was the guy I ended up marrying?

As I neared the bar, I passed by a tobacco shop. This was the first *real* first date I'd been on in nearly three years. I didn't count all of the set-ups and blind dates I'd gone on in the past few months. A cigarette would calm my nerves—I could just have one and then throw the rest away.

I was my usual fifteen minutes early, so I stood under the awning and inhaled. I'd printed out part of Glen's profile and filed those pages inside of an *Economist* magazine—to passersby, it looked like I was reading an article, not reviewing all of the details of my probable future husband. I wanted to impress him, so I tried to learn as much about Glen as possible. Without a last name I didn't get very far, but I at least wanted to remember his likes and dislikes for our conversation.

As I was looking at his photos, I saw someone coming toward me who looked like Glen's much shorter, much rounder, and significantly older brother.

"Are you Amy?" he asked.

Old photos. He'd used old photos and lied about his height and weight.

I smiled wearily. I could run away screaming or give this a shot. So what if he was a solid three inches shorter than me? Who cared if he was a little—okay, a lot—overweight? We'd connected so well during that instant message session.

He held the door for me as we walked inside.

Flynn's was only half-full, so we chose a booth toward the stage. There were two waitresses leaning on the bar, doodling something on a napkin, and the bartender was draped over his register watching a soccer game. A girl was teetering in too-high heels on stage, slurring the words to "Don't Rain on My Parade."

Because it was karaoke night, Flynn's had thick binders of song choices along with sharpened pencils and scraps of paper on each of the tables. As soon as we sat down, Glen looked at the bar and shot his arm in the air, snapping his fingers for attention. Mortified, I stared straight into the binder, trying not to make eye contact with anyone.

One of the waitresses came over with an empty tray and a notepad. "So I take it you're ready to order?" she sneered. I immediately wanted to apologize, but all I could do was ask for a Diet Coke and offer an empathetic smile.

"Long Island Iced Tea," Glen said. "But don't water it down with ice." What was it with men ordering Long Island Iced Teas on dates with me?

"What should we sing first?" he asked. "What do you like?"

Oh, what the hell. At this point, what did it matter? "George Michael," I said. "George Michael is an amazing musician. Most people just know him from his time in Wham! . . ."

Glen shot his arm in the air again, this time staring right at me. "High five!" he yelled too loudly.

I reluctantly tapped his hand with mine and kept talking. "'Careless Whisper' was one of the first eighties songs to really feature a saxophone like they used to do in the big band era," I said. "You could argue that most of the big ballads from the eighties borrowed from what he was doing."

The waitress came back with our drinks and put coasters in front of us on the table. Glen enthusiastically reached for his glass off of her tray. "Wait a minute, there, big guy," she said, pushing his arm out of the way.

"Okay, I'll give you the sax solo," Glen said, shooting his high-five hand in the air again. "I love that song. 'Careless Whisper'! Nice!"

Really? Do we really have to keep doing this?

"The point is, George Michael is a gifted musician," I continued. "Do you know that song 'Freedom'? But the 1990 version, not the original one," I asked, singing a few bars of the chorus. "That was his 'fuck you' song to the record industry. In the video, he set the jukebox and his leather jacket on fire . . . Anyhow, I also like that he's socially conscious. He was making a comment on the state of the industry. Did you know he originally wanted to be a journalist?"

"I did not know that," Glen said, resting his elbows on the table as he sucked huge mouthfuls of alcohol out of his straw.

"Actually, we never talked about what you do," I said, changing the subject. "You're an agent?"

"Nah, I'm one of the assistant managers of the Best Buy on Columbus Avenue," he said.

Stupid fucking Amy. Why did I pay attention to the username?

I knew there was nothing wrong with managing a retail store. My dad had made a career of managing large department stores—the hours were rough, but it was a good living. It's just that with his username, I'd imagined a talent or literary agent.

"Someday, I'm going to go back to school and finish my degree and then become a sports agent," he explained.

Someday? You're in your mid-forties!

"In college I played baseball, but I was also in a fraternity and I partied too much. Basically I just cared about sports. I flunked out my sophomore year and went to Best Buy. But the job is awesome. I get to control what's on the television sets, so when the Mets are playing, I can make this, like, wall of TVs showing the game!" he said, hand up in the air.

"High five," I muttered under my breath, tapping his hand again. Meantime, Bon Jovi's "Living on a Prayer" started playing while another woman got onstage.

"I effing love this song!" Glen said as she started to sing along with her.

Effing? Can't he say the word *fuck* like a normal person? I glanced down at my watch. It had only been fifteen minutes. How long did I have to stay? I wanted to be polite—Glen was clearly enjoying himself. But there was no *effing* way I was going out with this guy again.

While she finished, the bartender announced the next performer. "Let's welcome Glen to the stage next to sing A-ha's 'Take on Me,'" the voice boomed as Glen rushed up to the stage. The familiar electronic drum track started, followed by a bouncy synthesizer riff. Glen looked out at the crowd, swiveled his hips a little, ran his hand through his hair, and brought the mic up to his lips.

We're talking away . . .
I don't know what I'm to say. I'll say it anyway . . .

Some of the drunk girls were now standing right next to the stage, dancing along with him. He was working the whole area, singing directly to some of them and even stopping to kiss one woman's hand. The end of the song neared, and I clenched, thinking about the high note he'd have to hit. Glen ran back to the center of the stage, looked right at me, and belted out, exactly on pitch, "In a day . . ." Glen had transformed from a diminutive college dropout into a karaoke rock god.

The drunk girls screamed and even the waitresses seemed into it. The bartender came back over the speakers. "Glen, stay on that stage for your next number . . . ," he said.

I recognized that familiar saxophone intro. It was the big song at my bat mitzvah, when everyone finally got to slow dance. I'd seen the video a million times, with George wearing his black suit and holding on to a rope while singing "I'm never gonna dance again . . ."

"This next one is for my girlfriend, Amy!" Glen shouted over the crowd. "This is for you, baby . . ."

Wait. Wait . . . not me. I twisted my neck around—people were looking at me now, applauding. *Me, Amy?* No . . . I just met this guy. What the fuck is he doing?

I scrambled to find a five-dollar bill in my wallet, involuntarily shaking my head the entire time. I threw it along with some loose change on the table and ducked out the door before he saw that I'd left.

I got home and plopped my bag on the couch, and as I did, the Marlboro Lights I was supposed to throw away fell out. *After tonight, I deserve another one*, I thought. I grabbed the pack and my laptop and went out to the patio.

I sat down at the table and slid a cigarette out of the pack. As I lit and inhaled, I started an email message to Hilary, Juliet, my mom, and a few other assorted friends and relatives:

To: Mom; Dad; Hilary; Juliet; Liz; Jenny; Mary; Sharon
From: Amy Webb

Subject: Agent of Delusion!

You're never going to believe this date tonight. Agent120 seemed perfect. In his profile, he was attractive, looked athletic, and was dressed well.

So much for trusting online photos.

He's about six inches shorter and a solid thirty pounds heavier than he listed, and the photos were clearly taken in college.

But here's the best part. He took me to karaoke night at a local bar. After high-fiving me a dozen times, he went onstage and sang "Take on Me." (Surprisingly, he wasn't that bad.) He stayed onstage to start another song, and yelled, "This is for my girlfriend, Amy!" in front of the entire fucking bar!!!

Oh, and apparently he doesn't say the word "fuck" either. Just "eff."

What. The. EFF?!?

Miserable night,
Amy

As I hit Send, I considered the purpose of online dating sites. Wasn't the point to help filter through people like Glen so that I'd get to my future husband quicker? He and I had nothing in common besides a love of eighties music.

Then again, JDate hadn't actually set us up on that date. I'd looked at his profile and liked his photos. He instant messaged me, and without vetting him at all or even talking on the phone first, I agreed to go out with him.

Hilary was right—I should have taken more time to get to know him first.

4 | The Dates

Two hundred dollars for dinner and a
roadside flare of weed.

I spent the next several weeks going between JDate, eHarmony,
and Match.com. By now, all three were sending me matches,
and while I was insisting on having at least a quick phone call with each
potential date first, I'd followed the advice given to me by Hilary and
my friends and extended family. I was supposed to cast a very wide net
and date everyone, so that I didn't accidentally miss out on the perfect man.

The first several dates could not have gone more horrifically wrong.

Match.com set me up with Jim, an IT director at one of the local
universities. He'd reached out to me first, using the Match.com email
system. We sent a few messages, then talked on the phone. He had a
deep voice and made me laugh, but I didn't think we'd have any chemistry in person. He had thinning blond hair, had been raised Catholic,
and didn't like to read. That said, he was a foodie and liked to talk
about cooking, which I found somewhat interesting. He asked if I
wanted to have dinner with him at one of the nicer, white-tablecloth
restaurants in town, saying that he was an acquaintance of the chef.

The night of our date, I waited outside the restaurant, lit cigarette in hand. I now always had a pack of Marlboro Lights stashed in my bag. Unless he said something specifically negative about smoking or was someone who I thought might actually be husband material, I'd decided to allow myself one smoke before a date. I rationalized this by promising myself that it would be the only time during the week that I lit up.

As I stood outside smoking, I saw a portly man walking up the sidewalk. It was definitely Jim—I recognized his face immediately. But he was now significantly heavier than the photos he'd posted. As he neared, I saw that his button-down shirt was being pulled out of his pants as he walked, to reveal a swatch of skin just around his belly button. It reminded me of my high school chemistry teacher, who suffered from the same affliction. "The Triangle of Doom," we called it. And it was headed directly toward me.

"Hey, Amy," he said, wheezing a bit, hand outstretched.

I shook his hand back. "Thanks for asking me out," I said.

Jim opened the door for me and went up to the hostess stand. "There should be a reservation for two under Jim," he said. When the maître d' wanted to seat us upstairs, I grew concerned about his making it up the steps.

A waiter came to our table, relighting the candle in a little tea glass. Almost all of the wax had melted so that now there was just a wick and some metal left. "Thanks," Jim said to the waiter, smiling at him. He may have lied about his weight, but Jim was exceptionally polite to all of the restaurant staff, which I appreciated. When I worked at the Silver Moon diner in high school, all of the customers had assumed that I was uneducated and incapable of writing down their orders correctly. "Make sure that steak is done medium rare, honey. That means pink on the inside," someone would say. "You're ordering an eight-dollar steak at a shitty diner," I'd want to say back. "It's not even a half-inch thick. You're either getting it well-done or raw, you asshat."

Jim was nice. And he did seem knowledgeable about food. I decided to forgive his schlubby appearance and to give him an honest shot.

First he looked over the long wine list and ordered a bottle of red something or other. "What year is it?" he asked the waiter, since it was hard to find on the menu. As they debated vintages, I found the bottle and the price—sixty dollars seemed expensive for what would only be a few glasses of wine. I didn't know if I should be impressed that he knew what to order or embarrassed by what seemed like excess.

Then he insisted on ordering three appetizers: barbecue pork belly on top of salad, bacon-wrapped scallops, and a bowl of special olives that had a name I couldn't pronounce. I'd grown up in a family where each person got to order exactly one thing for dinner. If you wanted steak, you got steak. If you wanted the deep-fried cheese-stick appetizer or chocolate sundae dessert, they'd better be filling, because that's all you would get to eat.

"Then I'll have the lamb chops as my main," he continued. "She'll have the grilled Chilean sea bass special," he said, looking at me. "Trust me," he said. "You are going to love it!"

As the waiter started to bring out the first few dishes, Jim explained why the ingredients worked well together. "They do this with a dry cider and honey," he said. "There's a hint of a spice in here too," he said, taking another bite. "Can you figure out what it is?"

I did find the discussion interesting. I'd never eaten pork belly and was very relieved to learn that it tasted just like bacon.

We finished our main course, and the waiter came back to see if we wanted dessert. "I'm really too full," I said. "Can we skip it?" Jim agreed and asked for the check.

The waiter came back, sliding a black folder onto the middle of our table. Jim looked at me and smiled. "I'm going to the bathroom," he said. "Be right back."

The way Jim was ordering, I'd assumed that he was paying. He seemed so confident with the menu choices, not paying attention to prices or asking if I cared what came to the table. It seemed like a strange time to leave the table, I thought.

After several minutes, Jim came back and sat down, still not touching the bill. The waiter came back. "Can I take this?" he asked, motioning at the bill. Again Jim did nothing. It was fine if he wasn't paying for the entire meal, but shouldn't we both be reaching for our wallets?

During the nervous, awkward pause that lasted longer than it should have, the waiter and Jim both looked at me. The last bit of wax in the votive was now gone, and the candle flickered in defeat before surrendering and going out completely.

Fine, I said to myself as Jim stared at me, saying nothing. I guess I'm paying. I opened the bill and read the final amount: 160 dollars before tip. That was a fifth of my rent. I reached into my bag for my wallet and handed over my credit card.

I signed the receipt and stood up, expecting to shake hands with Jim and part ways. Instead, he put his meaty, pork belly–greased hand on the small of my back, as if to guide me out of the restaurant. Outside, he turned to face me.

"Well, good night," I said. "It was . . . interesting." I turned to the right and started walking toward my car, which was parked at a meter just up the street.

"Oh, I'm headed in that direction too," he said.

Great. Now I'm stuck walking—slowly—with this jerk.

"Do you smoke?" he asked.

Oh, what the hell, at this point I may as well have another cigarette. I knew I'd promised to have only a single smoke before dates, but I'd just blown two hundred dollars on dinner for some stranger I never wanted to see again. I could have saved myself the time and just lit a stack of money on fire.

"Yeah, I smoke," I said, searching for the pack of Marlboro Lights in my bag.

He reached into his shirt pocket. It was dark in the restaurant and I hadn't noticed the lump earlier. He pulled out what looked like a cigar, which only made me dislike him more. I hated their taste and tangy smell. He walked over to a bench just at the edge of a public park, struck a match, and sat down.

I smelled it instantly. Cigars have a certain stench, yes, but this was different. It was very familiar, acrid. And I hadn't smelled it since college. I looked up, and Jim was holding the biggest joint I'd ever seen. Like, a roadside flare of weed. He put it back up to his wet lips, took a very long, deep drag, and held it in.

That explained the wheezing.

I looked around in a panic. First he makes me spend two hundred dollars on dinner, and now we're both going to get arrested. Fantastic! *Fuck!! Where's my fucking car?*

"They say that pot can cause impotence," he said. "Do you want some?" he asked me, holding out the joint. I crinkled my brow and shook his hand away, trying desperately to locate my car on the street. "I mean, yes, I have a hard time getting it up lately. But how important is a hard dick? I can pleasure a woman in other ways," he said, holding up his chubby fingers, rotating them in concentric circles.

Speechless, I walked away in a hurry, zigging and zagging around cars so he wouldn't see which one was mine.

By date number seven, it was becoming too cumbersome to email all of my friends and family to regale them with what had happened each night. I'd have to go home first, sit down at my kitchen table, and try to remember all the horrible details.

I'd thought momentarily about setting up a blog and publicly posting the details of each date. Though I was pissed and hating most of these dates, I wasn't mean-spirited enough to embarrass all of these men. Also, I didn't want anyone to find out, knowing it could potentially make it more difficult for me to find my future husband. So instead, I created an email distribution list and decided to send a date-update message to the entire group rather than individually to my mom, sister, and friends.

As a result, I decided to only meet dates at Longshots, a pub near my house where there was an open WiFi network. Longshots was well lit, just dark enough to set a good mood without forcing everyone to squint in order to see. It was a bar with overstuffed couches and plush chairs, and it was just as well-known for coffee as it was for mixed drinks. Though it often got busy, there were always places to sit. Lots of people went there on first dates.

Longshots worked well because I could bring my laptop with me. I'd create an email template to rate the men I was meeting, and I'd then sneak into the bathroom during each date to send real-time updates of what was happening.

I drafted the email copy, explaining exactly how my new rating system would work:

High fives. If a guy wants to touch me, by all means he should. He can put a hand on my leg or on my forearm. But manufacturing a reason to wave his arm at me and then forcing me to slap him is just so juvenile.

Stupid sexual remarks. I had a hard time getting sleazy Silver Moon diner manager Chaz out of my mind and the line he'd used on Hilary to see if I'd sleep with him. A man should flirt, not bludgeon me with clumsy sexual comments.

Number of misused vocabulary words. I can't respect someone who abuses the language we speak. When a guy makes a stupid vocabulary mistake, he sounds dumb. If he uses a "myriad of" mangled words and phrases, I'll mark that against him, "irregardless" of how cute he is.

Times he checked his mobile. I want someone who's interested in me and who's present in our conversation. If he's checking his mobile phone every few minutes, that means his mind is elsewhere, possibly with another girl.

Units of alcohol consumed per twenty minutes. These idiots drinking Long Island Iced Teas and trying to get me drunk on first dates are not husband material.

Questions asked about my job. I love what I do, and I like to talk about it. Dates should be interested and engaged in what I have to say.

I had two goals: I needed motivation to continue enduring horrible date after horrible date, and going to the bathroom with my laptop to email everyone the details seemed like a fun way to entertain myself. My other and arguably more important goal was to convince my friends and family that just relaxing my standards and going out with everyone who asked was a bad idea. I knew that if I started collecting and sharing quantifiable data, I'd have empirical evidence to prove that it wasn't me. I wasn't the problem. The men of Philadelphia were.

Occasionally, dates started off well at Longshots and I didn't feel compelled to visit the bathroom. My hope was that I wouldn't have to go at all. I did, actually, want to find the perfect man. But when it was obvious that the date was headed nowhere—I could usually predict a disaster in the first five minutes—I engineered it so that every twenty minutes I'd excuse myself to the ladies'.

The women's bathroom at Longshots was surprisingly roomy and bright for a restroom in a bar. There were two stalls and a handicapped area, which included a toilet and sink. I'd set up shop there, first wiping down the sink and balancing my laptop on it. If I had a lot to write, I'd take out the ziplock bag of toilet seat covers I started carrying with me for just this purpose. I'd cover the seat and sit down, still wearing pants, to fill out my email template.

Most of the messages went like this:

To: Friends & Family
From: Amy Webb

Subject: John—Email #1

Tonight's Date: I'm out with someone who says he's an orthopedic surgeon. Supposedly Jewish. He's 6'2", bald, and good-looking . . . could be a stand-in member for the Blue Man Group sans makeup. Maybe it's the black turtleneck.

To: Friends & Family
From: Amy Webb

Subject: John—Email #2

Update: He's just spent the last 10 minutes explaining something about cabinetmaking and mitering wood. I'm currently examining him for sawdust.

High fives: 2
Stupid sexual remarks: 5
Bad vocab: 1
Checked mobile: 1
Units of alcohol: 1 beer
Questions about my job: 0

Back in a few.

To: Friends & Family
From: Amy Webb

Subject: John—Email #3

Update: Things are progressively getting worse. I'm pretty sure he's not a surgeon. He can't seem to pronounce "anesthesiologist" correctly and hasn't yet answered my question about which hospital he's affiliated with. I think he works at some cabinet shop somewhere. His hand is also scratchy, which I know because he's an aggressive high-fiver.

Time to sound the mobile phone alarm.

High fives: 4
Stupid sexual remarks: 5
Bad vocab: 3
Checked mobile: 2
Units of alcohol: 2 beers
Questions about my job: 0

I wanted to prove to everyone that while I was giving it the old college try, online dating was pointless for me. It hadn't made it easier for me to meet the right man; it only made it easier to meet a whole bunch of wrong men, the kind who lied in their profiles or who had major character faults. There had been a few I'd consider going out with again, but the overwhelming majority were comically bad.

For my own edification, I'd been keeping a spreadsheet and recording the data I was collecting in my email updates.

It was a small sample size, but I started to look for correlations and found that:

- The more times someone high-fived me, the more likely it was that he would misuse the English language.

First Name	Site	Stated Occupation	Actual Occupation	# High Fives	# Stupid Sexual Remarks	Highlights
Aaron	JDate	Doctor	General practitioner, MD	3	2	Said his last girlfriend refused to get a Brazilian bikini wax, which was another way she wasn't adventurous enough for him. So he broke up with her.
Andy	JDate	Lawyer	Lawyer—estates and trusts	0	1	He was trying to use some metaphor about me riding his motorcycle.
Brendan	Match	Teacher	Unemployed teacher, was mainly playing in a ska band at nights.	0	0	NA
Danny	Match	Advertising	Absolutely no idea. He wouldn't talk about it.	0	1	In the first 20 minutes, he asked me if I'd ever experimented with another woman.
Jamie	Match	Lawyer	Lawyer—insurance	4	0	NA
Jim	Match	IT	System administrator	0	1	Is the ability to get it up important?
John	JDate	Orthopedic surgeon	Definitely not an MD. Likely a cabinet maker or has other job in a woodshop.	4	5	Tits are more important than ass.
Kevin	JDate	Construction	General contractor, owns his own company	0	1	Had three kids he didn't disclose on JDate
Kyle	Match	Programmer	Coder for GPS company	8	0	NA
Matt	JDate	Journalist	Freelancer, doesn't seem to be working very much	0	7	He went on and on about a group of strippers he was supposedly friends with. Whole story seemed made up.
Matt #2	JDate	Lawyer	Lawyer—litigation	0	6	Referred to his penis as "The Captain" and himself in third person over and over.
Nick	Match	MBA student	MBA student	1	1	This chick dared me to pierce my cock, and I just went for it.
Ryan	JDate	IT	Data analyst of some kind	0	0	NA

# Bad Vocab	Word(s)	# Checked Mobile	Units Alcohol	Type	# Questions About My Job	Length of Date (in Hours)
0	NA	2	1	scotch	0	1
1	"mute point"	3	0	NA	0	1
0	NA	0	5	shots of something, not sure what it was	0	1.5
1	"for all intensive purposes"	1	2	beers	1	1
3	"irregardless" (said it three times)	6	2	beers	1	1
1	"a myriad of"	0	4	bottle of expensive wine	1	1.5
3	"anestethist" instead of "anesthesiologist"; "irregardless" (said it twice)	2	2	beers	0	1
0	NA	2	0	NA	3	0.5
2	"irregardless"; "expresso" instead of "espresso"	0	2	beers	1	2
1	"over-zealot"	0	3	1 buttery nipple, 2 kamakazis	1	1.5
1	"orientated"	10	1	scotch	1	1
1	"proactive"	3	1	red wine	6	3
1	"it takes two to tangle"	3	3	2 cosmopolitans, 1 gin and tonic	2	1.5

- Guys who ordered more than one shot during our date tended to lie in their profiles about what they did for a living.
- Scotch drinkers seemed to be more interested in kinky sex.
- Lawyers checked their mobile phones the most and were the least interested in what I did for a living.
- MBA students and graduates avoided saying "woman," instead using "chick" and "girl." They'd use "lady" for women older than twenty-eight.

Online, all of these men seemed great, and not just to me. Empirically, they were long-term-relationship material. But when we get together in person, it was clear we were a terrible match.

My mom would always call the morning after one of my email rants, and we'd laugh about how ridiculous my last date was. Still, she'd warn me about being too picky. "It's like you're going into it every time with a bad attitude," she said. "If you go out on dates looking for people's faults, that's all you'll see."

I often thought about giving up and canceling my subscriptions for a month or two, but then I'd meet a couple who had successfully found each other online. Between my mom, Hilary, and my other friends, I caved to peer pressure and agreed to continue dating. "The right guy will find you when you're least expecting it," my mom said over and over. "Until then, you have to think positively and create a situation where you have opportunities."

Meantime, I found that I wasn't the only one with this problem. I was discovering that lots of people had awful dating stories of their own. Sure, we all had plenty of dates—but where were the soul mates we were promised on all the websites and in the commercials now playing on TV?

5 | Bad Algorithms

Online dating sites are broken.

O kay. Let me step out of the story for a minute. I want to explain some important things I learned about the world of online dating, now that I have some perspective. Trust me—this is a worthwhile divergence.

At this point in our story, I've been going on lots of bad dates using JDate and Match.com, and I'm just about to sign on to eHarmony. All three of those sites promise that they have special formulas and algorithms that match members to their ideals.

I'd been growing curious about how these sites work, since none of them were doing a good job of finding me a husband. So I started doing some research. I wanted to know what was happening underneath the hood. I thought that if I had better information, I might be able to meet more qualified men.

What you're going to read next is an explanation of what I discovered. It's fascinating, I promise. So keep reading! Worst case, you'll dominate the dating-trivia category the next time it's on *Jeopardy!* . . .

———

What first lured me to online dating was the promise of using math to identify my perfect match. I'd seen commercials and magazine ads highlighting the technology behind the various websites, and to me it made perfect sense that data and math could do a much better job of bringing together compatible people than hope, fate, and a few Friday night cocktails.

That advertising has obviously worked. While most new couples meet at work or school or are introduced by friends or relatives, the third most common way that couples now meet is via online dating sites. More than fifteen hundred online dating services are operating worldwide, from general sites like Match.com and eHarmony to niche sites catering to vegetarians, devout Christians, full-time farmers, and even fans of Ayn Rand's *The Fountainhead*. It's a lucrative space too: The online dating market is worth an estimated two billion dollars annually.

One explanation for the explosion in online dating is that many of us aren't doing a very good job finding long-lasting matches on our own. Today, nearly half of all marriages will end in divorce in the U.S., and that's without accounting for the recent spate of celebrity sham-marriage outliers. In 1961, slightly less than 1 percent of married couples—one out of every 104—filed for divorce in the U.S., according to government statistics.

Now, I have a feeling you're already aware that during the past few decades, divorce rates have been escalating. You probably even know at least one couple that's recently separated. Let's stop for a moment and consider what might be going wrong.

It's more culturally acceptable for us to file for divorce now than it was in 1961. Our religious and governmental institutions have made it easier to legally untangle ourselves from marriage without dire consequences. Back then, if a couple wanted to divorce, they'd first have to argue before a judge that one of them participated in an act incompatible with marriage, and whatever that act was required proof. If the husband or wife had been accused of cheating, the divorcing party would need to produce some kind of evidence: a love letter, a set of photographs, or a private detective's official report.

Another common obstacle to divorce in the past was having to pay costly attorney fees. Today, however, there are a number of digital resources available that allow couples to file for a few hundred—rather than several thousand—dollars. In most states, if the couple agrees to a noncontested divorce, they can divide their assets and even custody of their kids via a few simple web-based forms.

Perhaps the most reasonable explanation for our high divorce rates is the most obvious one: We're simply choosing the wrong partners, and we no longer have to suffer through life in terrible marriages. Many of us fall into relationships because of early infatuation (high school sweethearts, college romance), convenience (work colleagues, same circle of friends), geography (small town and slim pickings), or internal or external pressures (biological clock), or because we've simply given up on finding someone who's insanely great.

I'd come very close to marriage twice, once with Allen and once with Henry. Luckily, both relationships ended before we had the chance to file for divorce. Several of my friends weren't as lucky. They'd gotten married in their twenties, and while some were separating amicably and cheaply, others were hung up in divorce court arguing over property and alimony. Yes, I was still single, but at least I wasn't trapped in a miserable relationship or arguing about who got to keep the cheesy hand-painted bride-and-groom champagne flutes we never used. I was actively dating and using online sites to meet new people.

In my case, it wasn't a lack of people to date, but instead an absence of real compatibility. I was growing impatient, and my Disastrous Dating Data chart had now topped fifty unique entries. I was no longer that college freshman looking to play around. Now I was the one looking for my soul mate, with whom I could settle down and get married.

As much as my mom was ready for a wedding, she constantly reminded me that I'd developed a bad habit of being completely impatient while simultaneously refusing to accept the options in front of me. Either I needed to consider the men I already knew who were interested in dating me and learn to accept some of their faults, or I'd have to be disciplined enough to trust that Mr. Right would eventually find me. "The moment you stop looking, he'll appear in your life," she'd often say. "It will happen when you're least expecting it."

Patience was a skill my mom had mastered. By now, she was in her third round of chemotherapy. Not her third session, but her third full treatment cycle. Most people complete a handful of chemo sessions along with some radiation to eradicate their cancer. That wasn't our situation. Since doctors were unable to find the primary site of her cancer, there was no way to pinpoint and attack it. Chemo was being used to slow the growth of the tumors she'd already developed. As it killed off the rapidly dividing cancer cells, it was also killing what was left of her healthy bone marrow, digestive, and immune system cells.

If I couldn't be there in person with her for her treatments, I'd call and talk to her on the phone. Her head wrapped in a scarf, she'd be lying back in a big, overstuffed reclining chair, covered in one of the knitted blankets her friends had made for her. An electronic pump with three bags of fluid would be wheeled next to her, and she'd spend six hours waiting for the toxic chemicals to drain into her frail body.

The oncology center she visited once a week didn't have individual treatment rooms. Instead, there were eight chairs positioned throughout a large sterile room. She got to know some of the other patients well, and it was always difficult when someone didn't show up for a weekly treatment. There were only two reasons a patient would stop coming to the center, and in the context of her reality, both were too painful to consider.

"It's never going to happen," I'd say. "I can't seem to change my situation no matter what I do."

"Honey, you're stressing out too much about this," she'd answer. Even with her weak voice and the ambient beeps of her electronic pump, our daily phone calls made me feel like everything would eventually work itself out. "This isn't like your career. You can't outwork everyone else in order to get what you want. You just need to relax and to stop thinking about it. Be patient," she'd say.

It was increasingly difficult to argue with someone for whom patience and acceptance were painful inevitabilities.

"I'm not advocating that you settle," my mom would often argue. Instead, she asked if perhaps I'd overlooked some good qualities in the men I was meeting. "Who cares if someone mispronounces a word? Have you forgotten that your own spelling was so bad all throughout elementary school that at one point, we were going to test to see if you had a learning disability? You need to give these poor men a break."

I considered the men I'd met recently. Most of our dates were so miserable that I wanted desperately to close the evening with a hand-shake and a promise never to contact each other again. Since that's not socially acceptable, I'd agree to check my calendar for the following weekend and get in touch over email.

Still, I knew I was coming off as disingenuous. I'm a terrible liar. I have no ability to mask the disdain I feel once someone disappoints me, regardless of the situation or personal dynamic involved. I once worked for an editor who, in a big staff meeting, was trying to describe the city of Chicago and actually hesitated mid-word before pronouncing the *s* in *Illinois*. He was an American journalist, and he should damn well know that the *s* is silent. That may sound petty to you, but it's akin to a die-hard hockey fan getting the Detroit Red Wings and Philadelphia Flyers logos confused. Or a trained chef not understanding the differ-ence between *béchamel* and *velouté* sauces. After his gaffe, my editor knew he'd made a big mistake. Everyone in the room knew it. But it was only me who stared him right in the face, squinted quizzically, and shook my head, embarrassing him and ensuring my early dismissal from that job.

Was it too much to expect a date to at least split the bill with me? To not smoke pot on a public sidewalk? Why was I even in a position to ask these questions? Clearly my standards weren't high enough, and I hadn't been using a strong enough filter to eliminate potential bad dates before they had the chance to begin.

Whereas I hid in bathroom stalls rating and ranking all of the dates I went on in order to mathematically prove what a miserable time I was having, it seems as though many of the people I knew had instead rationalized their ways through their own woebegone situations. One married couple I knew had met in their midthirties. They may have at one point been passionately romantic, but they were now in their late forties and bickered constantly. She had once confided in me that he probably wasn't "the one," but she wanted to settle down and have children, and she'd run out of time to be choosy. One day, the husband suddenly quit his job as a corporate lawyer and decided to pursue yoga—which meant no more private school for the kids and a serious change in their posh lifestyle. He moved to an obscure yoga colony for a month to study with a self-appointed guru. My friend contended that it was just a phase and that he'd eventually land on his feet at another firm. Midlife crisis or not, this was the kind of thing you should discuss openly with a spouse. The fact that he made such a drastic unilateral decision indicated that there were lots of other cracks beneath the surface of their marriage. And indeed, it turned out that the couple had been seriously arguing for years. She kept insisting that things would get better, while he just wanted out of the marriage. They were a bad match from the beginning, and now a fear of being alone and having to start over is all that was keeping them together.

For many of us, finding and meeting people isn't our biggest obstacle to long-term-relationship happiness. Yet historically that's the problem that humankind has attempted to solve. In nearly every culture and throughout every generation there have been matchmakers tasked with filtering communities in order to bring together two people and their families. In feudal China, a matchmaker would work on behalf of a man's family. The matchmaker would submit a prospective bride's name and birthday to a fortune-teller to determine whether or not the couple would be happy. If the match was deemed auspicious, the families would begin exchanging gifts and seek out a lucky date to tie the knot. In old Jewish culture, a *shadchen* acted as a go-between for young men and women, taking into consideration each family's standing in the community, shared values and character attributes, economic status, and even the amount of property owned.

In a way, these ancient matchmakers used their own formulas to determine whether two families should be united in marriage. A matchmaker's endgame was almost never to create a fulfilled, happy couple. It was about uniting two groups of people to ensure the survival of a bloodline and to grow a community. This process was so important that until recently, in many cultures it was impossible to get married without a matchmaker's involvement. That story arc in *Romeo and Juliet*? Shakespeare didn't invent a scenario where two lovers were kept apart because their families wouldn't allow a marriage. That was everyday life. Expectations of romantic love and the freedom to marry whomever we choose are relatively new concepts. With less emphasis on class and religion in modern societies, most of us now seek out love on our own and create unions just as miserable as all those formed by the matchmakers before us.

Once we were able to choose our own mates, we confronted another challenge: the difficulty of finding happiness. Thousands of doctors, academics, and others began researching romantic love in the hope of developing a set of rules for finding long-lasting relationship bliss. Pick your favorite method: zodiac signs, blood types, facial features, religion, emotional IQ. So-called relationship experts advocated their own methods and promised to help us identify the spouses of our dreams.

Of course, this didn't work either. For one thing, blood-typing and genetic screening turns out to be a great determining factor in successful pregnancies, but not such a great way to forecast whether someone's chronic messiness would eventually lead to nightly arguments. It was also too simplistic a method of cataloguing our millions of traits, nuances, and internal desires. We're complex beings, not produce. Sorting and filtering us so that we pair off with exactly the right mate was really too difficult for us to do on our own. It was a problem that could be tackled with math . . . and, as it turns out, computers.

So let me take you back to 1965 and walk you through a story that's going to sound strangely familiar to a plotline you already know well. Late one weekend night, two Harvard undergraduates, Jeff Tarr and Vaughan Morrill, were sitting in their room lamenting yet another lonely weekend. At the time, Harvard was still men only. Even with a college full of girls across campus at Radcliffe, Tarr and Morrill were perpetually single. Motivated in part by curiosity but mainly by a strong desire to meet girls, they started mapping out a computer system that could codify attractiveness and compatibility and then create matches based on statistics and probability.

Tarr and Morrill were joined by two more students, David Crump and Douglas Ginsburg, and together they drafted questionnaires that Harvard and Radcliffe students would answer. Then they paid a friend a hundred dollars to build a simple computer program that would match five students together who scored a high statistical probability of success. They called it Operation Match, and "computer dating" was born.

Using personality surveys that had to be filled out by hand (there were no websites or even personal computers in those days), would-be daters answered 135 questions, such as "Is extensive sexual activity in preparation for marriage part of 'growing up'?" and "Do you believe in a God who answers prayer?" Answers were inputted into punch cards that had to be manually fed into a room-size computer, which they had to rent and were permitted to use only between two A.M. and four A.M. on Sundays. The data was compared with and checked against all of the other answers to produce probable matches.

Students paid three dollars plus the price of a stamp—equivalent to about twenty-one dollars today—to participate and receive matches. They'd write answers to the personality survey by hand and then drop the survey in the mail. Then they would wait patiently for a response, sometimes up to a few weeks. Operation Match created a list of five potential dates, along with contact information, and sent the details back to the students. While the list included a personalized letter and descriptions of each date, there were no photos. Of every hundred Operation Match users, an average of fifty-two were women.

The service gained notoriety, and it wasn't long before students at many other schools sent surveys in to Operation Match. Once Tarr and Morrill began expanding to other single-sex schools, they customized some of the questions and added special comments for each campus. The new introduction to Harvard students read: "Have you any buxom blondes who like poetry?" The women at Vassar were greeted with: "Where, O where is Superman?"

At exactly the same time, a graduate electrical engineering student at MIT, David DeWan, started working on his own system, Contact Incorporated. He was just up the street from Harvard and was using his own set of IBM punch cards. Contact Incorporated ran nearly identically to Operation Match, except that it charged slightly more (four dollars) and used more clinical language in its questionnaires. Contact Incorporated collected vital statistics, geographic data, and demographic information, as well as tastes and preferences. Under Contact Incorporated's "two-way matches," DeWan argued that he could match ideal candidates to each other, rather than sending members a profile or two matching a list of desired qualities.

DeWan publicly criticized his rival, telling *The Harvard Crimson* that Operation Match's questionnaire was "less sophisticated, appealing to the big, Mid-west universities." Meantime, Tarr and Morrill gave a false tip to campus police that DeWan was planning to cover Harvard Yard in toilet paper. Things turned sour, and fast. Harvard officials prohibited DeWan from distributing questionnaires in Winthrop House—which was Tarr and Morrill's home base—citing a permit violation. They ejected him from the property, but it wasn't the first time someone from Contact Incorporated had been stopped. A questionnaire distributor was similarly thwarted by police on Yale's campus.

Back and forth they went. But with a strong lead and a growing national student audience, Operation Match became less distracted with Contact Incorporated and more involved in growing its business. Soon, Tarr and Morrill had amassed one hundred thousand users and millions in the bank. In the summer of Operation Match's first year, college students from as far away as California were signing on. They'd hired a dozen full-time staff to manage the service—someone had to create all those punch cards—and one of the early Wall Street firms dedicated to building tech companies, Data Network, came on board to advise. They established offices in New York in order to open the service up to the general, nonstudent public.

Tarr and Morrill became celebrities, appearing in a number of magazines and on television shows. Although DeWan's Contact Incorporated started to wither nine months into its existence, the success of Operation Match sparked a number of other early contenders. "Inevitably, the singles game is putting technology to use," *Life* magazine wrote in 1967, "and the computer-dating service is growing as steadily as the price of a share of IBM."

And then something interesting happened. It turned out that while kids at single-sex colleges were absolutely interested in using computers to find coeds to date, students in coed schools and others in the workforce had plenty of opportunity to mingle already. "It was easier when we had a captive audience, people at single-sex colleges with time on their hands and high hormone levels," Chris Walker, a founding member of the Operation Match team, told a reporter. "We all felt it was time to move on with real careers." Operation Match was sold to a student marketing company just two years after it launched, and its founders moved on to other projects.

If this story sounds familiar, it's because forty years later, another Harvard geek war broke out over a similarly groundbreaking new technology and thrust two feuding sets of students into the spotlight: Mark Zuckerberg and Eduardo Saverin, the founders of Facebook, and a pair known as the Winklevoss twins, who founded the now defunct ConnectU.

These nascent computer-dating services solved a crucial problem: College students wanted to meet others who were open to dating and who matched a certain set of desired criteria. While both Operation Match and Contact Incorporated used computers to achieve rudimentary matching for some of their members, neither managed to help everyone find their soul mates.

Nearly five decades later, online dating is once again popular, but the basic premise and architecture haven't evolved much from those original services. Operation Match promoted a "computer process" to introduce like-minded singles to each other. Today, dating sites use a different word—*algorithm*—to describe what is essentially the same basic system. The main difference is in sophistication.

Algorithm is really just a fancy name for the step-by-step process and calculations that are used while solving a problem. Think of an algorithm as you would a recipe for croissants. You need a set of ingredients: yeast, water, sugar, salt, flour, milk, oil, butter, and eggs. And you need a bunch of kitchen equipment: bowls, mixers, knife, baking sheet, oven, and some towels. Depending on how you put everything together, you could wind up with a flaky, delicate pastry or a hard lump of charred dough.

Algorithms are a shorthand way of writing out workflows. They're the step-by-step processes scientists use to think through complex problems, and the instructions that are given to computers to help process the results. In online dating, algorithms are what help sort through all of the data we're inputting, and they're what ultimately match us with others using the same service. In theory, whichever site has the best algorithm should be able to provide the best match.

If you asked a Jewish *shadchen* or a Chinese fortune-teller to write down their matchmaking methods, the resulting diagram would be a kind of algorithm. A *shadchen*'s formula might look something like this:

$$\text{Match Score} = \left[(C \times V \times E) \times .25 \right] + \left[(R \times K) \times .35 \right] + \left[\left(\binom{\text{Probability of}}{\text{Girl liking boy}} + \binom{\text{Probability of}}{\text{Families getting along}} \right) \times .40 \right]$$

Where: C = opinion of community
V = shared values
E = economic status of each family
R = Rabbi's approval
K = ability to have kids

It would be plugged into an algorithm that goes something like this:

```
For the entire community:
    match_probability := Compute_Match_Prob (person)
    if match_probability > max_prob:
        max_prob := match_probability
        best_match := person
return best_match
```

The *shadchen* would factor in a number of variables and would weigh each one according to priority. What did the community and rabbi think? Could the couple have children? What attributes did the families share? Then she'd consider how well the couple and their families might get along. Though she would never write down her decision-making process as a formula or use numerical values to predict a successful union, her blessing would be given based on how well a couple scored using the rudimentary algorithm she had in her head.

When friends asked me to introduce them to other friends or coworkers, I'd been using my own informal algorithm:

$$\text{Match Score} = \left[(S \times G) \times .55\right] - \left(P \times .45\right)$$

Where: S = Same interests
G = Ability to get along
P = probability that the date will go badly and the whole thing will become a total pain in my ass

Modern dating sites all promise top-secret magic algorithms that solve for what's referred to in the dating industry as the *tyranny of choice*. With millions of profiles logged in to online databases, there is a glut of choices. Surrounded by too many options, we become paralyzed, overwhelmed, and unable to make a decision. Some of us begin to think that we have infinite opportunities and become lured by the prospect of bigger, better deals. Others just want out, so they're willing to settle for someone who seems good enough at that moment in time.

The process of creating a successful dating site happens in many steps. Developing a set of algorithms is the start. Equally important is the data itself. It turns out that the design of a dating website and how it manages data collection is significantly more important than the algorithms alone in determining successful matches.

Dating sites require a steady stream of user data in order to function. They're hungry beasts that need constant feeding. How we enter our information and create our profiles is what differentiates each one of the dating services. While many still use the Operation Match–style basic questionnaire, a new crop of sites have emerged as alternatives to that original system.

One of the most popular online dating services, OkCupid, doesn't require a traditional profile at all and instead invites its users to create the questions asked of everyone on the site. Started by four students at—you guessed it—Harvard, the genesis of OkCupid was a collection of online self-quizzes and personality tests from a site the founders created called TheSpark.com, which also offered study guides called SparkNotes. Those quizzes begat SparkMatch, which allowed registered users to search for others with similar answers and types. The students sold SparkNotes to Barnes & Noble and used that money to begin working on a new kind of online dating service called OkCupid.

Unlike other dating sites, new users on OkCupid aren't required to answer a personality assessment or even to enter any vital statistics beyond gender and zip code. Once an account is created, users are offered sets of questions that are quirky and entertaining. The more questions you're willing to answer, the better your match outcome.

For each question, you provide three answers: your own answer, answers you're willing to accept from a potential match, and how important that question is to you. Example:

Question: Regardless of future plans, what's more interesting to you right now?
Sex
True Love

Plus: Answer I'll accept . . .
Sex
True Love

Plus: This question is . . .
Irrelevant

A little important
Somewhat important
Very important
Mandatory

OkCupid members have answered more than 250 million questions so far, and the average user voluntarily answers more than 200 questions while a member of the site. Others include: "Could you date someone who is really messy? (Yes / No)"; "What is the most exciting thing about getting to know someone new? (Discovering your shared interests / Discovering their body)"; "Do you enjoy intense intellectual conversations? (Yes / No)."

The system then starts to use some complex math to figure out how and when to match you with others. The nut they're trying to crack is a match percentage, and the process goes something like this: Let's say that you sign on to OkCupid and have answered 50 questions. Your answers are sorted and reviewed, and then the system evaluates your answers against a potential match to see how you've each satisfied the other person's preferences. Values are assigned to give each calculation the correct weight, with an emphasis on these two main variables: How much did the potential match's answers make you happy? How much did your answers make the potential match happy? OkCupid then calculates a match percentage by multiplying the answers that satisfied you and then taking the square root.

Some of the early OkCupid testers were the girlfriends and then wives of the four founders. As individuals, they would hop on the site to submit and answer questions in order to refine the algorithms they created. It turns out that OkCupid may have had a secret weapon. In 2004, Christopher Coyne married Jennifer Tarr, who herself was intimately familiar with the world of online dating and Harvard geekery. It was her father, Jeff Tarr, who cofounded Operation Match.

This wildly different approach earned OkCupid a spot in the U.S.

patent pool, and it caught the attention of InterActiveCorp (IAC), an Internet behemoth, which also happens to own *Newsweek* and Urbanspoon, as well as a competitor dating site: Match.com. OkCupid doesn't charge a subscription or membership fee; it instead relies on advertising. Since 2004, the site has earned an average of 1 million page views a month as well as a substantial amount of advertising revenue. In 2011, IAC acquired OkCupid for fifty million dollars in cash plus some other perks and benefits.

It's unusual for any algorithm-driven site to divulge its secret recipe. OkCupid is an anomaly in that way, partly because no other site has been built using such a complex framework of math and an active user community that voluntarily creates questions. The site now has patents pending to protect against others' stealing and using its code. Its competitors, eHarmony, Match.com, JDate, and the thousand other dating services, keep their algorithms under heavy guard.

Here's what we do know: Instead of using math, Match.com relies on lengthy profiles and tries to understand the gap between what a user says she wants and her actions on the site. Match.com observes not just what you select when you create your profile, but how you behave while clicking through other profiles on the site. For example, when you fill out your profile, you may say you're looking for a devout Christian Republican who doesn't smoke. But, if while using Match.com, you're most often clicking on apolitical Buddhists, Match.com's algorithm factors in what it calls your "revealed preferences." It identifies your stated and revealed preferences and behavior in order to make correlations using other user data on the site. It then creates a sort of internal profile and matches you with the person who seems to have similar revealed and stated preferences.

Match.com's algorithms calculate and score your revealed preferences, and the site changes how it weighs certain variables over time as you make connections. If it seems like occupation is really important to you, but you're not emailing, instant messaging, or favoriting people who fit your stated preference, it starts to give more preference to other variables going forward.

OkCupid relies on math, and Match.com adjusts for your revealed preferences. Many dating sites also hire behavioral scientists and relationship experts to help formulate their algorithms. All the doctors and scientists have their own sets of rules and criteria, for which they coin fancy names. Dr. Neil Clark Warren, a clinical psychologist who specializes in relationship research, spent three decades trying to identify the common traits of happy marriages in order to help people find better matches. He concluded that there was a correlation between a certain set of psychological traits two people must share in order to make a compatible couple. In 2007, using his "29 Dimensions of Compatibility," Warren launched eHarmony. On the site, those "dimensions" were further categorized as "Core Traits" and "Vital Attributes."

eHarmony now commands one of the largest pools of daters worldwide and employs psychologists and other scientists in its "relationship lab." Rather than relying on user data or math alone to refine its algorithms, eHarmony observes couples in the real world as they interact in order to inform the surveys and quizzes they use on the site. One of eHarmony's research projects involves conducting a five-year study of 301 married couples, 55 of whom met on eHarmony. They're asked to fill out questionnaires and diaries and then to visit the lab to participate in four interactive sessions.

The lab has four windowless interview rooms, outfitted with hidden cameras and decorated sparsely with a basic living room set and some flowers. Researchers are stationed in a control room down the hall, where they observe behavior such as flirtation, humor, empathy, conflict resolution, and more. They hope to learn what personal characteristics align well in order to tweak the matching algorithms used.

After creating profiles on JDate and Match.com, I signed on next to eHarmony. It promised a painless system and touted its matching algorithm. I was sitting in a coffee shop with my laptop, finishing a dry cappuccino, when I made the decision to give it a shot. I knew that I'd have to create a profile, but I was shocked at the number of questions I was forced to answer.

eHarmony started with basic vital data: What was my gender? Birth date? Ethnicity? Level of education? Occupation? I was asked to describe in less than twenty words what I do for a living.

From there, I had to clarify my answers. How important was my match's age to me? How important was his education? How important was income to me? How important was height? Would I be willing to date someone with a different ethnicity from me?

I was asked to both upload a photo and also describe my appearance. I thought this was clever, because certain semantic tools could be used to analyze the words I chose, which should further enhance the matching process. I was to rate myself on stylishness, attractiveness, athleticism, weight, healthiness, and overall sex appeal. Was I satisfied with my appearance? How important was physical attractiveness to me?

When I clicked on the Submit button at the end of the page, another twenty questions were listed on my screen.

Question: Which of these descriptions most closely describes you?
I love to help others
I seek adventure
I waste my time
I love order and regularity

Question: Look at the following 50 words. Choose all of the words that you feel describe your true nature.
Warm
Dominant
Clever
Resilient

Optimistic

Reflective

I clicked on the Submit button again, only to be faced with yet another screen of questions. This time, I got a new set of personal characteristics to evaluate that were based on my answers from the previous pages.

> Question: What are the personal characteristics that describe you?
> I have a high desire for sexual activity
> I view myself as well-adjusted
> I ask questions in search of information
> I enjoy a good joke
> I care a lot about the physical shape I am in

As I sat there, in the coffee shop, I started to feel frustrated. I wanted to click through and get to the end to see my matches. But that wasn't how eHarmony worked. On other sites, users could browse and sort dates the same way they search for shoes on Zappos.com. At eHarmony, a limited number of matches are delivered to each user. There was no searchable database. This means that unless I paid careful attention to how I was answering, I might wind up with a crappy hand of potential dates. Even so, there was no status bar. When would the questions end? As I clicked through page after page of questions and multiple-choice answers, I thought back to a Myers-Briggs personality-type exam I was forced to undergo with a previous employer. The longer I sat and stared at the test, the harder I found it to answer the questions.

Myers-Briggs Test Question: I prefer to have matters settled or keep decisions open.

Would my boss rather that I'm decisive or flexible? Depending on the situation, I can be both. How would a CEO answer this question? Decisive. Probably decisive. *Argh!*

I not only charted as an ESTJ (extroverted, sensing, thinking, judging), but I scored the maximum number of points in each category. Myers-Briggs doesn't reward you for high scores—this wasn't a situation where I aced the test. Instead, my score put me in an outlier position. (Employers typically look for scores more in the middle.)

Deep into page 7 of eHarmony's oppressive questionnaire, I started worrying that I was once again overthinking each answer.

Question: Do people let me down often if I depend on them?

Of course they do. Wait—does that mean I'm too anal-retentive?

It's obvious that some people enjoy being asked a lot of very personal questions that force introspection and deep thought. I am not one of those people. I never took the quizzes in *Cosmopolitan,* and I could care less how the CNN.com poll of the day charted my political leanings.

Question: Am I a smoker?

On the screen, no. In real life, yes—sometimes I was. I decided to be optimistic and answer "No."

Question: Do I view myself as well-adjusted?

Yes, *I* did, given my breakup with Henry and my mom's cancer. I'd managed not to become an alcoholic or run up huge credit card debt shopping to make myself feel better. That said, I'd been having panic attacks. Bad ones, where sometimes I blacked out completely, both at home and in public. Someone I knew and trusted recommended a local psychologist, and I was eager to get rid of my anxiety without medication. Ultimately, though, I knew I needed help preparing for the end stages of my mom's life.

Friends told me that the first few sessions would require us getting to know each other. There would be idle chatter, a genteel chess game of pleasantries and bullshit, before we could get to the actual work of sorting me out. But I already knew what my problem was, and I just wanted to fast-forward to the part where we got to fixing it.

I decided to make a binder with spreadsheets listing every major and minor moment of my life, in chronological order. I tagged each one with a few descriptive keywords from a standardized list I'd made: mother, father, sister, work, school, achievements, losses, health, weight, friends, cancer, breakups, death. Then I described each event. I created a short list of people in my life and tagged each using that standardized list. I also included all the panic attacks I'd had, noting time of day, location, immediate response (did I black out, or did I just feel anxious?), events leading up to the attack, and what happened right after. I mapped some of that data looking for trends, and I color-coded the results I saw. I made two copies of the binder, one for me and one for the therapist.

At the first meeting, I brought both binders with me. I handed the therapist a copy and asked her to start on page 7, after the introduction, and deep into the spring of 1993. I mentioned that I'd be going quickly but that if she managed to follow along I could get through significant highlights in the sixty minutes we had.

Just as I was getting to 2003 and describing my relationship with Henry, she stopped me. She quietly and gently closed the binder and handed it back.

"Don't you need this for your records?" I asked.

"I think you should take this home, along with yours, and keep both in a very private place," she said. Then she scribbled something in her own notebook.

I suddenly realized that she thought I had a very different problem.

So . . . yes. Yes, eHarmony, I did see myself as well-adjusted. Incredibly well-adjusted, actually. How many other people could find the strength and discipline to document all of the painful moments of their lives, then codify and sort them for the sole purpose of efficiency? I'd saved the therapist several weeks of idle chitchat!

But my worldview was different from the therapist's worldview. The question was, what was the worldview of the algorithm?

eHarmony's algorithm did a terrible job of finding me matches. Although I was very clear about my views on religion—namely, that I was a nonbeliever—eHarmony set me up with an orthodox rabbi and a Jew for Jesus. The only "dimension" we shared was a zip code.

eHarmony, JDate, Match.com, and all the other players in this space tout their super-fantastic algorithms. Contact Incorporated and Operation Match promised amazing computer matching too. If technology has become as sophisticated as we know it to be today, why is it still so difficult to match us with our soul mates?

It turns out that one key variable—and this is a big one—is still just as capricious and as undependable as it was five decades ago. It's us. You and me. The people entering data into these systems are precisely what make them not work.

When I started answering eHarmony's endless stream of questions, I was being blunt, honest, and direct. Then my patience started to wear thin, so I clicked on what I thought sounded good. *Sure, I like strong men who work with their hands.* And then I started questioning my interpretation of the questions, as well as the answers I'd been giving. *Is eHarmony really asking me if I'd be willing to date a lumberjack? They're strong and work with their hands. But I don't want to marry a lumberjack. I don't even like trees that much.*

Many of us answer the questions on dating sites aspirationally rather than honestly. We think about idealized versions of ourselves and paint a skewed profile, often not on purpose, but because these sites are designed to make us feel great about ourselves. If we don't enjoy the experience of entering our own user data, then the system will have less information to parse and ultimately too little content to push through its algorithms. That said, if we want a stable, happy long-term relationship, we can't answer questions as the people we hope to be five years from now, but instead we must answer them as the people we are right now, regardless of how overweight / flat chested / not well traveled / whatever we are in the present.

Think about the way you've set up your Facebook profile. And if you don't use Facebook, instead think about how you've described yourself to new people you've met recently. You list your favorite foods, bands, books. You talk about cities you want to visit. These aren't meaningful data points; they're stylized nuggets of information meant to personify ourselves in a formulaic way to others. A Facebook profile is in many ways an outfit we wear and the accessories and lip gloss we put with it: we're hoping to project a particular image in order to socialize with (or avoid, in some cases) a particular group of people.

Dating sites and the algorithms they advertise purport to sort through our personalities, wants, and desires in order to connect us with our best possible matches. Which means that we've outsourced not just an introduction, but the consideration of whether or not that man or woman is really our ideal. We're putting our blind trust in a system that's meant to do the heavy lifting of figuring out what it is that we really want out of a mate, and what will truly make us happy. This job is being processed using the information that we, ourselves, have entered into a computer system. Bad data in equals bad data out. Algorithms that dating sites have spent millions of dollars to refine aren't necessarily bad. They're just not as good as we want them to be, because they're computing our half-truths and aspirational wishes.

For these dating sites, it's possible that creating perfect algorithms and ideal matches isn't actually the goal. Think about how these sites earn their revenue. OkCupid uses an advertising model, so the more times you visit the site and click around, the more money is generated.

JDate, Match.com, and eHarmony rely solely on subscriptions to make money, and they all offer three-, six-, and even twelve-month memberships, with a hefty discount for paying in advance.

The profit model for dating sites relies on retention, even though our desire as members is exactly the opposite. We want to find true love so we can be finished with dating altogether. Once we're in relationships, we're theoretically off the market. We cancel our memberships and spend our money elsewhere. Fresh new crops of daters should cycle through the various dating sites just as current members are leaving, but that's not always the case. And besides, the more members or page views a site can count, the more money there is to be made. Algorithms may try to connect people on a maximum number of compatible data points, while bean counters are likely tasked with ensuring that we go on good—just not great—dates.

If I was going on horrible dates and if I knew the system had numerous faults, why did I keep paying membership dues at JDate, eHarmony, and Match.com? Why didn't I suspend my online dating activity, even temporarily, and take my mom's advice to be patient? I suppose it's because deep down, I'm an optimist. I didn't need to rely on the matches the sites were delivering to me. Instead, I could keep searching on my own using each site's database as a repository of possibilities. Someone who made me laugh, challenged me to think hard, and understood my points of view would turn up in the search results at some point.

There was a high mathematical probability that at least one man in these databases would be my perfect match. I was certain.

6 | The List

Must not like Cats*!*

It was now July, a few weeks since my date with Jim, the weed smoker who refused to split our dinner bill. I knew matching algorithms weren't perfect, but I kept dating and decided not to cancel my memberships with eHarmony, Match.com, and JDate. The majority of dates I'd been going on weren't horrible, they just weren't great. I was an optimist rooted in math and logic. I knew that if I spent enough time searching through each site and going out with a large enough group of men, I could increase the probability of my finding the right one. And besides, even if I canceled, I knew how Internet marketing worked. All three services would continue to email me new profiles every day.

Subject: Hot Match!

Message: We have a new match for you! LegalTruth20 is 34 and lives just a few miles away from you! You haven't logged in recently. Don't keep LegalTruth20 waiting!

I was sitting at my desk at work when Match.com sent me a similar reminder message, this time highlighting MenchTastic, and his profile immediately grabbed my attention. He was thirty-three, was a nonsmoker, and said explicitly that he wanted kids. He was also a journalist covering the city hall beat for one of the local newspapers. I was intrigued enough to click through and read the rest of his profile.

In his About Me section, MenchTastic wrote, "I'm a journalist, which sometimes means long hours at work but always means I have fantastic stories to tell." Looking at his profile, I thought that I might know his byline. Even so, we shared enough similarities in our personal and professional lives that it felt as if, even as strangers, we'd been a part of each other's social circles for many years.

I moused over his photo gallery and started clicking through. He had thick, dark curly hair and wore modern horn-rimmed glasses. In one picture, he was wearing white slacks (linen maybe?) and a navy long-sleeve shirt. He looked serene and content, standing with a very tan, old sailor behind the wheel of a large yacht. In another shot, he was sitting at his desk at work, surrounded by stacks of newspapers, file folders, and paper. On his desk were a coffee mug and a pile of reporter's notebooks along with two giant computer monitors. Dozens of press-pass badges were hanging on his cubicle. In the next photo, he was out at an event, dressed in a black fitted shirt and dark slacks. He was slender, tan, and seriously attractive.

As I clicked back to his profile, an instant message window popped up on my screen:

MENCHTASTIC: Hey there

"Shit!" I said aloud. He's caught me looking at his profile. What do I say?

YOZORA: Hi . . .

I waited to see what he'd write back.

MENCHTASTIC: I don't have a lot of time to chat now. On deadline at work. What do you think about getting drinks sometime this weekend? Or tonight? Technically the weekend starts in a few hours . . . Are you free?

I immediately heard Hilary's voice in my ear. "You can't go out with him tonight! You can't make yourself that available." But he's so good-looking. And he's a journalist. And he's asking me out. Aren't I supposed to date everyone right now? Cast a wide net and see what I catch?

YOZORA: Sure. Want to meet at Longshots on Fairmount Avenue after work?

As soon as I hit Send, I felt a strong tingle in my stomach. Then instant regret. Did *I* just ask *him* out by accident? Shit! I bet I just came on too strong. I should have . . .

MENCHTASTIC: 6pm tonight. I'll meet you there?

YOZORA: Sold.

I rifled through the piles of paper on my own desk looking for my mobile phone. Where did I put it? Not under the file folders . . . There, underneath my laptop. I dialed Hilary and waited for her to answer.

"So I met this guy on Match," I said. "He's a journalist. He sort of looks like Jeff Goldblum, but the *Independence Day* Jeff Goldblum. Not modern-day Jeff Goldblum. He seems really smart. He looks smart."

"Yes, I can talk even though I'm at work and this isn't an emergency," Hilary said back.

"Sorry. Can you talk? Great. So anyhow, he seems normal," I continued.

Hilary sighed heavily. "What does he do again?"

"Journalist," I said, taking a big gulp of coffee. "I actually think that I know who he is already. I'm pretty sure he's a friend of a friend of Juliet's."

"Do you think that's a good idea?" she asked. "Won't you both be too competitive, trying to get scoops or whatever? We all know that you'll assume he isn't smart enough for you."

"Very funny," I said. "He wants to go out tonight."

"Uh, you can't go out with him tonight. It's Friday night and you're available? He's going to think you're desperate," she said.

"Why can't he just think that I happen to have some free time on the night that he happened to ask me out?" I said, taking another drink of coffee.

"What are you going to wear?" she asked.

"I was planning on going straight from a client meeting, so black pants—"

"You can't do that," Hilary interrupted. "If you like him, you need to go shopping. Your black pants and black or gray top or whatever you're wearing isn't good for a first date. Jeff Goldblum isn't going to date someone who wears what you wear to work."

"Well, I don't have time to go shopping," I said.

"That's another reason you shouldn't go out with him tonight," she said. "Listen, I've gotta go. I'm busy at work."

My date with MenchTastic kept me preoccupied the rest of the day. I sat through a client meeting discussing the usability of a website, and all I could think about was his photo gallery. Where was that boat? Did he know how to sail? I bet he has sexy hands—strong, veiny even, but soft. I looked at my watch more often than I should have, waiting for the meeting to end. We finally wrapped up our discussion, but without enough time to head home first, I went straight to Longshots and decided to wait at the bar for him.

I ordered a club soda with a twist of lime, which looked like my usual first-date drink but contained none of the potentially dangerous alcohol. MenchTastic would likely order a drink once he got here, and since I actually liked him I didn't want to get accidentally drunk at the very beginning of the date. Since it could happen so quickly, I usually didn't realize I was drunk until something bad had already happened. It could just take one strong drink for accidentally drunk and unwittingly aggressive Amy to rear her ugly head, and the bartenders at Longshots were too unpredictable to entrust with this very important first meeting.

Drink in hand, I commandeered my usual position at Longshots: the overstuffed leather sofa in the back corner. It was dim but not too dark, and it was the one place in the bar that didn't cast the kind of bad shadows that could add a week of sleepless nights plus another twenty years to my face. I threw my gigantic bag, packed with my laptop and dating data, next to me as I sat down and sunk into the cushion.

By now, the waitstaff and bartenders knew me by name. For the past few months, I'd been having drinks at Longshots with different men at least twice a week. I never stayed more than an hour and always made at least two trips to the bathroom. They must have suspected me of something, though they weren't quite sure of what. Was I a drug dealer? A prostitute for men with a haggard-office-lady fetish? What was in that huge bag of mine?

Just as I was taking a sip from my glass, I saw MenchTastic walk through the door. He was just under six feet tall and solid but not overweight. Even in the dim lighting, I could see that his olive skin had a healthy glow, as if he'd just been to the beach. With his black pants, dark blue button-down shirt, black overcoat, and messenger bag slung across his chest, he looked like he'd walked right out of a J.Crew catalogue. So far, his profile was accurate. A good sign. He seemed to recognize me instantly too and walked straight toward me.

"Hey! Thanks for meeting me tonight," he started. "I'm Jay."

"Hey—I'm Amy," I said, smiling back at him.

Jay removed the messenger bag from his shoulder in one smooth movement and put it, along with his coat, next to my gigantic bag on the couch. Our conversation flowed easily. He'd been on a deadline that day, working on a story about how a city councilwoman may have misappropriated campaign money for her own personal expenses. He'd managed to get a coveted interview with one of the investigators, a primary source, which meant that he'd be able to go through documents together with the councilwoman and have her explain what the audit showed. I mentioned that long ago when I was a reporter, I'd used a pocket scanner I bought in Japan to make copies of documents. He'd been using a digital camera to take photos but thought the scanner was a much smarter idea.

As we talked, I noticed our voices overlapping and moving in cadence together. We weren't quite finishing each other's sentences, but I mirrored his enthusiasm and found myself thinking faster and grinning more. I'd moved in closer to him and hadn't once thought about my laptop or email rating system. I was too eager to hear what he would say next.

The waiter came by and asked if Jay wanted to order a drink. Longshots offered an extensive menu with pages of specialty drinks and, in the back, several more pages of coffee roasts and flavors. Jay said he wanted coffee. He'd just filed his story, and he wanted to be alert in case the copy desk called with questions. "I'm looking for something that has a rich flavor, maybe even nutty or chocolaty," he said. "What do you recommend?"

Our waiter seemed genuinely delighted to share his knowledge. He explained that he helps to select which small coffee-bean purveyors Longshots uses.

"The El Salvador Verro de los Ranos Peaberry is delicious. And it's sustainable, which is awesome," he said. "The fair-trade Guatemalan Huehuetenango—"

"Wait. Say that again?" Jay asked, smiling.

"I know, it's a mouthful, right?" the waiter said. "Hue-hue-ten-an-go. It's on the spicy side. For that, I'd recommend double espresso, without any sugar if you're able. I can serve it with a few twists of orange peel to bring out the citrus notes."

"Well, I don't think I have a choice, right?" Jay joked. "Hue-hue-ten-an-go, with peel!"

What a shockingly different experience from my ill-fated date with MrJim1971, who wanted to be the know-it-all expert on food and wine during our insanely expensive meal. He wasn't interested in taking recommendations or even in asking my opinion. I loved how, in contrast, Jay was so genuinely, naturally inquisitive. At least at Longshots, he wasn't making assumptions. He was asking thoughtful questions and paying attention to the answers. Curiosity was one of the hallmarks of a good journalist.

As we waited for the coffee, our conversation began to wander from city hall to China. He'd been fascinated with Asian culture and was hoping to travel to the outer edges of the Great Wall. I told him that I'd once been to Dalian, a small city in the northeast. I was on a reporting trip, trying to learn about how China's hyper-productive manufacturing scene was affecting nearby countries. One day, it was so brutally cold that I wandered into a tea shop to warm up. The owner knew English and didn't have a chance to practice it often, so he was thrilled to see me. We spent the next two hours tasting every one of the thirty-eight teas he had in his shop. He explained that he sold thirty-eight teas because eight was a lucky number in Chinese, and the three in front of it meant "triple prosperity."

And then Jay's phone rang. He looked down at the screen and rolled his eyes. Cupping his hand over the receiver, he whispered, "I'm really sorry. I need to take this. Two minutes?" he said, holding up two fingers. I rolled my eyes back at him to commiserate as he walked back toward the bathrooms.

I knew what it was like to get those calls and to be available at all hours. Journalists, especially those on a daily desk, were never really off the clock. Copy editors would want clarification on the spelling of a name, or to say they'd cut several key paragraphs out of a story because there wasn't enough space. It was an infuriating but necessary part of the job. If Jay's story was as controversial as he'd intimated, this would be only the first of many calls he'd receive throughout the night. I understood completely.

Jay walked back toward me, phone in hand, the corners of that warm smile not quite as outstretched as they were earlier. He pushed our bags aside and this time sat down right next to me, propping his elbow up on the back of the sofa.

"Okay, sorry about that. So tell me more about Japan," he started. Had I ever eaten puffer fish? Was I worried about getting poisoned? What about Japanese *onsen*—the hot springs? Were the coed baths awkward for me?

It was a subtle opening I'd been waiting for, an opportunity to be flirty without flirting. Yes, I loved visiting hot springs. Most were no longer coed, but even so, I wasn't bashful or embarrassed. Communal bathing was a deeply rooted part of Japanese culture. It was a matter of understanding how to bathe properly. In a large room, I'd undress completely and neatly stack all of my clothes into one of the wicker baskets provided at the *onsen*. Then I'd walk naked toward a washing area. There were little stools, mirrors, and showers positioned so that I could lather every area with soap while sitting down. Once completely clean, I'd go over to one of the hot pools, dip my toes in first, and inch the rest of my body in as I acclimated to the heat, I explained.

"I'm sure all of the men stared at you," Jay said. "What was that like?"

"I don't know that they were staring . . . ," I said. I could feel my cheeks growing warm.

"You're beautiful," he said. "I'd stare. Plus, you have American breasts!" he laughed, putting his hand on my knee in a way that wasn't forced. Suddenly, I had a strange inclination to high-five *him*.

Jay's phone lit up again. This time, it was a text message. I shot him a knowing glance. The copy desk, no doubt, had yet another question.

"Ugh," Jay said. "Sorry, I just need to make a quick call. Do you mind?"

"Of course not," I said back as he punched some numbers into his phone and put it up to his ear.

"Yes?" he began. "Yes, that's right. It's what I said earlier."

There was a long pause, then a sigh. "Yes, that's exactly what I meant."

Another pause.

"Fine. Yes, that's correct," he said. "Okay, bye . . . ," he trailed off, putting his phone back in his pocket.

"Sorry," Jay said. "That was my wife."

I had no knowing glance for this.

Jay immediately qualified what had just happened with a long-winded, confusing explanation: Technically he was still married, but he and his wife were on a trial separation. They'd been seeing a therapist who recommended that they each see other people. He was sure their marriage was over, so he decided to use Match.com to look for new companionship. But since there was no checkbox for "trial separation," he listed himself as single.

As he continued to rattle off various other issues and concerns, I felt increasingly numb. *Did he just say that he's married?* What just happened? Maybe the bartender accidentally used real gin in my drink? I stared at the glass, looking for signs of alcohol.

"We got married too early," he rambled. "We don't have any kids, so I think now's the best time to split up." As he carried on and on, complaining about how she didn't understand his stress at work, I noticed a strand of long blond hair clinging to his shirt, just above his wrist. Farther up, there was a pale band of skin around his ring finger. They must have spent the weekend together at the beach, out in the sun, I imagined. She's probably very pretty. Nice, even.

"She's just prying like she always does," Jay said. "We are supposed to date other people!"

I shook my head, involuntarily trying to unhear what he'd been saying. "You're fucking married?" I shouted. "Married?" I couldn't look at his face as he whined about his wife. This time, I skipped the bathroom. I didn't bother with the email, since I hadn't built "Forgot to tell me he's married" into my rating system. I reached across him, picked up my bag, and bolted toward the door.

Once outside, I pulled out my iPod and scrolled through to find George Michael performing "Don't Let the Sun Go Down on Me" live with Elton John during a 1991 show at Wembley Stadium in London. I turned up the music as loud as it would go, shoved my hands in my pockets, and started walking.

Fucking Match algorithm! The one fucking time Match sets me up with someone who I am actually compatible with, I get screwed by the user data. *Fucking married asshole!*

As I neared the steps to my apartment building, I fumbled for my keys, which by now were tucked in one of the dark pockets of my massive bag. I pushed aside my laptop, realizing that it had never occurred to me to visit the bathroom to track date data. Instead, I'd fantasized about showing him my spreadsheet of horrible dates. We'd laugh about what I'd done, but as a journalist he would appreciate the thought and dogged reporting I'd applied to my data analysis.

I walked up the flight of stairs, put my key into the lock, and opened the door to my dark apartment. I'd been duped into falling for a cheating liar. What was the point of this exercise?

I threw on the lights and stood in the kitchen, staring at my reflection in the glass-paneled cabinets. Jay hadn't tried to high-five me. He drank espresso instead of beer. He asked thoughtful questions and seemed genuinely interested in my answers. He seemed so fantastic, so eerily perfect. Except that he was *fucking married.*

"All things come to she who waits," my relatives would tell me every time I saw them. Maybe they were wrong. Maybe my mom was wrong. Wasn't it possible that patience has no bearing on whether or not someone finds love? Everyone I knew was giving me the same advice: *Date everyone! See what's out there! Give these men a few chances before telling them no!* A new chart came to mind:

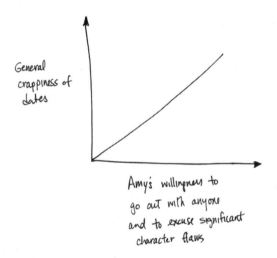

"What if Jay was the one for you?" I could hear my grandmother asking in her wobbly old Jewish-lady voice. "So what if he's married? He's not happy. He's not happy, he gets a divorce. Then he gets married to some other girl, who has *your* babies with *him.* And then what? You have no family. You have no husband. You have no life. Was he Jewish? What kind of a *fercockta* name is Jay?"

I watched my reflection contort as I thought about Jay and this other woman and their perfect children. Just beyond my crumpled brow, I noticed a glint of foil wrapped around the neck of a wine bottle. The previous tenant had left it for me as a thank-you for helping her out of her lease. It was still decorated with the orange ribbon she'd curled and tied around the foil. The bottle had been collecting dust for months. I didn't typically drink by myself at home, and I never brought any dates here. But after Jay, I wanted a corkscrew.

I rifled through the utility drawer first, pushing aside a pile of rubber bands and some old pens to see if I could find an opener. A lighter with a transparent green case was stuffed in the back along with a pack of matches.

"I'll need that," I muttered aloud and shoved both into my pocket.

I looked back up at the cabinets, realizing that even if I did find a corkscrew, I no longer owned any wineglasses. Henry had kept all of them, along with most of our kitchen equipment. I'd taken our television and bedroom set, which seemed like practical choices at the time. I'd been too busy at work to replace my glasses and plates. And anyway, most nights I either picked up dinner on the way home or met up with friends. Alone on the shelf was a sixteen-ounce Three Peckered Billygoat Coffee travel mug I'd bought a year ago during a family trip to Alaska. It was better than drinking straight out of the bottle, I figured. As I reached for it, I saw the corkscrew hiding in the very back of the cabinet.

I unwrapped the foil, shoved the corkscrew into the top, and tried to pry the cork out. *Why are these things so fucking difficult to open?* I pushed and shoved until half of the cork broke free and plopped into the wine below. I didn't care. I filled my mug halfway, stopping just beneath the third pecker, and watched bits of cork slosh around as I walked toward my patio.

The pack of Marlboro Lights was just where I'd left it, between a hurricane candleholder and a mostly dead aloe plant. I'd bought cigarettes last week, vowing to have just one. The pack was now a quarter empty. I tipped it over and slid one out. I reached into my pocket for my mobile phone, dialed Hilary, lit my cigarette, and inhaled.

"Weren't you supposed to go out with Jeff Goldblum tonight?" Hilary answered. She was at a dinner party at a friend's house. Her fantastically amazing friends, Eric and Ralph, had slaved away cooking a lovely meal for eight sophisticated guests, who also happened to be wildly interesting and fabulous.

"Just go somewhere quiet," I sighed.

"Okay, just give me a minute," she said. I heard the brush of her clothes against the phone and muffled conversations coming and going as she passed by her dinner companions. She pulled the door shut behind her.

"So what happened?" she asked.

"He's married!" I said, getting right to the point.

"No!" she shouted. "Journalist Jeff Goldblum is *married*?"

"Fucking married!" I shouted. I told her all about how good he looked. How we'd bonded over our shared irritation at the copy desk. He asked the waiter thoughtful questions about espresso! He thought it was amazing that I'd lived in Japan!

"You're right," she empathized. "Match doesn't really have an option for 'lying about my relationship.'"

"Lying asshole is more like it," I said, exhaling smoke into my phone by accident.

"You're aware that our mother has cancer, right?" she asked.

"It's just once in a while," I said. "Don't I fucking deserve a cigarette after tonight?"

"I'm just saying . . . You should lay off. It's not good for you," she said. I could hear a toilet flush, then water swirling violently in the background.

"Are you peeing? Are you going to the bathroom while I tell you the tragic details of my life?"

"You said 'go somewhere quiet'!" she said. "I did. Eric's bathroom. I'm at a dinner party."

"I don't have the endurance to go on any more dates," I sighed. "I'm done. I'm canceling all my memberships to every fucking dating site."

"Don't do that," she said. "Listen, you just have to keep trying. I promise you, there's someone out there who's great and good-looking and not married. And he'll somehow appreciate your very bizarre fashion sense and weird neuroses."

"Doubtful," I replied.

"Do you remember how we used to watch *Mary Poppins* when we were little?" she asked. "Those two kids, Michael and Jane. They can't get along with any of their nannies. They go through one after the other—they hate all of them. Does that sound familiar?"

"I'm not a fucking child, and I'm not trying to find a nanny."

"Just hear me out," she said. "Remember how one night, they write an . . . *advertisement?*" she asked, drawing out the *ver* with an exaggerated British accent. "They wrote *The Perfect Nanny* at the top and then made a big list of everything they wanted?"

We'd watched that movie a million times when we were little. One week, we decided to re-enact the Supercalifragilisticexpialidocious scene using our stuffed animals. So we rewound, listened, paused, practiced, and repeated the song over and over until we finally warped the VHS tape. Perched on the toilet, Hilary started singing as quietly as an opera singer is able: "Have a cheery disposition. Rosy cheeks, no warts, play games, all sorts . . ."

I was humming along with her at this point.

"Remember?" Hilary said. "They make the list; then Mary Poppins appears."

"Right . . . ," I started.

"So maybe you just need to make a list and a husband will magically appear," she said. "With a fabulous black satchel and a top hat and cane. Actually, that sounds just like Eric. He would totally wear a top hat . . ."

In that moment, I realized why I wasn't finding a good match, and indeed why all single people in the online dating world were struggling. Algorithms weren't at fault. Neither was bad data. We weren't making Mary Poppins lists. We'd never sat down and made a giant comprehensive list of exactly what we wanted—required!—in a mate.

Dating sites relied on rudimentary information. Do I smoke? Do I want kids? Do I prefer a specific level of education? Then the sites matched us with others who had similar data points. But in attempting to make dating sites applicable to the widest possible user base, all of the questions had been made far too generic. I wasn't going on great dates because I wasn't being specific enough about what would make me happy in a long-term relationship. And I wasn't exhaustively vetting each potential date before going out with him.

I needed a comprehensive list.

"Are you there?" Hilary said, interrupting my thoughts.

"Hey, I'll talk to you later," I replied, taking another drag from my cigarette.

"Good. Just go to sleep. When you wake up tomorrow this will all be behind you," she said. "Ooh . . . Eric is just about to start the second course."

I gulped down the rest of the wine in my plastic mug and then ran back inside to my kitchen table. I grabbed a legal pad and a handful of Hi-Tec-C pens, my trusted companions in Japan. Each was a bright color with a .25-millimeter ultrafine tip. I picked up the remaining book of matches and bottle of wine and went back outside. I had another two hours of summer sunlight and, at this point, nothing to lose.

I sat down at my patio table, arranging the notebook and pens in front of me. I poured another mug full of wine, lit a cigarette, and inhaled deeply. Suddenly, everything made perfect sense. How could anyone possibly look for long-term relationship potential without speci-fying all of the necessary traits in that person? Everyone—not just me—needed a list. I started to scribble down notes:

I stared at my notebook, flicking the ashes from my cigarette. *Smart? Funny? That could be anyone,* I thought. I started doodling on the bot-tom corner of the page, drawing three-dimensional cubes, when I saw some writing a few pages deeper in the legal pad. I flipped through and found an old grocery list from when I was still living with Henry:

Produce.
- Lemons (Meyer only)
- Mushrooms
    · Shiitake
    · Enoki
- Heirloom tomato x 3
- Roma tomato x 6
- Washed Romaine lettuce
- Organic garlic x 2
- Sweet basil x 1 bunch
- Vidalia onion x 2

Meat
- organic chicken breast
- organic salmon

There was a logic to my grocery list. I always started in the produce aisle, so I began by listing the precise type of vegetable or fruit I needed, along with the variety. A tomato wasn't just a tomato—there were dozens of options. Thinking about it now, I realized that I'd probably spent more time thinking through what to buy at the grocery store than determining what, exactly, I desired in a husband.

If I was really making a Mary Poppins husband list, I ought to be as honest and detailed as possible. I needed to get much more granular.

What did I really want? In the movie, the list was torn up by the children's father and sucked up into the chimney. What if I was able to magically create the man of my dreams? I didn't have a chimney. But why risk a half-assed husband? I would have to list every single possible trait I could imagine.

1. Smart. He has to be a little smarter than me, and outwit me some of the time. He should have the kind of mind that hears something once and remembers it forever.

2. Funny. Someone with an acerbic, intellectual wit: Larry David created and writes *Curb Your Enthusiasm,* and along with Jerry Seinfeld also co-created the *Seinfeld* TV series, launching a whole new genre of observational comedy. Woody Allen: He used to write extensively for *The New Yorker* in the sixties, critiquing popular culture through the lens of Archimedes or Freud. Judd Apatow: His *Anchorman* was hilarious because it was so true. So your basic pantheon of Jewish comedians. Plus Steve Martin, whose *New Yorker* essays and novellas are wry and clever. Steve Martin and the Jews. That's what I want.

3. Jew...ish. I need someone who was raised in a Jewish household. He should know what's kosher and what's not, what all the holidays are, the lore, and the history. He should know how to survive long *shul* services on nothing more than a few hard candies from his bubbie's

purse and a promise that if he will just sit still for five minutes, everyone can stop for ice cream on the way home. He has to understand all the inside jokes and have the same set of shared experiences. But he can't be religious at all. It will be too difficult for me to fake a belief in God. If we don't have exactly the same point of view on religion, it will absolutely cause problems during marriage. I know it may be a rare breed, but he must be a cultural, emotional, linguistic, intellectual, gastronomic, nonreligious Jew.

4. ~~Not short~~. Between five-ten and six-two. Any shorter and I won't be able to wear heels. Any taller and we won't be able to snuggle in bed.

I felt my cheeks and the skin on my throat starting to burn. Could I be this picky? A man can't help his height. Maybe there's a guy on JDate right now who has the perfect sense of humor and dizzying intellect, just in a smaller package. I'm not exactly petite and thin myself. Was it fair to be this demanding?

Henry was very attractive. I was smitten the moment he turned around at the airport and answered me in English. He was funny, outgoing, and smart. But we were the same height, and deep down, that had always bothered me a bit. I liked the idea of being physically submissive in a relationship, when the timing and mood were both right. I wanted someone to overpower me, who could wrap his entire body around me in a hug, but who could also throw me down on the bed and ravish me. I was too tall for Henry to throw me anywhere. Someone who's smaller may be wonderful, but in my case he will never make me feel like he's in control.

Fuck it, I thought. If I'm making a fucking list, I'm making a fucking list! I took another drink of wine out of my coffee mug and continued.

5. Body hair: Yes on arms, legs, chest. But not too much. No hairless balls or egregious manscaping. Since when did American society decide that a man's hotness is achieved through aggressive chest waxing? Or "boyzilians"? If it was the 1600s and there were uncontrolled lice breakouts or other diseases in the village, fine. I can see getting rid of body hair. But I live in a city and I want a masculine-looking man. I know there's a theory that getting rid of hair makes a guy's penis look bigger, but in reality it makes him look like a prepubescent little boy. Unfortunately, I'd seen one up close. What woman wants to have sex with a giant-little-boy-man-penis?

6. Head hair: Curly and dark. As a teenager, I'd spent multiple summers at Olin-Sang-Ruby, a Jewish overnight camp in Wisconsin. Every year, there was a delegation from Israel, and invariably they were all cute. My first kiss was with one of those olive-complected, curly-haired Israelis, and I've been attracted to that type ever since. But I also have another, less obvious type: stylish balding with high-end glasses. (No male-pattern balding in the back. No surprise balding that's obscured with a baseball or other hat.) On TV and movies, they tended to play the supersmart, if slightly nebbishy, lawyers and doctors: Evan Handler, Jeffrey Tambor, Stanley Tucci. My astronomy professor in college looked just like Stanley Tucci. He was from the East Coast, had a bit of an accent, and wore glasses. He was wickedly smart, had a dark sense of humor, and was incredibly sexy.

7. ~~Likes musicals~~. Likes selected musicals: *Chess*, *Evita*. Not *Cats*. Must not like *Cats*! Yes. There, I've said it. I'm

not going to listen to show tunes cranked up to a maximum decibel level like when I lived with Henry.

8. Must not be in debt. At this point in our lives, he should be done paying off loans and shouldn't have massive credit card debt. Mortgage is acceptable.

9. Must make enough money to be comfortable and should have a sustainable income. He doesn't need to be wealthy. But he should have a source of secure income and some kind of bank account. If he loses his job or can't work, he should be able to float for at least a year. I don't want to be in a situation where we're living paycheck to paycheck.

10. Must not smoke. Must insist that I don't smoke either. I need to stop my one smoke several-cigarettes-a-day habit, and that's only going to happen if he is an ardent nonsmoker.

11. Must not do drugs. I tried to experiment in college, but the one time I smoked pot I felt nauseated and fell asleep on my roommate's friend, who was visiting from somewhere in West Virginia. The whole process seemed like a waste. I certainly don't want someone who is into drugs now.

12. Must have an actual career. Cannot be an aspiring writer/chef/artist/whatever. If he says he's a doctor, he needs to produce actual ID on the spot. I can't go through another date like the one with John, the fake orthopedic surgeon.

13. Career must be important but not all consuming (like mine). He has to understand a sensible work-life balance,

since I don't. I need him to teach me how to cultivate hobbies and how to not work constantly.

14. Must understand how important my career is and be willing to support me in it. If I have to spend a Sunday working, or if a client needs me at their office for a few days, he must be able to give me space and should not feel threatened.

15. Age: between thirty and thirty-six. I suppose there are twenty-five-year-olds who are interesting, but they're in a different place than I am now. Too much older than thirty-six will be a big gap. I need someone close to my own age, and if I'm being totally honest, I want someone who's only one or two years older than me so we can make the same pop culture references.

16. Never married before. No crazed ex-girlfriends either. No children. No insane mother or other mother issues. And not fucking currently married!

17. Wants to have two kids with me. This is non-negotiable. I'm going to want to be pregnant within the next three years, so we may as well agree to this at the beginning.

18. Doesn't drink all the time. Just occasionally. Doesn't "need" a beer or a cocktail in order to eat dinner. I have friends who insist on only going to BYOB restaurants so they can bring their own wine. Other friends complain if a restaurant doesn't offer a certain beer on tap. We're there to eat, not get drunk.

19. Likes the outdoors. But only enough for a picnic or grilling in the backyard. Doesn't want to spend the day golfing or reading on the beach. Isn't compelled to do

overnights at rustic campsites. Driving a car up and down a mountain range should count for "hiking."

20. Likes dogs. Preferably not big, shedding, slobbery dogs. He should like smaller dogs, like beagles or dachshunds. Doesn't necessarily want to own one right now.

21. Likes to watch TV, movies. Acceptable "good" TV/ movies include: *Cheers, Coupling* (UK version only), *Arrested Development, Curb Your Enthusiasm, Deadwood, Six Feet Under,* and *Seinfeld.* He should also hate to watch sports. Especially golf.

22. Appreciates my quirks and neuroses. Should be both impressed and entertained that I took a color-coded binder full of spreadsheets to an introductory therapist session.

23. Challenges and stimulates me. Should have good, long discussions. We shouldn't agree all the time, but we should be able to have amicable disagreements.

24. Has lots of integrity. Highly ethical. He should be competitive, but not someone who cheats to win. Clarifications: Driving twenty miles per hour over the speed limit may technically break the law, but I'd argue that many speed limits are set too low. Speeding = Okay. Lying on a tax return or cheating on a wife is unethical. Tax fraud = Not okay.

25. Has a positive outlook on life. He should be in a good mood most of the time, seeing opportunities rather than obstacles. I don't want any complainers.

26. Is mature . . . is a grown-up. Doesn't lose his mind if he doesn't get his way. Henry often got upset when we

didn't do exactly what he wanted. He'd mope around or angrily go off on his own and do something else.

27. Likes computers and gadgets, like me. Interested to learn more.

28. Appreciates the beauty of a well-crafted spreadsheet.

29. Can fix anything. If not, is willing to tinker to figure out what the problem is. And if he can't do that, then he should have someone on speed dial who can come and solve whatever the problem is. I have curly hair that constantly gets coiled around drains and plumbing. During the halcyon big-hair days of the nineties, our college bathroom was a wreck. None of my roommates knew how to take apart a toilet or snake a drain. We'd let the water pile up in the shower until it neared our shins, and only then would we reluctantly make yet another call to the plumber.

30. Really appreciates and understands me. Knows my motivations without explanation.

31. Is genuinely able to crack me up. He should be inherently funny without having to make fun of other people. Like Jerry Seinfeld, he should make hilarious observations about the present situation.

32. Lightning-fast thinker. Witty. Brilliant, but not professorly. He should make me feel like I'm a few clicks behind him on the IQ scale.

33. Adventurous. Doesn't want to sit still. He should be willing to take a day trip to go tour a historic house or hang out at a street festival or try a new restaurant.

34. Is willing to move, to not be stuck in one place forever. But he can't want to drift. He should be in the process of establishing long-term roots.

35. Loves to *really* travel. Not cruise-ship travel. I want to visit Petra, Jordan, and walk through the ancient ruins. I want to bring him to visit my friends in northern Japan. I want us to reenact my favorite scene from *The English Patient,* when Count Almásy and Katharine wander around the souks in Cairo.

36. Be from Chicago or willing to fly there often to see my family and to spend time with my mom.

37. Be able to advise me on matters of business and everything else. As a business owner and as a wife, I need to have a partner in life who can help advise me.

38. I have to think he's smart enough and savvy enough to then take his advice. He should be right most of the time. (But he shouldn't necessarily know it.)

39. Mac person preferred over PC person.

40. Be very good with money. Understand how it works. Make it work for us. Ideally, he should manage his books, and he should know how to make sound investments for the long term. I don't want any petulant day traders or emotional investors. He should also be humble and have the good sense to never talk about money publicly.

41. Be willing to go out on romantic dates. Plan fun getaways, surprises.

42. Feel compelled to woo me. But in a restrained way. I don't need my name on a billboard or skyscraper. He

should pay deep attention to me, remembering the various details of the things I've told him. He should notice the little things, like if I've cut a few inches off my hair or that I prefer dark roasted coffee.

43. ~~Likes jazz~~. Likes jazz only from the 1920s to the late 1940s. Growing up, we always listened to my dad's record collection, which included Sidney Bechet, Cole Porter, Artie Shaw, Ella Fitzgerald, Benny Goodman, Billie Holiday, Django Reinhardt and Stéphane Grappelli. Also acceptable (but later): Vince Guaraldi.

44. Like classic movies: *Casablanca, The Philadelphia Story,* anything with Peter Sellers.

45. Be an excellent trivia partner.

46. Enjoys *Jeopardy!*. He shouldn't make fun of me if I don't know the answer to a question. Henry used to say "nice job" with this horribly condescending tone, like he was shocked when I answered a question he didn't know.

47. Be a reader. Own books. Preferably stuff from Fitzgerald, Hemingway, Heinlein. Also Michael Lewis, Steve Martin. He should have a bookshelf overflowing with an eclectic mix of well-worn Fodor's and Lonely Planet travel guides.

48. Either like to dance or be willing to dance with me. Looking like a complete ass while dancing is totally acceptable.

49. Be willing to listen to George Michael, and never make fun of me for loving his music. Endure me singing along

to the *Listen Without Prejudice* album often. Attend George Michael concerts when asked.

50. Dress well, in a way that I can appreciate. Nice shirts, well-fitted pants and suits, unusual, quirky socks. He should care about his appearance and strive to look good for me. Note: no athletic team shirts or jerseys.

51. Be of medium build. Not fat, not skinny.

52. Must weigh at least twenty pounds more than me at all times, whatever I happen to weigh at that moment.

53. Should not be supermuscular. I don't want a former athlete who's trying to reclaim his eighteen-year-old body. No protein shakes or other nutritional supplements should ever make an appearance.

54. Must be very accomplished. Should be on boards and seen as a leader in his industry. He should be a humble polymath.

55. Be secure and quietly confident. But not arrogant.

56. Should not succumb to jealousy of me, of colleagues, of family members.

57. Genuinely like and appreciate my giant, loud Jewish family.

58. Likes cities, hates suburbs. I want to live in a place full of excitement, culture, and opportunities. Ideally, we'll walk to the market together for groceries and try a new restaurant once a week. He should abhor chain restaurants and the McMansions of suburbia.

59. Must share most of my interests: touring historic homes, playing with new technologies, attending seminars and conferences. Of course, he should also share my noninterests and have apathy toward long road trips, mall shopping, wine culture, hanging out in bars listening to local bands.

60. Is willing to participate in or try some of my activities: learning about cooking and cuisine, going to museums, seeing new places, etc.

61. Shouldn't get angry. He should never feel compelled to punch a hole in the wall. Henry had a really bad temper and once got so angry at me that he slammed his fist into the wall about six inches away from my face.

62. No history of cheating. Not on a test, not in a game of poker, and certainly not on a girlfriend.

63. Be totally devoted to me. He must listen well, pay attention, and love me intensely.

64. Be physically affectionate but not overbearing. I want him to hold my hand in public, not deep throat me at Sunday brunch.

65. Be adventurous in bed. He should be willing to try new things, new places, new techniques, without my prompting. He should be confident enough to pull off whatever that sexual adventure is.

66. Be very, very, very good in bed. I cannot stress this enough. He has to be amazing—so amazing that I'll feel sheepish talking about him to any of my friends.

67. Must be very friendly (but not in a fake way) to wait-staff. He should be like Jay on our date, before he became a lecherous asshole.

68. Should be easygoing, adaptable. If plans don't work out his way, he should be able to move on without whatever it was ruining his entire day.

69. Must get along well with Hilary. Non-negotiable!

70. Must be unflappably dependable. He should never forget dates and can't flake out on our plans. If he says something, he should mean it and follow through.

71. Must have an excellent vocabulary. He should feel comfortable correcting me if I misuse a word.

72. Should never have the instinct to high-five me. No high-fiving allowed!

I sat back in my chair. I was no longer angry at Jay and lamenting my decision to go out with him. No, at this point I felt empowered, and proud of myself for being honest enough to develop such an impressive list of seventy-two data points. This Mary Poppins Husband List was exactly who I needed to make me happy. He was right there, detailed in black ink. None of the men JDate, Match, or eHarmony had introduced me to resembled anything like the man I'd just created with this list.

I lit another cigarette, celebrating my accomplishment. Then it dawned on me that I'd inadvertently created a small problem. What was I supposed to do with three pages of hand-scrawled notes? I needed to make sense of what I'd written. Reviewing my list, I noticed some duplication, so I'd need to fix some of what was there. I couldn't really use the list as it was—I needed to codify the traits and characteristics.

<u>What I Want</u>

MARY
POPPINS

1. Smart
2. Funny
3. Jewish, but Jew-<u>ish</u>. Not religious!
4. ~~Not short~~ 5'10 - 6'2"
5. Hair: Yes on arms, legs, chest. <u>No hairless balls!</u>
6. Head hair: Curly + dark or balding on top. Must be stylish balding.
7. ~~Likes B'way musicals~~. Likes selected musicals: Chess, Les Mis.
8. Must not be in debt (mortgage = ok)   <u>NOT CATS</u>.
9. Must make enough money to be comfortable. Have sustainable income.
10. Must not smoke. Must insist that I stop smoking
11. No drugs
12. Must have actual career. Cannot be "aspiring" writer/chef/etc.
      If he says he's a doctor he must PROVE
         it on the spot w/ real ID.
13. Career is important, but he shouldn't be obsessed
14. Must understand how important my career is + support me in it
15. Age: 30-36
16. Never married before. No crazed ex-girlfriends. No children.
      Also, no insane mother! — No insane mother issues.
17. Wants 2 kids with me.
18. Doesn't drink all the time. Occasionally = ok. Doesn't <u>need</u>
      a beer or cocktail in order to eat dinner.
19. Likes the outdoors. But isn't compelled to go rustic or to camp.
      Driving a car up + down mountain range = "hiking"
20. Likes dogs
21. Likes to watch TV, movies. But only good TV + movies.
22. Appreciates my quirks + sensibilities
23. Challenges + stimulates me

24. Has lots of integrity. Highly ethical.
25. Has a positive outlook on life.
26. Is mature... Is a grown up.
27. Likes computers + gadgets, like me.
28. Appreciates the beauty of a well-crafted spreadsheet!
29. Can fix anything. Or is willing to figure out the problem.
30. Really appreciates + understands me.
31. Is genuinely able to crack me up.
32. Lightening-fast thinker. Witty. Brilliant, but ≠ "professorly"
33. Adventurous. Doesn't want to sit still.
34. Is willing to move. Doesn't want to be stuck in one place forever.
35. Loves to really travel. NO CRUISE SHIP TRAVEL!
36. Be from Chicago or willing to relocate there or visit often.
37. Be able to advise me on matters of business, life, etc.
38. He must be smart enough + savvy enough for me to take his advice
39. Mac person > PC person
40. Be very good w/money. Understand how it works + make it work for us.
41. Be willing to go on romantic dates
42. Feel compelled to WOO ME
43. ~~Likes jazz~~ Likes jazz from 1920s-1940s
44. Likes old movies
45. Excellent trivia partner
46. Enjoy Jeopardy. Don't be condescending or make fun if I don't get an answer
47. Be a reader. OWN BOOKS.
48. Either dance or be willing to dance with me. OK to look like an ass.

49. Must be willing to listen to George Michael. Attend concerts.
50. Dress well, in a way I can appreciate.
51. Be of medium build. Not fat. Not skinny.
52. Must weigh at least 20 pounds more than me at all times!
53. Should ~~be~~ not be super-muscular. No former athletes.
54. Accomplished but humble.
55. Secure + CONFIDENT.
56. Will not succomb to jealousy of me, friends, colleagues.
57. Must genuinely like and appreciate my family
58. Likes cities, hates suburbs
59. Share most of my interests in common
60. Is willing to participate in/ try some of my activities
61. Shouldn't get angry. Shouldn't punch holes in walls.
62. No history of cheating.
63. Be totally devoted to me.
64. Be physically affectionate. But not overbearing.
65. Be adventurous in bed.
66. Be VERY VERY VERY good in bed!
67. Must be friendly to wait staff. Not fake friendly.
68. Easygoing + adaptable.
69. Must get along well w/ Hilary.
70. Must be dependable
71. Must have excellent vocabulary.
72. Should never high-five me. NO HIGH FIVING ALLOWED!

In order to use it to judge future potential dates, I needed to prioritize the various data points. Was every one of the seventy-two traits I'd listed a deal breaker? Honestly, I could live without a husband as devoted to George Michael as I am. And it was probably okay if he wasn't a classic-movie fanatic.

I decided that the list had to be sorted and tagged, using three frames of reference: traits in partners from previous serious relationships, traits demanded by my family, and traits I considered to be top priorities in order to please myself.

Thinking about Henry, I could see that there were some things that worked in our relationship. There were also plenty of issues that seemed to be problematic in other past relationships. For example, I wasn't good at social drinking. My body seemed to transition from sober to drunk without warning, and as a result I didn't like hanging out at bars. Sure, I was smoking as I made the list, but I didn't want an occasional or social smoker. Instead, I wanted an avid nonsmoker who would force me to stop.

Was there a pattern to the men I'd dated previously? What were the common traits shared by men from my past relationships? I lit another cigarette.

Next to my legal pad were several Hi-Tec-C pens in different colors: red, green, blue, purple, and black. I decided to color-code the list for each set of traits, marking a small dot next to the list entry. I rolled the green pen toward me and at the top of the paper wrote: "Traits in Partners from Previous Relationships."

I thought about Henry and about all the other relationships I'd been in that lasted more than a few months. I marked a green dot next to each trait that was relevant:

- Smart
- Funny

- Interesting
- Between five-ten and six-two

That's it? That can't be right, I thought.

I scanned the list again, objectively evaluating each trait and holding my green pen close to the paper. I'd just made a comprehensive list of everything I demanded in a husband, and of everyone I'd dated—even casually—there were only four traits that previous partners had? No wonder those relationships didn't work out. I put my plastic mug back up to my lips and tilted my head back as far as I could while still focusing on the paper, but there was nothing left. I licked the rim a bit. The wine, Chateau LaFou–something-or-other, wasn't very good, but the taste was starting to grow on me. I put the mug down on the table, reached for the bottle, and poured.

I rolled the blue pen toward me and wrote "Traits Demanded by My Family" at the top. Then I combed through the list, marking blue dots next to each one of the traits that qualified:

- Smart
- Jewish
- Must not smoke
- Must have actual career
- Wants two kids
- Has a positive outlook on life
- Is mature, a grown-up
- Lightning-fast thinker
- Be from Chicago or willing to relocate there
- Be very good with money
- Must genuinely like and appreciate my family
- Shouldn't get angry
- No history of cheating
- Be totally devoted to me

This, of course, made sense. My parents, sister, grandparents, aunts, and uncles all wanted me to find someone who would treat me well, who would keep me interested, and who would fit into our existing family structure. They wanted me to be in the kind of relationship where I became a better version of myself.

Now, I thought about what was crucially important to me. What were the traits I'd need in a husband in order to make me truly happy? I brought the red pen up to the paper, at the top wrote, "What I Need to Make Me Happy," and judiciously awarded red dots:

- Smart
- Jew . . . ish
- Career is important
- Wants two kids
- Challenges and stimulates me
- Is genuinely able to crack me up
- Be very good with money
- Must genuinely like and appreciate my family
- No history of cheating
- Be very, very, very good in bed

Now that it was dark outside, I had to use the light from my computer to review all of my markups. My list was now covered in different colors. It made basic sense, but a spreadsheet would help me to visualize what was really important. As I pushed my chair back, it rumbled against the wood of the patio deck. I knocked against the table a bit as I stood up. I was dizzy, and the backs of my legs tingled. I checked the time on my mobile phone. It was ten P.M.? How had three hours passed?

I brought my bag back outside and arranged my MacBook on the table next to my list. I opened up a basic spreadsheet and entered all of the traits from each color:

88Data, A Love Story
119

RED	BLUE	GREEN
My Traits	My Family's Traits	Previous Relationships
Smart	Smart	Smart
Jew . . . ish	Jewish	Funny
Career is important	Must not smoke	Interesting
Wants two kids	Must have actual career	Between 5'10" and 6'2"
Challenges and stimulates me	Wants two kids	
Is genuinely able to crack me up	Has a positive outlook on life	
Be very good with money	Is mature, a grown-up	
Must genuinely like and appreciate my family	Lightning-fast thinker	
No history of cheating	Be from Chicago or willing to relocate	
Be very, very, very good in bed	Be very good with money	
	Must genuinely like and appreciate my family	
	Shouldn't get angry	
	No history of cheating	
	Be totally devoted to me	

Using the red list as a base, I decided to narrow the pool down to a prioritized list of ten deal breakers. Since no drugs and no smoking should both be assumed, I disqualified them from consideration. Ten seemed like a good round number. I didn't feel like I was being too greedy, and I was focusing on the things that mattered most.

I started a new spreadsheet, typing my ten deal breakers in priority order in one column. In the next column, I gave each a score to weigh each trait: 10 = highest, 1 = lowest:

TOP-TIER TRAITS	SCORE
Smart	10
Be very good with money. Understand how it works. Make it work for us.	9
Be very, very, very good in bed. So good that I'll feel sheepish talking about him.	8
Jew . . . ish	7
Career must be important, but not all consuming (like me).	6
Wants to have two kids with me.	5
Challenges and stimulates me.	4
Is genuinely able to crack me up.	3
Genuinely like and appreciate my giant, loud Jewish family.	2
No history of cheating. No smoking. No drugs. (All of these should be understood—automatic.)	1

I took a sip of wine from my coffee mug and thought about what was on my screen. I'd just ranked what traits in an ideal husband were most important to me and to the people in my life. These ten deal breakers made perfect sense, but there were other data points on my list that I knew were also significant. Ten was just an arbitrary number, I figured. So why not create a second tier of almost-as-important traits, and change the weighting system? Deal-breaker traits would receive a distribution of the ninetieth percentile of points available out of 100. Then I could give the second-tier traits much less weight by allocating fewer than 50 points per category:

TOP-TIER TRAITS	SCORE
Smart	100
Be very good with money. Understand how it works. Make it work for us.	99
Be very, very, very good in bed. So good that I'll feel sheepish talking about him.	98
Jew . . . ish	97
Career must be important, but not all consuming (like me).	96
Wants to have two kids with me.	95
Challenges and stimulates me.	94
Is genuinely able to crack me up.	93
Genuinely like and appreciate my giant, loud Jewish family.	92
No history of cheating. No smoking. No drugs. (All of these should be understood—automatic.)	91

SECOND-TIER TRAITS	SCORE
Never married before. No crazed ex-girlfriends either. No children. No insane mother or mother issues.	50
Must not be in debt of any kind.	50
Must have an actual career. Cannot be an aspiring writer/ chef/ artist/ whatever. And if he says he's a doctor, he needs to produce actual ID on the spot.	50
Feel compelled to woo me.	50
Has a positive outlook on life.	45
Likes computers and gadgets, like me.	30
Appreciates the beauty of a well-crafted spreadsheet.	30
Adventurous. Doesn't want to sit still.	20
Loves to *really* travel. Not cruise-ship travel. Travel to Petra, Jordan, and walk through the ruins. Travel to northern Japan to visit my friends. Wander around the souks in Cairo.	50
I have to think he's smart enough and savvy enough to take his advice. He should be right most of the time. (But he shouldn't necessarily know it.)	50
Be of medium build. Not fat, not skinny.	30
Dress well, in a way that I can appreciate.	20
Is willing to participate in or try some of my activities: cooking, going to museums, seeing new places, etc.	20
Between 5'10" and 6'2". Any shorter and I won't be able to wear heels. Any taller and we won't be able to snuggle in bed.	50
Head Hair: Curly and dark or balding on the top. Stylish balding. No male pattern balding in the back.	50

It would be highly unlikely that someone who scored a maximum number of points in the second-tier category would not also score at least several of the more heavily weighted deal-breaker traits. Glen would have scored a 50 if I was feeling generous, and I would have given Jim about 150 pre-date.

Looking at my list now, 150 points shouldn't have qualified Jim for a date. Karaoke night with Glen should never have been an option. What was a good number? Doing some quick math, I decided that from here forward, anyone I'd consider going out with would have to score an initial 700 points. He could get extra credit in any category up to 10 points too. This would ensure that I would eliminate bad dates before I had the chance to go out on them. In order to score a potential date accurately, I'd have to use email or instant message and also talk to him on the phone long enough to determine whether he'd met the 700-point threshold.

And then, after the first few dates, I would force myself to rescore him. In order to enter into a relationship—a semiserious one, even— he'd have to score a minimum of 1,000 points. That would mean he'd met at least seven of the top-tier traits and most of the second-tier list.

I resolved to honor my list and scoring system from that point forward. I grabbed my phone and called Hilary. I knew it was late. I didn't care.

"Hello?" she said. I expected her to be at home in bed, but she was still at the dinner party. I could hear just a few men talking, laughing a little.

"I did it," I said, nearly shouting. "I made the list!"

"What list?" Hilary asked.

"The Mary Poppins husband list you told me to make!"

"No . . . ," she started.

I started rattling off each data point. "One . . . smart. Because, you know, he has to be brilliant. Two . . . funny. He has to completely crack me up . . ."

"Wait a minute," she sighed, exasperated. "Let me get somewhere quiet." During the short pause, I imagined her excitedly scurrying to the bathroom again, as giddy as I was about what I'd just created. In reality, she was probably rolling her eyes at her friends and making that pointed-finger crazy gesture at her head. "Oh, it's Hilary's poor deranged sister again," fabulous Eric was saying from his charming black leather sofa.

"Okay," she said. "I'm in the bathroom. Go ahead."

I read Hilary the entire list, all the way down to number seventy-two. Then I explained how I'd prioritized and color-coded it, assigning numerical values to each trait. I told her that I would refuse to go out with someone until he reached a minimum score of 700, and how any future husband had to score at least 1,000 points.

"It's a flawless plan!" I concluded, waiting for a response. A few seconds went by. "Are you still there?"

"Amy, you need to destroy that list," Hilary said. "Or fold it up and put it somewhere where no one will find it."

"But don't you see the beauty in what we did?"

"*We* didn't make a list with seventy-two different things you're demanding in a husband," she reminded me. "I was just trying to make you feel better."

"But the reason I'm going on all these bad dates is precisely because I didn't have a detailed list of what I need to make me happy," I said. "It all makes perfect, logical sense now. It's just math. I can see it!"

"There's no way you're going to find someone who scores—what was it?—like two thousand points on your scale. This is just going to make things harder for you," she said. "Trying to find a husband who fits the exact list of what you want is going to be like looking for a needle in a haystack. You're never going to find him."

"That's where you're wrong," I said. "It's dead easy to find the needle. You hack the haystack. Knock it over, scan it with a metal detector, find your needle."

7 | The Mirror of Truth

I am not Cameron Diaz.

I hung up with Hilary, confident now about the data points on my list and excited to start using my new scoring system. I pushed my chair back from the table, jutting my hips left and right to stretch. As I started to reach down to touch my toes, I noticed I was still wearing my clothes from my date with Jay, and my black pants were lightly dusted with flecks of gray ash.

It seemed like it was a week ago that I was sitting at Longshots with Jay, being drawn into his ridiculous story. *Was that tonight? What would he have scored?* I wondered, leaning back in my chair. I plugged him into my spreadsheet, doing quick calculations. I'd give him a 600, which seemed too high knowing what I do now. Should I add in a section for faults and assign negative numbers for any potentially disqualifying attributes? I decided to start using negative points, since any list deficiencies should be counted too.

I squinted to focus on the top of my screen. What time was it? The clock showed twelve forty-five A.M.—had I been outside that long? My little epiphany had lasted most of the last five hours. I rolled my head to stretch my neck and shoulders. Why did it feel like the floor was spinning?

I peered inside my bedroom window and stared at my pillows. Was I tired or drunk? I couldn't tell. I could try to fall asleep, but it felt like I'd stumbled upon some rare, creative magic. What if it was gone tomorrow morning when I woke up?

No, I should power through and keep going. I'd built an ingenious scoring system—I don't care what Hilary says—and it was time to test my hypothesis. If I date only men who reach a minimum score, then we will like each other enough to eventually get married.

I couldn't go to sleep now. I needed to start evaluating profiles methodically and putting each one through my system.

In the background, iTunes was ambling through a Django Reinhardt and Stéphane Grappelli mix of French gypsy jazz on guitar and violin. I needed better music for this next step of the process. I swiped through the hundreds of albums I had stored on my computer, searching for my level-up anthem. *Giant Steps . . . Dirt . . . Girls on Film . . . Buena Vista Social Club . . . Purple . . .*

Where were the Beastie Boys?

There, sandwiched between Wham! and Erasure, were Michael Diamond, Adam Yauch, and Adam Horovitz, three funky-ass Jews from Brooklyn. I tapped on my keyboard's speaker button until it maxed out and then hit Play. The smack of a drum was followed by a slow-driving electric guitar riff. Then Ad-Rock faded in: "I . . . can't stand it. I know you planned it. I'm gonna set it straight, this Watergate. . . . I'm tellin' all y'all it's a sabotage."

I walked back into my bedroom and threw open the closet doors. I wanted out of this shirt and pants and into something more comfortable. Inside were neatly arranged stacks of my other "work" clothes: dozens of threadbare T-shirts, hoodie sweatshirts with frayed sleeves, and five identical pairs of faded black yoga pants. I took the top pair of pants and then thumbed through the shirts, looking for the perfect one as I started the next part of my quest.

"It has to be R.E.M.," I said aloud and with confidence. I'd gotten that shirt in 1989, when they were playing the Rosemont in Chicago. My parents didn't want my group of friends to drive into the city alone. Everyone else got to go, and all I got—literally—was a lousy concert T-shirt that a friend brought back for me. It was now faded and soft from a decade and a half of constant use.

Next I selected a hoodie. I owned several—some plain and without lettering, one from the Gap, one from Columbia, and some vintage hoodies I'd found in resale shops. But for tonight, I needed the MIT. It was gray with maroon lettering across the chest, and I'd bought it after my first visit to the Media Lab, a top-secret facility where the far-out future existed right there, in the present. Researchers were developing paper-thin electronic screens, building self-aware computers, and creating algorithms to solve every complex problem you've never thought of. Every time I wore that hoodie I felt inspired to dig deep and do something amazing.

I tossed my shirt and pants onto the bed and suited up, zipping my hoodie and sliding into my faux-fur slippers. I went back outside to my computer, stumbling a bit over the threshold, and sat down at the table. I slowly pulled the hood over my hair, struggling a bit to tuck it all in, and tugged on the strings tightly. It was time to get to work.

Everything I'd done tonight made perfect sense. The list? Genius. How could anyone possibly rely solely on a dating site's generic questions to evaluate their perfect mates? My scoring system? Super-genius. That would allow me to emotionally distance myself and judge each potential date using objective criteria. And math! I would no longer be swayed by good looks. A potential match must have the same tastes, points of view, and ambitions as me. I'd have to figure that out by reading between the lines of his profile, and then via at least a few interactions over email and instant message.

I pored over my spreadsheets and scoring system and flipped through the pages of notes I'd been keeping. This would work. It would absolutely work. I just had to be disciplined enough to deploy the scoring system every single time, without forgetting or being too generous with points.

I signed back on to JDate, knowing that because I was specifically looking for someone Jewish, I should use that site as my control group. eHarmony wouldn't allow me to search its members on my own, and anyway, its matching process was taking far too long and producing poor results. In Philadelphia, Match didn't seem to have enough Jewish men registered, and since that was a top priority on my deal-breaker list, I put my membership on hold.

Now back on JDate's familiar screen, with the blue star and red heart at the bottom of its logo, I started evaluating profiles. I assessed photos first, and looking now with scrutiny, I realized that pictures do make a critical difference. Someone might be hilarious, brilliant, and friendly, but a bad gallery would derail my ambition to click through and learn more about him.

In some cases the photos were grainy or fuzzy. Or cropped strangely. Or obviously posed. Some photos had absolutely gorgeous women in them, women who were far better looking than me. That was problematic. Even if it was only a sister or best friend, I'd always feel insecure knowing she's around.

The photos I found most appealing were those that looked as if they were shot spontaneously. One that stood out was of a guy talking to a group of friends. He was animated, laughing, seeming to have a great time. I wanted to know more about him. As a result, I wanted to be a part of his great time too.

This wasn't about me being superficial (but let's face it, looks do matter, at least a little bit). Instead, JDate was accosting its users with an incredible amount of information. On one screen, there were banner ads blinking at me; a navigation bar at the top with dozens of clickable options; a secondary navigation area with buttons for emailing, instant messaging, flirting, and so on; buttons for social media; a drop-down menu to view and sort my matches; five text-heavy content boxes on the right-hand side of the screen; and a lot of fine print covering the bottom of the page. In the center section were twenty large profile photos.

Our brains are designed to interpret and recognize faces—it's how humans thrive in our social groups. When encountering a webpage like this, our eyes are naturally drawn to the chunks of data that are most easily processed. On JDate, that meant pictures.

While I did find some of the men attractive, I had a difficult time getting over their chosen usernames. Doc4U might have been good-looking, but I couldn't stand text-message-style abbreviations. So many usernames seemed forced or desperate: WhyNotMe, Ready4Marriage, FunTymes.

I clicked through the pages, surveying my options. Eric1971 looked interesting. His gallery included photos of him on a Jet Ski, posing on the beach with a dog, and wearing a tuxedo at someone's wedding. He had light hair and bright blue eyes, and he looked genuinely relaxed and content.

I ripped a sheet out of my legal pad and sketched out a quick matrix, breaking apart his profile and plotting all of his key attributes and points. I was also looking for more subtle clues that might indicate whether or not he would score high enough in my system to warrant a "Flirt" or "Secret Admirer."

Eric1971 was thirty-four, and that fell within my acceptable age range. In his profile, he met my basic criteria: culturally Jewish, non-smoker, occasional drinker. Under "The things I could never live without," he wrote: "The Internet, cell phone, DVR, Curb Your Enthusiasm, Arrested Development."

But he started bleeding points for what he wrote in his About Me section: "I'm creative and artistic. I've had several jobs, lots of pets and a whole bunch of cars that I've bought and sold. Don't worry I bought/sold the vehicles with all cash. I don't need a cosigner just a real woman! Preferably one who owns a jeep, pickup or muscle car."

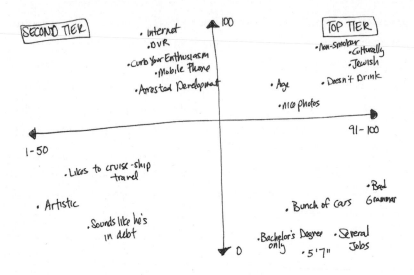

Too many of Eric1971's profile attributes fell below the middle line. Yes, a handful of my deal-breaker traits had been satisfied, but they were the generic ones. There were plenty of nonsmoking, nondrinking, culturally Jewish, thirty-two- to thirty-five-year-olds who also had nice photo galleries on JDate. Data points above the line didn't trump the fact that he didn't meet my height criteria and that he'd had far too many jobs in too short a timeframe. There was either something wrong with Eric1971's abilities and work ethic, or he was incapable of getting along with others in an office environment. Regardless, his "I don't need a cosigner just a real woman" line doomed the whole profile for me. And to think . . . he's someone I would have gone out with before I made my list!

I went back to the main screen and kept clicking methodically, making sure to evaluate every profile and to survey all galleries. TitaniumM4's photos were of him in full combat gear; 48237126 had a bird on each shoulder; JaJimDC looked fantastic in his photos but then said he was a sports fanatic. Kenny68 was too old; Avi402 already had three kids and two ex-wives; ScooterM didn't own a passport.

Wait a minute . . . who is JewishDoc57? He listed himself as six-two, and in his photos I could clearly see a thick head of dark curly hair to match his dark friendly eyes. He wrote that he wants kids, is culturally Jewish, and never goes to synagogue.

I tore out another sheet of paper, retightened my hoodie strings, and started a matrix.

About Me:

I'm a plastic surgeon, but I've done well enough and worked long enough that I no longer spend every waking moment at work. I have affiliations at a few hospitals, and I'm now in surgery three days a week. Don't get me wrong, my career is very important. But I've come to learn that pursuing outside interests, people and places are all paramount to a happy life.

Under Travel, JewishDoc57 got specific: "I'm keenly interested in exploring other countries and their cultures. I've traveled alone, with tour groups and with friends. I've hiked Mt. Fuji, walked along the Great Wall and took a bike tour through the south of France. I travel light, take lots of photos and pack as much as I possibly can into each day. I'm game for just about any kind of adventure, as long as it doesn't involve a cruise ship."

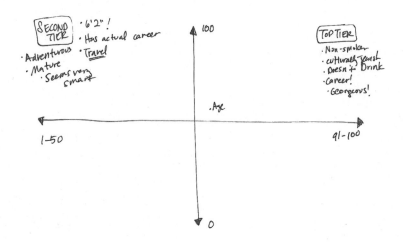

Jackpot! We were perfect for each other!

JewishDoc57 would love the fact that I'd lived in Japan and Hong Kong. We could compare Great Wall photos. He'd no doubt love to hear about my job and the company I was trying to build. Oh . . . and I bet he'd enjoy reading through trashy magazines and showing me which celebrities have had what kind of surgery!

Without even reading his entire profile, JewishDoc57 had already crossed the magic 700-point threshold. I gazed at his photos, clicking through his gallery multiple times. He was stunningly attractive. I could imagine him in scrubs, visiting the bedside of a fire victim, telling her everything was going to be okay in his capable hands.

His hands! I bet he has gorgeous, well-groomed surgeon hands. I stopped on a photo of him wearing a dark suit and tie and thought about me standing next to him, in some kind of shimmering black Diane von Furstenberg wrap dress, attending a charity dinner. We'd be a power couple, brokering good and exploring the world together.

Without looking away from my screen, I reached for my plastic mug. I tipped my head back, trying to cajole the last drops down to my mouth, but it was dry. Where was that bottle? "I'll just have a little bit more," I said aloud, trying to get the very last bit out and splashing a bit on my screen as I poured. Looking at the mug now, it occurred to me that maybe I should switch to water. What if JewishDoc57 was online now too, looking at my profile, and decided to instant message me? I didn't want to be that sad, lonely single woman drunk messaging JewishDoc57 in the middle of the night.

I wandered back into my apartment and stopped in the bathroom on my way to the kitchen. Even in my loose yoga pants, the pressure on my bladder had become uncomfortable—I probably should have gone the first time I got up to change clothes.

I flushed and turned on the faucet, letting the water flow over my fingers. I brought my still-wet smoking hand up to my nose—the stench of tobacco had seeped into my skin. I shouldn't have smoked so much tonight, I knew, and I squirted more soap into my palms, eager to scrub away what was quickly becoming my new habit.

The Beasties were still roaring on my computer. "Got to straighten my thoughts, I'm thinking too much sick shit . . . I've got to contemplate . . . ," I sang along, reaching for the towel.

With my system in place, I'd pinpointed JewishDoc57, my future husband, in under ten minutes. Looking at his point total, he was obviously a better match for me than Glen or Jim. It was just a matter of time before we were making each other laugh over a fabulous dinner. What would I wear? For JewishDoc57, I'd dedicate four whole units of time to go shopping.

As I went to flip off the light switch, I caught a glimpse of myself in the mirror. My hoodie was still pulled tight, but there were tufts of very frizzy hair sticking out near my ears and forehead. My glasses were sitting diagonally on my nose, brushing up against my left eyebrow. How long had they been like that? My eyes drifted down to my stomach, which looked rounder because of the pockets, but turning to the side, I detected a definite paunch. I kept turning, cranking my head to look at my backside. I hadn't pulled up my pants all the way—they were loose and always fell down as I walked anyway.

But . . . my ass. What had happened to my ass? It was rounder and fuller than I'd remembered. And what was with the wide swatch of bright green peeking out from the waistband? Since when did I own big green underwear?

I turned back around, my eyes now darting from my face to my arms to my thighs. I wasn't the glamorous future wife of plastic surgeon/world traveler JewishDoc57.

I was JewishDoc57's schlubby aunt Esther.

"He's going to laugh at me," I said to that mess in the mirror.

I suppose Hilary was right, for a change. I looked like shit. I could legitimately say that post-Henry breakup, I didn't have the energy to do my hair and makeup every day. If I was being honest, though, I'd have to admit that I'd stopped really trying to look good about a month after I'd met him. It took a lot of effort and multiple fancy-sounding products to defrizz my curls. My current routine was to rub a blob of gel through and hope for the best. A full face of makeup now meant a few swipes of mascara and some Vaseline to coat my lips. And I'd gained six pounds. I could still wear all of my clothes; they just didn't fit quite as well as they used to. My yoga pants hadn't seen a single downward dog in more than a year.

I sat back down on the toilet, propping my head up on the sink, coming to terms with my reality. I'd just had a revelation that defied everything I'd ever been told about landing a long-term relationship. That vision had led me to JewishDoc57, who was perfect but who was obviously out of my league. So now what?

To be fair, I could clean myself up. I could get a haircut, buy some new clothes, and put an effort into my appearance. But there was a bigger problem. I didn't have any context. What was my target? Should I sound friendlier, or more professional, or should I try to tell a story? What about my profile would grab JewishDoc57's attention as strongly as he had grabbed mine?

And then it dawned on me: If I found JewishDoc57 that attractive, and if he'd already scored 700 points without my even meeting him, I couldn't possibly be alone. Other women on JDate—a lot of them, probably—felt the same way.

Who were they? What did they look like? These women probably weren't wearing hoodies and crooked glasses. How did they describe themselves? Which ones would pique JewishDoc57's interest? How did they compare to me?

I rushed out of the bathroom, forgetting about the lights and accidentally catching my little toe on the corner of the door. It throbbed, but I stumble-hopped through my room and back out to my patio. I sat down at the table, wincing as I massaged the pain in my foot, and looked at my screen. Why hadn't I thought of this earlier? I went back to JDate's home screen, and next to my username I clicked the Log Out button.

It was a simple, obvious solution—the kind that scientists always hope to discover. *Simple* and *elegant* were words used to describe some of my favorite technologies. And now I'd finally happened upon my own creative breakthrough.

In order for JewishDoc57 to pick me over the other women, I needed to outperform all of the possible profiles in JDate's database. I had to know what kind of women were my competition, what they looked like, what they wrote, and how they interacted with him.

In short, it was time to join JDate as a man.

Fuck You, Impostors!

You are a: man seeking woman.

I logged out of my JDate profile, immediately cleared the cache on my browser, and turned on the privacy setting. I needed to start a new profile with a clean page and with all of the keystrokes I'd been using removed. With the pack of cigarettes and bottle of wine now churning through my system, I felt exhilarated, confident . . . and paranoid. Was someone on the other end watching me? I didn't want JDate to autofill responses based on my Yozora profile. What if they traced my old account and linked it to my new one?

I'm just buzzed, I thought, comforting myself. I looked at the clock on my computer. It was now two A.M., and although it was early Saturday morning, I was wide-awake. The Beasties mix I'd been listening to had finished an hour ago, and I needed something in the background to help me focus and concentrate on the tasks at hand. I quickly scrolled through all of my music and found a 2003 recording of the London Symphony Orchestra playing Holst's *Planets*. I fired up "Mars" and got to work.

I went back to the home page, as if I'd never seen it before. "Meet Jewish Singles." *Would I like to join and meet thousands of Jewish people*

138   Amy Webb

in my area? I asked aloud, reading from the site. "Why, yes, JDate. That sounds wonderful!"

The first window asked what had previously been a simple question.

You are a:

Man seeking woman

Woman seeking man

My eyes darted around my patio and over to a nearby bush. *This is ridiculous,* I thought. Nobody's in the fucking trees watching me do this. No one's going to know. I highlighted the first choice and clicked "Continue."

What kind of relationship am I looking for? And what's my current relationship status?

☐ Marriage

☐ Single

I methodically clicked through, answering each of the questions again as when I'd first signed on to JDate. But now I was taking my time to craft this fake profile. He'd be just like JewishDoc57: six-two, 175 pounds, and just about to celebrate his thirty-sixth birthday. He was a nonsmoker who drank occasionally and wanted kids.

I clicked through to the next screen, which asked for his education. What did JewishDoc57 have again? I scrolled through the list, selecting "postdoctoral," since that was the highest level offered. What kind of doctor should he be? Cardiologist? Sure, that sounded good.

Under religion and lifestyle, I entered "Culturally Jewish but not practicing" and said that he went to synagogue only on major holidays. Next I had to write a profile. I tried to make mine as similar as Jewish-Doc57's as possible, but I gave it a few flourishes:

I'm a cardiologist in private practice with affiliations at a few hospitals. I've reached enough seniority now that I don't work 80 hours a week. I manage to take three or four vacations a year, and I typically work four days a week. My career is vitally important to me, but I'm now able to pursue outside interests. Whether it's visiting the Henry Ford Museum in Detroit, the magnificent Rem Koolhaas–designed Seattle Public Library or some far-flung mountain retreat in India, I'm looking for a partner to share my next set of adventures.

On the final screen, it asked for a username. I thought for a moment, then started typing . . .

Username: JewishDoc1000

"It's not like you're competitive or anything," I could hear Hilary yapping back at me.

I clicked the maroon Finish button on JewishDoc1000's new profile page, and suddenly I didn't feel so bold and fearless. Why were my cheeks flushing? I knew that on my screen were a whole bunch of women waiting for me. All I had to do was look.

Still, I averted my eyes, stopping to fixate on an exposed nail in my patio railing. I wanted to look back at my computer, but it somehow felt dirty, like I was twelve again and in a movie theater watching a kissing scene with my parents sitting next to me.

What was wrong with looking at the online dating profiles of women? Wouldn't I do the same thing—scope out other women, listen to them talk, size them up—if I was at a party or out with friends? JewishDoc1000 wouldn't just let me see other women on the site, he would allow me to experience online dating as a man.

Yes, if I were to tell someone later what I was doing, it might seem a little strange. But fuck them for not appreciating the genius of my plan. This was a perfectly obvious, rational solution. If I wanted to find a perfect 1,500-point man, I probably could with enough elbow grease and time. But even if I found him, that wouldn't necessarily mean that he'd want the version of Amy he saw in my profile.

Who were the women on JDate? What did they look like? What did they do for a living? What did they write in their profiles? I needed to solve for the variable I couldn't control: my competition. This wasn't predatory; it was a socio-anthropological experiment!

Yet there I sat, distracting myself with . . . *how far was that nail sticking out of the railing?* Half an inch? No, three-quarters of an inch looked more accurate. Why was it protruding from the railing like that? A nail couldn't just decide it didn't want to be part of the railing anymore.

I'm being ridiculous, I thought. I shook the pack of Marlboro Lights upside down, trying to find another cigarette. One last crumpled cigarette fell out on my MacBook, along with flakes of tobacco like sad, dried-up glitter that'd given up on trying to sparkle.

Okay, but I wasn't sad or pathetic. I was about to triumph over a system that had been working against me. In the background, my playlist was now about four minutes into "Jupiter," a song I'd performed many times as principal clarinet. That was a hard fucking part, and it always caused the audience to erupt with applause. This moment, this next step in my journey to find a husband, was my ovation.

I rolled the last, bent cigarette toward me and put it up to my lips. I'll light this, inhale, and look back at the screen.

I blew a ring of smoke in the direction of my computer and clicked Continue. There, through the middle of that grayish-white cloud, my JDate competitors were revealed to me for the first time. I took another puff while my eyes focused on the screen. In front of me was a trove of shockingly pretty women. More blondes than brunettes, all with shiny, long, straight hair. They were well dressed, at least from their rib cages up, and they seemed genuinely happy.

If someone was on the home page, there was a high likelihood that she was popular. The first twenty spots were coveted, marquee positioning. Those profiles were there for a reason. When new users signed on for the first time, they needed to feel a pull, a draw to stay on the site. Without the promise of gorgeous, interesting people who were accessible through a simple mouse click, users might leave and join another service. I knew that was the first, and probably most important, value proposition of this or any other dating website.

JewishDoc57 would be too intimidating for me to approach in person—he was so handsome, he might already be in a relationship, or he might just outright reject me. But online, he was suddenly accessible via an innocent little button. If I clicked through to look at his profile or to start a conversation, there'd be very low risk. Unlike in real life, there would be no mangled cheesy first line or inevitable face-to-face embarrassment. If JewishDoc57 didn't want to pursue me, he could simply not respond. Silence bruised the ego far less than meeting the eyes of someone who showed disdain before I'd even had the chance to say hello.

It's obvious that the goal of any dating site is to establish an easily accessible popular crowd of attractive profiles and to allow new users to create a basic profile so they can look around for free. Letting everyone in for free is critical; otherwise, a site would have no members. But additional services—like the ability to message other members, save members to favorites, see additional photos, and so on—require paying a monthly fee ranging between twenty and seventy dollars, depending on the site. If a new user sees lots of profiles of attractive people right away, she'll be more willing to upgrade her account. Like the other dating sites, JDate selected a handful of profiles to feature. The rest showed up via algorithm: the more men who clicked on a profile, the more popular it became.

I started combing through the first page of women's profiles. As I scrolled up and down, one key characteristic stuck out for me. All of the women looked oddly similar. Not particularly Jewish, but also not *not-Jewish*. They were very pretty, petite, and youthful. They simultaneously seemed approachable and sexy. It looked as if someone had snapped a photo during the apex of the most amazing day of each one's life.

I clicked on MaddeGirl first. If you had called Central Casting and ordered the nicest, prettiest girl next door, that was her. She was an elementary school teacher, liked camping, and was "really into sports cars." She looked tiny—couldn't have been more than five-two—and had long blond hair and bright blue eyes. MaddeGirl probably finger painted by day and played beer pong on the weekends.

Would JewishDoc1000 date MaddeGirl? She was attractive, sure. But she seemed like she was trying too hard. "Really into sports cars?" It seemed obvious that she was just vying for JDate clicks. What are you, nineteen, MaddeGirl?

Actually, I hadn't looked at her age. Or what she'd listed for religion.

Age: 26.
Religion: Other.

Okay, that makes sense, I thought. You're cute, but you're not Jewish. Are you on JDate for a reason? Or were you just uploading your profile to every dating site to cast the widest possible net?

I went back to the home page and to the list of featured and popular profiles. MaddeGirl had likely been favorited by a number of men. Next to her was EaglesFan32B, a nice-looking blonde who described herself as "petite," "adventurous," and "fun." I clicked through to her profile page, which offered a number of really attractive photos. In one, she was standing in a bikini on a beach somewhere, volleyball in one arm. Her arms were toned, and her hips and waist seemed to achieve that athletic-but-feminine ratio. I'd thought that maybe the 32B in her username was meant to reference her breasts, but it was clear she was closer to a full C. In another photo, she was wearing a little black dress that fit snugly across her hips and waist but was more billowy on her torso. It had a keyhole opening, showing off a youthful cleavage.

I clicked on a third photo, which featured a very tight close-up of her face. We were eye to eye now, staring at each other. I pictured EaglesFan32B at the beach, showering off after an intensive coed volleyball game. I could see her walking toward an outdoor changing area. She had 10 percent body fat, and all of it was in her gloriously perky breasts. She didn't need to reach for a towel. Molecules of air fought for space and the honor of covering her cellulite-free skin. She looked in the mirror, admiring her impossibly taught butt. As she twisted to gaze over her shoulder, she instead caught the eyes of a frizzy-haired Jewish lady, perched on a green patio chair with a MacBook balanced on her unusually large thighs . . .

"Fuck!" I shouted at myself. Okay, they can't all be like this. I took another drag of my Marlboro Light and kept reading through her profile.

EaglesFan32B liked to spend her free time "hitting the gym, dancing, cycling, and reading."

Reading. Yeah, right, I thought.

About Me:
I'm addicted to lattes, smoothies, sunshine, spinning class, and cashmere sweaters. I find myself spending most vacations on a sun kissed beach wearing a teeny bikini. I prefer watching football over chick flicks any day of the week. If you want to know more, just ask, LOL. :-)

Here's what I'd like to know, EaglesFan32B. Who's laughing out loud wanting to learn more about you? Would that be me? Am I the one laughing-out-loud-smiley-face?

These women didn't seem real. I went back to the home screen, only to realize that EaglesFan32B was also listed in the featured section. Hers was one of the most highly rated, popular profiles on the site.

I scrolled to the next row of women. SmileyGirl1978, a dark blonde, was also "petite," and a "Fun girl who is Happy and Outgoing."

I looked up at her photo gallery. There were multiple photos of just her alone, from the waist up. She'd mastered the Victoria's Secret model pose. I could tell that she didn't need one of their bras for support—she was one of those horrible women for whom gravity has no consequences. She was probably tiny—spindly, even. And yet she'd contorted her torso to minimize her waist and amplify her breasts. In every photo, her straight blond hair cascaded just over her cleavage. Her left hand was resting with purpose on her hip, and it highlighted what looked like a disproportionately small waist.

SmileyGirl1978's About Me section said:

> I am silly, nice and friendly. I love to make people laugh and to laugh alot. I love to have a grate time. I would like to meet someone with a Genuine sense of humor. My ideal date would also go with me to football games in the Fall, basketball games in the Winter and baseball games in the Summer. I'm looking for my beshert. Is that you?"

Ugh, who is this horrible woman? I thought. *Why can't you spell?* I moused over her details.

> Height: 4'11"
> Weight: 110 pounds

Of course, I thought. There must be a rule on JDate against women who can ride the big roller coasters by themselves.

Wants kids: Yes.

Pets: Cat, Dog.

Smoke: Nonsmoker.

Drink: Socially.

Education: Will tell you later.

Annual Income: Will tell you later.

Religion: Culturally Jewish.

Okay, that's strange, I thought. I'd never seen so many "culturally Jewish" women in one place. Were they actually Jewish at all?

I considered the last sentence of SmileyGirl1978's profile. "I'm looking for my *beshert.* Is that you?"

Beshert isn't a fashionable foreign word you throw around, like *tapas.* No one I knew actually used the Hebrew word for "soul mate" in casual conversation.

I clicked back to the home page. MaddeGirl, SmileyGirl1978, and EaglesFan32B were clearly all attractive, and now I saw that they were also very active on the site. It dawned on me that there was a popular crowd on JDate, and I wasn't in it. I wasn't even a part of it in spirit.

What else do you three have in common? I wondered. None of these women seemed to have any higher education, or if they did, they'd left that section blank and for some reason didn't want to talk about it. If you've spent seven years in school and you're now an MBA, why not list it?

I clicked on another featured profile, Tammy4337. Pretty, thin, blond. Surprise, surprise, surprise. She was also vague in her profile, listing "Design" as her career. What do you design, websites? Tractors? Tell me something about your real skills and interests! At least my Yozora profile was descriptive and thorough. The men who looked at me knew exactly what I did for a living, and to be perfectly honest, what I did was pretty cool. I used to jet in and out of countries on reporting assignments. I'd shared a snack of deep-fried silkworms with a toothless Korean woman on the side of a mountain! I'd embedded with the Japan Self-Defense Forces and taken part in a forty-eight-hour combat training session!

And by the way, Tammy4337, I happen to speak three languages. And I can *spell* in all three! In fact, I don't just speak Japanese like some *gaijin* expat, who mispronounces *miso* as "mee-zoo" and winds up ordering water instead of soup at a restaurant. Don't believe me, Tammy4337? Check the hobbies section of my profile, paragraph three, second bullet point!

All of these JDate profiles were so generic, so pointless. Jen80 likes to have fun. Don't we all like to have fun? Sparklez "loves to laugh all nite long." Who doesn't like to laugh?

And what was with this outpouring of sports fanaticism? You're telling me, Happy1979, that you'd honestly rather spend the afternoon trapped between some JDate guy and a sweaty, drunk baseball fan, pretending to care about the world's slowest game being played in miserable summer heat? I see what you're up to, Happy1979. And I'm not buying it.

And yet there was Happy1979's profile, all sunshine and rainbows. She was popular, favorited, and had a prime spot in the middle of the top row.

I noticed that my right knee had been bouncing up and down, and by the pain I was now feeling in my hip, I'd apparently been fidgeting for a while. I reached for my pack of Marlboros, knowing it was empty but feeling that the universe owed me one last bonus smoke.

It just didn't make any sense. Yes, these women were all beautiful. But they seemed so juvenile, so incredibly boring. In the real world, all of my male friends—even the ones who'd score above 900 points—dated short, vapid women like these, but they didn't stay together long. My friends would quickly tire of them and move on to another possibility.

I worked through JewishDoc57's logic and his possible motivations for preferring the top twenty profiles on JDate's home page. Maybe there were primal urges beyond his control? But I thought Darwin had solved for that sort of thing. If JewishDoc57 was an actual doctor, that meant he'd endured at least eight years of college and medical school, plus at least another two or three years to specialize in plastic surgery. Assuming that med school is at least somewhat challenging, he must be smart. Smart men usually need lots of stimulation, so he'd have a wide array of interests, things he liked to do outside of watching football and drinking beer directly from a spigot. Smart, attractive doctors were confident. They would welcome the opportunity for meaningful conversation and certainly wouldn't see a smart woman as a threat. Alpha males like Jewish-Doc57 would have to know that genetically, they needed to mate with smart, alpha females. Instinctively, hormonally, karmically they were compelled to further their genetic line, to produce super-smart, alpha children with someone like me! Happy1979 might have perky tits and be good in bed, but she couldn't co-create an alpha baby with JewishDoc57!

I clicked back to the home page, no longer shy about looking and certainly no longer driven to avert my eyes.

Click.

> Stephanie9999
> 5'2"
> 110 pounds
> Occupation: Other
> Annual Income: Will tell you later
> Religion: Reform

Click!

> LizzieM
> 5'1"
> 109 pounds
> Occupation: Graphic Arts
> Annual Income: Will tell you later
> Religion: Culturally Jewish

CLICK!

Randi2281
5'3"
118 pounds
Occupation: Legal Services
Annual Income: Will tell you later
Religion: Reform

CLICK!!!

HottieDC
5'1"
110 pounds
Occupation: Business
Annual Income: Will tell you later
Religion: Culturally Jewish
"I'm looking for my beshert to spend the high holidays with."

Fuck you, impostors! Two women using the word *beshert*? The high holidays aren't like some winter break where you and your "*beshert*" rent a cabin in Breckenridge and drink hot toddies by the fucking fire! You don't cozy up in warm sweaters during the day and then have wild, Waspy hot tub sex all night long. No, the high holidays are where your grandmother and aunt Rita complain about the temperature every five minutes and the rest of your relatives argue about what time sunset actually is so that everyone can eat already! And eat? Do any of these women eat? Because they can't all possibly be anorexic midgets with ambiguous jobs and secret incomes! I call bullshit! Bullshit!!

I shoved my chair back and walked to the end of the patio.

I felt like I was back in high school all over again. Now that I was starting to reverse-engineer JDate, I realized that in my case, the opportunity to "poke" and "flirt" with gorgeous men would yield me no better results than staring at the back of Dave Peterson's head in environmental biology class. He was the most popular kid in school and held the usual credentials: tall, muscular, good-looking, captain of the basketball team. Somehow I used to think that if I stared at his head and sent all of my adolescent energy his way, that he'd eventually turn around, smile back at me, and ask me to the prom. But it didn't matter how much I stared then, or how much I poked and clicked now. Guys like Dave would always be staring at HottieDC, the thin, blond cheerleader sitting two rows up.

I took a deep breath. I've definitely had too much to drink, and I'm definitely amped up—but clearly I'm missing something, I thought.

I started to put what I'd seen into an equation and to work backward, assessing all of the variables. I may not be a short, Popsicle-stick woman with huge boobs, but I also wasn't unattractive. It's not like I'd never been approached in a bar before. In fact, I usually wound up talking to at least one new guy if I was out with friends. Before Henry, I'd dated plenty of men, and I'd rarely initiated contact. I was outgoing, I was smart, and I was funny. Online, I may not be as immediately competitive as EaglesFan32B, but that was simply because I wasn't going to upload a photo of myself standing on the beach in a bikini.

What did all of these women share in common? I wondered. They were all very active on the site, had been favorited many times, and were highly rated profiles. Maybe it was language? I considered how they described themselves:

- "petite," "adventurous," and "fun"
- "addicted to lattes, smoothies, sunshine, spinning class, and cashmere sweaters"
- "loves to laugh all nite long"

Nothing they wrote was controversial, committed. How can you rally against laughing? Who feels politically opposed to sunshine? It seemed that the profiles were all upbeat, positive, and fairly generic. Maybe there was a secret formula the popular crowd used, possibly without even realizing it? Were these women the same way in real life? When you met them, were they enthusiastic without being overbearing? Were they agreeable, nonspecific, perpetually cheery?

It occurred to me that I'd actually had this conversation before, more than a dozen times. When a male friend would introduce me to a HottieDC or a Happy1979, I'd politely chat with her for a few minutes and then immediately find a way to escape the tedious, tired small talk. Obviously, my friends were looking to get laid—what else could they possibly want with women like that?

The answer was easy, and it was the same every time, regardless of which one of my friends it was. These women were approachable. They weren't a challenge. They seemed easy to date. Easy to get along with. Friendly, outgoing, and fun.

It's what I called "Cameron Diaz Syndrome." Think about her movies, I'd say. In *There's Something About Mary,* she played the cheery, optimistic, girl-next-door-who's-also-a-model archetype desired by men everywhere. She loved football and was so egregiously nice she got duped into dating an Australian con man and a psychopath with a skin condition. Under no real-world circumstance would a woman this gorgeous, this successful, and this hilarious spend the majority of her time with such a sad group of misfits. But Hollywood would have us believe otherwise.

Cameron Diaz tends to play a likable, spontaneous, easy-to-date woman on screen. Hell, even in still photos of her, she seems carefree. Ready to be everyone's best friend. She can hang with the guys but is still secure enough to spend lots of time apart when asked. Also—importantly—she's thin, blond, and always showing skin.

The problem, of course, is that Cameron Diaz is a movie star playing a well-honed type of character. In the real world, Cameron Diaz was thirty-three and had been bouncing from man to man while gossip magazines ruminated on whether or not she'd ever get married. Even Cameron Diaz couldn't land a committed relationship.

Were the men of JDate suffering from an acute bout of Cameron Diaz Syndrome too?

I knew that while genetics played a big role in how we look, that sense of ease and quiet confidence was something that could be cultivated. Most of us—especially women—tend to undersell ourselves. We're taught that being direct about our achievements is tantamount to bragging. And as women, we're reminded that men aren't interested in competing with us. That we should admire what they do overtly, but keep our accomplishments private.

I didn't want someone who would be intimidated by who I was and what I did. Surely there was room for honesty?

I wondered how JewishDoc1000 might perceive the Yozora version of me, based on the original JDate profile I'd posted and within the context of all these other women. I sat down, grabbed my notepad, and started sketching.

On the right, I wrote my name and copied down the most prominent highlights from my profile. On the left, I wrote HottieDC and listed the major points of her profile.

As I looked at both sides of my paper, it didn't take long to see how what I'd written might be off-putting. (See chart on next page.)

And then I considered my profile photos. I'd used three.

I'd made a conscious decision to select these three photos. In the first, I was snuggling our family dog, which I thought made me seem like an easygoing pet lover. But now, looking at that photo on the JDate page, all I could see was Bailey's dirty, strange fur and wonder what it was attached to. I knew the second wasn't flattering at all, but it showed me at work, speaking at a prestigious conference to a huge crowd of people. In the third, I was still in grad school at Columbia University,

Hottie DC	Amy
Height: 5'1"	Height: 5'6"
Weight: 110 lbs	Weight: Tell you later
Occupation: Business	Occupation: Consultant. I'm an speaker, author, future thinkers, adapting current technologies for use in communications *(Keeps going)* ↓
Annual Income: Tell you later	Annual Income: Tell you later
Religion: Culturally Jewish	Religion: Culturally Jewish
About:	About:
"I'm looking for my beshert to spend the high holidays with"	• Japanese (Full proficiency)
	• Chinese (Elementary proficiency)
	• HTML, CSS (Full proficiency)
	Graduate School: Columbia University MS, Journalism Concentrations in narrative nonfiction and international reporting. Studied under Sam Freedman, Michael Shapiro, Ari Goldman, Seymour Topping
	Undergraduate: Indiana University BA, Political Science Concentration in economics ← I was originally on a performance scholarship at the Jacobs School of Music. (Classical clarinet)

standing next to the *Alma Mater* statue. I'd done my makeup well that day and my skin looked really radiant. I'd received a few compliments from strangers, and one woman even asked me where I got my facials. Looking now with a fresh perspective, I realized that my photos were yet another detriment.

I went deeper into JDate, clicking beyond the popular profiles and through to pages 19, 20, and 21, where the listings become more random. As horrible as I knew my photos were, I could now see that my profile wasn't as awful as some of the others. One woman blathered on and on about how important fitness was to her. She was attractive, maybe a little too muscular. She listed thirty-seven different activities that she participated in regularly: kayaking, water polo, water aerobics, spinning, step aerobics, interval training. She said that her goal was to run ten marathons that year. Obviously being active was important to her, and any partner would have to be fit too. But the detail and breadth to which she described everything had to have been off-putting to anyone who wasn't some kind of Olympic athlete.

Another woman kept her profile very succinct: I'm single. I'm not a weirdo. I have a steady job. I'm looking for someone I won't be embarrassed to introduce to my friends.

Saying that she wants a man who won't embarrass her sounded really aggressive and negative to me. And the very fact that she said she wasn't a weirdo made her sound like . . . kind of a weirdo.

I could see that the vast majority of online daters don't agonize over building their profiles as much as they should. I certainly didn't. I hastily copied and pasted content from my résumé, assuming that what really mattered was not some digital profile, but the first few interactions. While I'd included way too much specific, sterile information, others had written the minimum number of characters just to fill space and had relied instead on what they thought were great photos.

But even for really attractive women, photos were problematic. Many women uploaded photos with a phantom shoulder in view. Whose shoulder was it? A recent ex? A current boyfriend? It was rarely someone's brother or best friend. Some photos were grainy and dark, so it was difficult to see what the woman really looked like. There were disasters too: photos that were obviously really old, drunk photos, and photos that looked like they were bad outtakes from a *Maxim* shoot.

That said, at least slutty, cheesy *Maxim* photo women seemed like they were ready for fun.

I looked at HottieDC's profile again. She had uploaded five uniform photos. In each, she was standing at a slight angle and looking straight at the lens. She wasn't drunk. There were no furry animals or other people's body parts in the frame. Her smile didn't seem forced. In fact, I got the feeling that she'd been laughing just before the photo was taken. Her hair and makeup didn't look overdone, but she had definitely spent time on both. She was showing skin—her décolletage and shoulders—and each photo was cropped such that I could see just enough of her arms to assume that she also had beautiful hands and well-manicured nails. Really, the only difference in HottieDC's photos was the color of camisole she was wearing in each. She could have been a catalogue model, but one that seemed friendly and approachable enough to ask out to dinner.

I compared my photos to HottieDC's, EaglesFan32B's, and some of the other photos I saw on JDate:

There was absolutely no competition. I'd been bested by HottieDC and all the others right and good. I'd thrown my JDate profile together quickly in between work meetings because I wanted to see the men on the site. I hadn't planned a strategy for my profile. Forget strategy—I was irritated by the whole profile-building process, seeing it as an obstacle to just meeting the men that I'd want to date.

It seemed strange now, that I'd just slap together my online dating profile, when I'd spent days agonizing over my résumé, tweaking and massaging it to land the perfect job. Sometimes I could read, edit, and reread email messages for an hour before sending them. Yet here I was, husband hunting and armed with only a handful of half-assed bullet points and what was one of the stranger assortments of photos on JDate. I hadn't stopped to consider how badly I was representing myself during that critically important first-impression stage. If JewishDoc1000 saw what I'd written, he wouldn't want to date me. For that matter, neither would the real JewishDoc57.

HottieDC's profile may have seemed insincere and shallow to me, but then I thought about all the other popular profiles I'd viewed. Were these women really that shallow, or did they instead reveal just enough information to pique interest? Maybe HottieDC was smarter than I was giving her credit for. Online, she was definitely more enticing than me. She was open, less competitive, and more eager to date.

I supposed that I could just copy her profile and use a version of it as my own. But I also needed to take new photos. And as long as I was using HottieDC's profile as a comparison to mine, maybe it made sense to evaluate other popular profiles from the home page as well. There were no doubt patterns and similarities. I could figure out what these women shared in common, at least digitally. I could collect data, study it, and learn how to edit my profile so that it would be more competitive.

"Uranus" was now playing, and I turned up the volume. As the French horns, cellos, and tympani drove along at a familiar, recognizable pace, I started thinking about how to organize patterns in online dating. In order to make sense of all that data, I'd need a spreadsheet to keep organized. And some whiteboards. Colored markers too. I imagined myself walking through a nearby Staples store picking out supplies. There were ultrafine-tip black pens and fat neon highlighters that I could use to visually map the data.

It was time to fall back on what I knew. I'd start tracking metrics. After all, data is what I knew. It wasn't emotional. It was clean, it was evident on dating sites, and I could use it to determine what made the perfect woman, at least in the online dating world.

I started to feel my stomach rumble and twitch with an excited, nervous energy. I knew that collecting profile data was only the start. Eventually, people started interacting with each other on dating sites. What were these women doing differently from me? Were they making the first move by winking or poking another user? Were they sending an email first? I wondered how long they were waiting to contact someone back. Was there a secret formula to the first few instant messages?

In order to uncover why these women were successful, I'd have to interact with them.

I could keep JewishDoc1000 active and test the waters . . . favorite a few women, maybe even send a quick email. Did communicating with them cross a line?

I swallowed the last sip of wine from my coffee mug. My left leg was tingling a bit. How long had I been sitting here? It must be going on six hours.

I glanced over at the Mary Poppins list I'd made earlier that night.

JewishDoc1000 met many of my criteria. He scored more than 900 points, but I could do better and create an entirely different profile that met even more criteria. With two profiles, I could potentially test more interactions and learn more about who these women were. I could aim for not just the best possible profile on JDate, but what would constitute an ideal husband in the real world. If I've gone this far, why not set a higher baseline?

I'd already written JewishDoc1000's profile, and I could easily go back in and mold it into exactly what I wanted. But instead, I invented a new profile with a much higher point value. I could call him Eric2336.

I started sketching out his personality, his goals, and his hobbies:

> *Eric Wasserstein. A civil litigation attorney who's just made partner at a large law firm. He loves Woody Allen movies, he's seen every* Seinfeld *episode at least once, and he agrees that* Arrested Development *is the best American sitcom of all time. He's six-one, with short black hair, dark eyes, and a medium build. He uses a Mac at home and a PC at work . . .*

Eric2336 started sounding formidable. He could also be the man of my dreams, the man of any woman's dreams, I reasoned. So let's see how HottieDC likes him. I went back to her profile, clicked Favorite, and waited to see what happened.

9 | Gaming the System

In which I outsmarted the algorithms.

I clicked Refresh and waited. Eric2336 was everything I wanted in a man, so why weren't any women clicking on him? I was losing patience.

Click! Refresh!

Nothing changed. No beeps, no flashes. Nothing. I counted slowly to three, then clicked again . . .

Why won't the damn thing change?

I kept refreshing over and over, staring at my JDate inbox, confident that the next time it loaded, I'd see a new message waiting for me. But each time, there was nothing but a welcome message from the service, thanking me for my paid membership.

"Why is nobody clicking on Eric's profile?" I said aloud, clicking to refresh the window again.

I'd designed Eric2336, now known as Eric Wasserstein, specifically to attract HottieDC and women just like her. He was a near-perfect specimen: a tall, handsome lawyer at a famous firm, who loved Woody Allen and once meditated at an Indian ashram. Surely at least a few women should be clicking on my profile? I hit Refresh again, this time glancing at the clock at the top of my screen. How was it four A.M. already? I'd been at this for the entire night. Clearly, I'm not thinking clearly . . . I'll go to sleep for a few hours, wake up, and check my inbox again.

I closed my MacBook, collected my paper and pens, and stumbled back inside, yanking the power cord out of the wall as I walked into my room. I was too tired to pull the door shut behind me.

I threw everything onto one side of the bed, then pushed back the covers and collapsed into my pillows. As I shut my eyes, I felt my temples throbbing against my glasses, which I'd forgotten to take off and place on the nightstand. My whole head felt as if it was being compressed. It could have been the wine and all those cigarettes, but I decided that in my breakthrough tonight, I'd been concentrating too hard. I needed to defrag and spin down my mind. Instead, I drifted off to sleep, just as the birds outside started their early-morning ruckus.

Soon I had the feeling I was lying in a bed that was much softer than mine, one with decidedly fluffier pillows. I felt a warm leg against mine, then a smooth but firm hand glide across my stomach. "Good morning, beautiful," a deep voice whispered in my ear. "You fell asleep with your glasses on again."

I rolled my head toward him and felt his lips against my forehead.

"Eric Wasserstein, the civil litigation attorney who's just made partner at the big law firm?" I asked, looking into his gorgeous eyes.

"Shhhh," he said, bringing me toward him.

As he started kissing my neck, I noticed a rather large robin perched on the doorknob. It must have flown in because I didn't shut the door all the way, I thought.

"I'm six feet tall and twenty pounds heavier than you are," he continued, nibbling on my ear.

But all I could focus on was that bird, which was staring at me with its beak open. Then it let out a piercing but familiar ring, which sounded more like a banged-up pay phone than a robin's call . . .

I blinked several times, thrashing my head against the pillow, and then saw my mobile phone glowing.

"Fucking phone," I mumbled. "Who's calling this early?"

I sat up, trying to focus on the digital clock next to me. It was already noon, a full six hours later than my usual wakeup time.

It was the start of the weekend. My lungs burned from all the cigarettes I'd smoked, and I probably could have used another few hours of sleep, but this particular morning (okay, afternoon), I was waking up with a new purpose. I was empowered to cruise JDate as Eric2336 and to start studying how my competition was using the site.

I walked into the kitchen and put a kettle on the stove. I had two full days off with no plans and no dates lined up—an exhilarating feeling—and I could devote the entire weekend to tweaking Jewish-Doc1000 and Eric2336, along with my scoring system. As I waited for the water to boil, I thought about my next steps. I'd happened upon a critically important discovery—the need for a list—and then built a scoring system to prevent against future bad dates. And I'd had the foresight to log in as a man not only to check out my competition, but also to study how women interacted with my ideal mate.

JewishDoc1000 and Eric2336 were good first steps, but I didn't want them to just be simple copies of what was already out there. Plus, I wasn't allowing for any variation. In the real world, the men of JDate offered an entire spectrum of acceptable possibilities. I'd listed *Arrested Development* and Woody Allen specifically to highlight a particular sense of humor—namely, one that suited mine. To be fair, though, I had a few close friends who were very funny and hated Woody Allen, but who thought that rambling bro-comic Dane Cook was a genius. I also had two wildly divergent physical types. Jeff Goldblum: curly, dark, Mediterranean; and young Larry David: East Coast Jewish, funky glasses, bald.

HottieDC may love the Jeff Goldblum version of Eric2336, but not the Eric2336 who watched *Crimes and Misdemeanors* five times trying to decide if nice guys might someday finish first.

The kettle started whistling, so I wrapped a towel around the handle and poured the water into my French press. As the mixture of coffee grounds frothed, it occurred to me that I ought to be more explicit. If I'd already created these two profiles, why not turn this into a real experiment? Instead of two profiles with limited information, why not a minyan? I could construct a network of ten men who each shared common characteristics but were different enough that together, they'd attract a critical mass of women.

Press in one hand, I walked back into my room, picked up my laptop, notebooks, pens, and power supply, and headed back out to the patio.

I sat down at the table, arranging my supplies just as I had the night before. Layers of cigarette butts filled the ashtray, and loose tobacco flakes were still scattered everywhere. My Three Peckered Billygoat coffee mug was right where I'd left it. It was completely dry, but when I reached for it, a sticky maroon ring held it securely to the table. I sniffed it, hoping enough of the wine had evaporated that I could pour my coffee in without having to go back into the kitchen. It seemed clean (clean enough?), so I pushed the knob of my French press all the way to the bottom of the glass and poured myself a fresh cup. It didn't taste good, but it was hot and caffeinated.

I thought about variables and what I needed to accomplish. I had ten top-tier attributes and fifteen second-tier attributes in my scoring system, which meant that I had a whole bunch of potential husband combinations. I opened up my computer's calculator app to do some quick math:

$$(10!) + (15!) =$$

$$(10 \times 9 \times 8 \ldots \times 1) + (15 \times 14 \times 13 \ldots \times 1)$$

$$= 1,307,677,996,800 \text{ possible combinations}$$

JewishDoc1000 didn't have to be a plastic surgeon, and Eric2336 didn't have to be a lawyer. I was really only looking for someone who had a career and was gainfully employed. He could be a lobbyist or a professor, or he could work in business.

I needed to solve for extra variables. But ultimately, this exercise was about understanding two audiences: my competition and my potential matches. If that was the case, there was no reason for me to reinvent the experiment wheel. This was no different from doing a standard user-profile list for one of my clients at work. If a company wanted to attract more visitors to its website, or launch a new application or build out its social network for a marketing campaign, I'd model user profiles based on all possible audience targets. What would entice these people to accomplish the set of tasks we wanted them to complete? What behaviors could we expect? What challenges might they face? What would motivate them to reach our goal?

If I created model user profiles inside JDate and knew each character well enough, I could inject them into a situation to simulate their actions. My goal in this experiment wasn't just to observe other women on JDate. It was to understand them deeply enough so I could model their behavior. I didn't want to try to hide who I was or to pretend to be someone else—I just needed to learn from the masters and present the best possible version of myself online. I'd use these profiles to collect data and to learn from the women with whom I would soon interact. Then I could build a super profile—a sort of amalgam of the popular girls and my own data.

I knew now what was possible. It was the ultimate solution for which I'd been searching, for which everyone had been searching. I could game online dating.

I took another sip of my coffee, thinking for a moment about how to get from Yozora with bullet points to an amalgam of popular women . . . a sort of super profile worthy of JewishDoc1000. Besides creating the ten male profiles, I'd need a whole bunch of data, which would take time to gather. I should probably also define the experiment, set some rules, and create a framework for collecting information.

And office supplies. I needed lots of office supplies.

I closed my laptop and brought everything—my notebooks, pens, power cord—inside. Just around the corner from my apartment was a small but well-stocked office supply store. I decided to run out and pick up the essentials: two of the largest whiteboards I could carry, a set of dry-erase markers in different colors, Post-it notes, legal pads, tape, and file folders. I also needed my version of a little black book: a vinyl binder with 5-inch rings.

Back at home, I started rearranging furniture. I put the leaf in my kitchen table and pushed the longer side flush against the wall before positioning the two whiteboards on it. I cleared off the books, magazines, and light on the end table next to my futon and moved it to the corner of the kitchen. It would make a much more stable base than the cardboard box I'd been using as a printer stand, and I was about to force the machine into overdrive. I grabbed a bowl from the cabinets and placed all of my pens and markers, along with the Post-it notes, inside.

With my new workspace ready, I kept the black marker in hand and started writing notes on the whiteboards. I began with a question near the top of the left-hand board:

WHAT AM I TRYING TO FIGURE OUT IN THIS EXPERIMENT?

Below, I brainstormed a big list in no particular order:

- What am I doing wrong with my own profile?
- Is there a correlation between vocabulary used in a profile and that profile's popularity?
- Do profiles with fewer words do better than those with more words?
- What are the physical attributes of the photos in popular profiles?
- How is humor used in popular profiles?

- Is there a correlation between hair color and popularity? Or hairstyle and popularity?
- How much do popular profiles reference specific information about current/aspirational career?
- What is the tone and gist of the first contact?
- What is the tone and gist of subsequent contacts? Does tone evolve quickly or slowly?

I started imagining the data I'd find. I bet that HottieDC didn't send the first message. She was too attractive for that. And she was probably popular because she was blond.

"Wait a minute," I said aloud. I knew that just because a few facts or data points seemed to align, that didn't mean that one thing was the cause of the other. If HottieDC wrote the word *fun* multiple times and also had a popular profile, it was entirely possible that she was popular for other reasons. I grabbed the red marker and at the very top of the whiteboard wrote CORRELATION ≠ CAUSATION to remind myself to be careful about making assumptions.

On the other board, I started sketching out a workflow to determine the best way to surface some answers. That meant creating ground rules and expectations for my experiment. I started writing:

1. I will message people only using the website, via instant message, or via a disposable Hotmail account I'll create for each persona.

Since I didn't need anyone's real identity, it would make better sense to keep interactions as anonymous as possible. Also, with ten male profiles to manage, it would be most efficient and make the most sense to streamline as much as possible.

2. I will have introductory conversations only.

My goal was not to unfairly lead any women on to think that we might actually meet in person. Instead, I was only interested in learning about what made a great profile and what happened during the beginning of an online relationship. Who messaged whom first? What was the protocol? What got revealed? I only needed information from what happened during the first few interactions. Regardless of how I ultimately changed my profile, I'd still be *me* in the relationship. I'd therefore cap all interactions at three per woman. I would not make future plans to meet, give out a fake phone number, or make any promises. If, after the third interaction, things seemed to be continuing, I'd politely apologize and say that I didn't think things would work out.

3. I will not initiate any contact.

Because I was trying to be as respectful as possible, and because I didn't want to unfairly raise anyone's hopes, I decided to interact only with women who messaged me first. Meantime, I would still click through the site to observe and catalogue what other women were writing in their profiles.

I realized these restrictions automatically made my data collection dirty, and a scientist or statistician would balk at my methodology. I wasn't trying to prove a theory or get published in a scientific journal. I just wanted answers to my questions, and to the ultimate question, really: How could I game online dating sites to find and attract my ideal husband?

I sat down at the table, looking at the whiteboards and then at the time. I'd now spent forty-one hours—that's a whole fuckload of units—developing labor-intensive solutions to my problem. It was going to take many more hours to collect the data I was after. It might have been possible to write some code to scrape profile data off dating sites and then to crunch numbers on the back end, but an algorithm couldn't observe behaviors and infer meaning in a way that made sense within my own context. Also, I wasn't a programmer.

I looked at the whiteboards and then at my laptop. I'd need a place to store the data I'd be collecting. Starting with one big workbook that included multiple tables and spreadsheets seemed reasonable. I'd go after qualitative and quantitative attributes. Quantitative data would be relatively simple to gather and would be the easiest to analyze, since I was only asking how many times women daters do/say/post different variables. Pulling vocabulary in from profiles would be easy enough. I could simply copy and paste all of the self-entered profile content. Same with emails and chat transcripts.

I knew it would be trickier to deal with qualitative data and assign a number to the kinds of qualities that made a woman seem funny or smart or likable. The problem with my collecting and analyzing this data was that I knew I couldn't always be a good judge. Given my sardonic, dry sense of humor, could I assess someone who didn't laugh at the same things I did?

I also knew that vocabulary could be an issue. I'd personally never use the word *fun* to describe, say, a physical object. But Hilary did all the time. In her world, a couch, a Barbra Streisand song, and a plate of spaghetti could all be "fun," and that didn't make her boorish or laconic.

How could I qualitatively judge personality? I could define each category by *x* number of types, like sense of humor. I started mapping out labels for humor types:

> **Dumb:** Doesn't get the joke quickly, needs explanation, isn't able to be funny in her written profile. Also, someone who uses the word *silly* in the wrong context.
>
> **Apatow:** Smart but also appreciates gross-out humor.

Sarcastic: Uses sarcasm in her written profile and messages
   but isn't mean.

Seinfeld: Makes sharp jokes and dry references in her profile,
   is quick to the punch line, seems a few steps ahead.

Bitchy: Makes fun of other people/places/things, tries to
   one-up others, is generally not a nice person.

Then I could apply a 1 to 10 rating scale to the descriptions so I could do analysis later on in the process. That would allow me to describe a woman's use of humor as a 7-Apatow with a 9-Seinfeld, which may not have made sense to an outsider but helped me understand instantly how a woman was communicating.

I also knew that I needed to improve my timing and my approach in those critical first few emails and instant messages. Each time someone clicked on or messaged one of my male profiles, I'd start a timesheet, noting lots of different granular attributes. What time of day was it best to send an email? How often did successful daters send messages? How long did it take for them to respond?

Successful timing, I knew, also had to do with who said what and when. There is a certain rhythm to courtship. What was said in that first contact with the popular women? How quickly did they reveal personal information? How often did they want to talk about their feelings, wants, and expectations? Did they seem pushy or docile?

I also needed to collect passive information. Some women might be very interested in one of my profiles, but they might be waiting for me to make the first move. They could favorite me or simply click a few times a day to get my attention. My experiment's rules wouldn't allow me to contact them first, but I didn't want to discount these women in my analysis.

If I wanted to evaluate this much data, it was going to take significant time to collect. The more data I had, the more accurate a super profile I could create. A week would be too short . . . while six months seemed like overkill. Would it take the average woman a few days to contact me after seeing one of my profiles? I had no idea, but it seemed unlikely that we'd max out our three interactions in less than several days. I tapped my fingers on the keyboard without actually typing anything as I thought through how much time to devote to the experiment.

A month? A month should be enough time to both gather all the information I needed and schedule time to get a haircut, go shopping, and maybe sneak in a manicure. Within a month I should be able to launch my super profile and my real-world makeover.

Now that I had rules, a schedule, and a framework for the experiment, it was time to refine JewishDoc1000 and Eric2336 and to create the other eight profiles. I started scribbling possible names in one of my notebooks: LawMan2346, ProfAndy, Jay12207, Ming850, Book-Maniac, Ari1971, IdeasMan88, DrDNA . . .

I knew from my client work that I'd need to create a full description for each user profile, right down to insignificant details. If these profiles were going to be successful, they'd need to be as authentic as possible. Each would be based in Philadelphia, though many would be transplants from other cities. I had to know what these men liked to eat for breakfast, whether they preferred beer or wine, even their favorite brands of potato chips. I needed to know their hobbies: would Prof-Andy rather visit a Smithsonian museum or tour a historic home? Which kind of old movies did Jay12207 like better—madcap comedies with Danny Kaye or American classics with Jimmy Stewart? How many brothers and sisters did LawMan2346 have? Was BookManiac a pet owner, and if so, dogs or cats?

I opened a new document on my laptop and started typing. LawMan2346 was a lawyer who scored 750 points:

NAME	JASON
USERNAME	LawMan2346
TOTAL SCORE	750
AGE	32
HEIGHT	6'1"
WEIGHT	200
HAIR	black, thick, curly
JOB	Lawyer—specializing in litigation. Already partner. Doesn't have horrible hours—can control his own schedule. Has worked at three firms. This is probably his last job unless he goes off on his own, which he isn't sure about. He would only launch his own firm before getting married/starting a family. He has a great reputation in his field—is feared and respected.
GRAD SCHOOL	Harvard Law
COLLEGE	Columbia—majored in philosophy, minored in Spanish
HIGH SCHOOL ACTIVITY	Debate team (two-man, policy). Was also on the student newspaper, which was called *The Eagle Reporter*. He wrote a weekly opinion column. Was really good at math, not as great at chemistry, biology. Hated his sophomore year English teacher, who insisted they read *Moby Dick* twice, at the beginning and end of the school year.
PARENTS	Married for 38 years. Dad is a lawyer. Mom is an economist working at the Federal Reserve. They have a great sense of humor—he talks to them daily.
SIBLINGS	One younger brother, Mark, who is an investment banker. They're three years apart. They didn't get along great as kids, but they're best friends now. Mark is totally opposite of him—plays sports, drinks beer. Typical man's man kind of guy.
FAMILY TENSIONS	His mom is pressuring him to settle down and start a family. He's feeling nervous about parenthood, since it will disrupt his whole life.
HOBBY 1	Cooking. He loves learning about what flavors go together, how to properly cook meats, the science behind great food. He's been to Thomas Keller's restaurants, and got the dinner prix fixe at Per Se. Loves to cook for people, throw dinner parties at his house.
HOBBY 2	Tech, gadgets, computers. Apple instead of PC. Owns a MacBook.
HOBBY 3	Traveling. In college, he spent the summer between his junior and senior year backpacking through Europe. He takes a wild adventure every year and has been through parts of Asia, Africa, South America. Does not like cruises, thinks they're for people who don't like to travel-travel.
INTEREST 1	Certain TV shows: *Curb Your Enthusiasm* and *Arrested Development*. Thinks both are hilarious. Also thinks that *Cheers* is one of the best sitcoms ever.
INTEREST 2	Movies. Thinks that *Godfather II* was just as good (if not slightly better) than *Godfather I*. Hated *Godfather III* with a passion.
INTEREST 3	Historic homes. He loves to take tours of historic homes and mansions and has been in amazing places all over the world: Hampton Court Palace, Mark Twain's house, the Biltmore Estate.

NAME	JASON
MUSIC 1	Likes music, but not country, metal, or rap. Sort of ambivalent about the rest.
MUSIC 2	Appreciates music from the '80s.
PETS	Doesn't own any, but would someday want a medium-size dog. Okay with adopting one from the pound.
FOOD	Ardent carnivore. No food allergies. Doesn't do fried foods, mainly because they upset his stomach. Eats bacon, but would never eat a ham sandwich or pork chop.
IRRITANTS	People who don't signal before making a turn. People who take too long to explain something. Dell (computer) customer service.
POLITICS	Not too involved or interested in politics. Leans left, but has voted Republican. It depends on the candidate.

I would absolutely date LawMan2346. I liked the fact that he talks with his parents every day and is close with his brother. That mirrored my relationship with my family. We had debate team in common, and if he'd been successful, that meant he and I would also share the same kind of work ethic. I could see us visiting the Hearst Castle and the Metropolitan Museum of Art.

ProfAndy's user profile was next, and I needed to significantly alter what he looked like, as well as what he did for a living and his hobbies. Even with these variations, he still scored 850 points.

NAME	ANDY
USERNAME	ProfAndy
TOTAL SCORE	850
AGE	36
HEIGHT	5'10"
WEIGHT	185
HAIR	balding, very close-cut hair
JOB	Investment banker. Specializes in mergers and acquisitions, focuses mostly on emerging technology and start-ups. Already partner. Doesn't have horrible hours—can control his own schedule. Has worked on Wall Street, is now tired of NYC living. He's thinking about starting an Angel investment fund.
GRAD SCHOOL	Wharton MBA

NAME	ANDY
COLLEGE	University of Chicago—majored in business (finance). Interned at Lehman Brothers his junior and senior years.
HIGH SCHOOL ACTIVITY	Went to Northside College Prep High School. Did Academic Decathalon, which was actually cool there. President of Student Council. National Honors Society and Microfinance Club. Very good at math.
PARENTS	Married for 42 years. Dad is a corporate finance guy. Mom is also a CPA. He talks to them a few times a week.
SIBLINGS	One younger sister, Ilene, who is a lawyer. They're four years apart. They get along well, but he doesn't like her current boyfriend, Frank. Frank isn't Jewish.
FAMILY TENSIONS	The family doesn't like that Ilene is dating Frank. They're not very observant, but Frank's family is very Catholic.
HOBBY 1	Though he no longer lives in NYC, he still has many friends there and tries to visit a few times a month. He likes to spend a few hours on Sundays walking through Central Park. Has favorite coffee shops on the Upper West Side and in TriBeCa near his old office.
HOBBY 2	Loves going to museums. He's a member of MoMA and the Metropolitan Museum of Art, even though he doesn't live in NYC anymore. He has a few favorite paintings at each (*Boating*—Manet, and *Number 1*—Pollock)
HOBBY 3	Traveling. He's been throughout Asia already, and particularly likes China. He hasn't spent much time in Western Europe yet, but he wants to.
INTEREST 1	Certain TV shows: *Six Feet Under, Deadliest Catch*. Also really liked *Northern Exposure*.
INTEREST 2	Interested in technology. Uses a smartphone. Is an expert in hardware and set up his own home office.
INTEREST 3	Fencing. He took a fencing class in college for fun, and still keeps up with it now. He belongs to a local fencing club and practices once a week.
MUSIC 1	Likes music, especially southern classic rock.
MUSIC 2	Appreciates music from the '80s.
PETS	Doesn't want to own pets until he has children who are at least in elementary school. Wants a dog to be a part of teaching them responsibility. Allergic to cats.
FOOD	Will eat anything. Prefers watching what he eats during the week so he can splurge on the weekends. Does not like energy drinks, but does love coffee.
IRRITANTS	When people mess up simple finance tasks, like balancing a checkbook. Doesn't like people who speak really loudly on trains or airplanes.
POLITICS	Conflicted. He'd vote Republican, but he doesn't agree with their social politics. He'd vote Democrat, but he doesn't agree with their budget and fiscal planning. Usually he votes for whoever seems to have the best financial plans (taxes, spending, budgets).

I worked for another two hours, building spreadsheets with detailed user-profile information. Each one initially scored between 750 and 950 points, which aligned with what I thought was a realistic range given what might happen in real life. In order to achieve a higher score, certain nuances, like quick wit and whether or not he had integrity, could only be judged after at least one in-person meeting.

I clicked to print all the profiles. My next step was to create the JDate memberships.

I pushed my chair back and stood up, bringing each ankle up behind me to stretch my legs. I was dreading this next step of the process—I didn't enjoy the tedious work of manually entering all that data the first time I created my profiles, and I now had to endure answering questions, copying and pasting content, and verifying email addresses eight times in a row.

I sat back down and opened a browser window. I typed in JDate's web address and clicked to create a new profile. I was now very familiar with the screen and what was going to be asked of me.

You are a:
Man seeking woman

What kind of relationship am I looking for? And what's my current relationship status?
☐ Marriage
☐ Single

When I clicked the maroon Continue button, I was taken to a final screen where I was asked to upload at least one photo.

"Fuck!" I shouted. I'd gotten this far into my extremely complicated, ingenious project only to be thwarted by this one irritating little oversight. I'd completely forgotten about photos. When I was logged in to dating sites as myself, I skipped all the profiles that didn't have pictures. Without photos, I knew my J-men wouldn't get any hits.

I rocked back in my chair, balancing on its two rear legs, and pulled my hoodie up over my head. Where was I going to get photos? I stared up at the ceiling, looking for inspiration. Instead, I found three brown-gray splotches. Was that mold? Or smoke stains?

I could try to Photoshop friends and family members, and maybe try to meld their faces together or something . . . but that seemed unlikely to work. I could ask some of my friends if I could temporarily use their photos as is, but I only knew two single men. The ones in relationships would never agree.

"Fucking photos . . . ," I said, sighing. I glanced from the ceiling back down to my computer and saw a folder on my desktop labeled "Images."

Of course! My stock photo service account! I always needed images for presentations and reports, so I'd licensed photos from an online service. I could just buy each one a face!

I logged in to my account and, at the top of the screen, did a quick keyword search on "man." I also discovered that I could refine by physical characteristic. Searching on "man, curly hair" gave me more than 1,000 options. "Man, curly hair, glasses" returned 466 photos. "Young man, bald" returned 2,636 photos.

I clicked to initiate a download when a window popped up with the license agreement. "Okay . . . ," I said slowly. "This is not a problem. I bet you don't list anything about online dating profiles . . ."

I scrolled through, reviewing the lengthy document. "Do not distribute the photo or resell it . . ." No problem. "Do not print it on a poster . . ." Not an issue. "Do not incorporate it into a trademark . . ."

I read through the agreement again, looking for any mention of use on an online dating site. There was none. I clicked to download, accepted the license agreement, and printed each photo out in color. I wanted to have a complete visual picture of each man and tweak the details before finalizing their profiles on JDate.

I sat down at the kitchen table, rereading all the user profiles I'd created. Each fit my criteria, and though each had scored the required minimum number of points, they really were very different kinds of people. We are all so nuanced, with an infinite number of possible likes and dislikes, tastes and preferences. Hilary argued that with my list, I'd been too specific about what, exactly, I was looking for in a husband. From my point of view, that haystack didn't have just one needle. There were potentially thousands of needles waiting to be found, sorted, analyzed, and dated.

I opened my wallet and slid out four plastic cards. I assumed that JDate would allow me to create only one profile per credit card. I had two credit cards and two bank debit cards, which meant that I'd be able to experiment with just four paid accounts. The others would have to be free accounts with limited functionality, which I realized also meant restricted messaging.

I needed to accomplish one last step before building out all the profiles. Each would need a valid email address. I lined up the pages on the table and created an email account for each one at Hotmail. LawMan2346 would use LawMan2346@hotmail.com, JewishDoc1000 was JewishDoc1000@hotmail.com, and so on. To my surprise, of all the usernames I created at JDate, only ProfAndy was unavailable on email. That wasn't an issue. He'd be ProfAndy12.

So that I didn't have to continually log in to JDate and all of those Hotmail accounts to look for messages and activity, I brought all ten email addresses into a single program on my computer. I labeled each account with the correct JDate username and set the system to automatically push new messages to me every 30 minutes.

I decided to spend the rest of the day creating each of the profiles. I trudged through, copying and pasting text. As I worked, I realized that

I'd neglected to incorporate some of JDate's required data fields into my spreadsheets. As I added elements, like zip code, I had to go back and correct the data on my own computer. What I'd entered in JDate had to exactly match my user-profile list's descriptions, in order to ensure proper tracking. I started with LawMan2346 and then moved on to ProfAndy. By the time I circled back to JewishDoc1000 to tweak and correct his profile, my forearms were cramping badly and my eyes were straining to focus on the screen.

Using and collecting meticulous data was the only way I could improve my chances of finding the right person, and I knew that the only way I could fundamentally change my experience was to spend a month learning from my competition. They would unwittingly make me over and teach me how to be a popular girl. I couldn't pull an all-nighter again. I could cast these profiles out into the world and check to see which bait took in the morning. It was time for some much-needed rest.

I awoke the next day and went straight into the kitchen to start water boiling for coffee. My table was now covered in ten dossiers, neatly arranged, with each male profile labeled. I'd left my Mac-Book there too, recharging. I sat down at the table and pushed open the lid. JewishDoc1000's profile was still logged in, right where I'd left him.

I glanced at the icons at the bottom of my screen, thinking about that net I'd cast. Did I catch any fish? Hovering next to the mail program I'd configured the night before was a red notification bubble—I had new messages. This was it, a critical new moment of truth. If I clicked through and there were lots of messages, that meant my experiment had worked. If the messages were just JDate spam and I hadn't heard from any actual women . . .

I let out a deep sigh, not wanting to think about an empty inbox. I rolled my pens back and forth against the table. It's only eight hours since the profiles went live. Surely a few women would have looked at them and responded, right? I hovered over that icon for just a few seconds longer.

"Fuck it," I said, and I clicked.

Right there on my screen, in black-and-white, were thirty-seven new messages. More than three dozen messages!

I grabbed my phone and started dialing.

"Hey," Hilary answered.

"Where are you?" I asked.

"Brunch with Christy and Julie," she said. "Where are you?"

"In the kitchen," I said hurriedly. "After I made the list and scoring system, I knew that I could use them to find the perfect guy. But obviously other people would think he's perfect too. Then I realized that I needed to keep going."

"Okay . . . ," she said. "What did you do?" she asked slowly.

"I logged in to JDate as a man," I said.

"Of course you did—"

"Ten men, actually," I interrupted. "I started out by making a profile of the perfect man, someone who'd score more than seven hundred points. Then I went into the site with his profile and started looking around. There were all of these fucking women. All of them were thin and showing way too much skin, if you ask me . . ."

"Wait, when did you do this?"

"I don't remember. It's all a blur now," I said. "So after I saw what my competition was, I knew I had to do something."

"Amy, do you know what day of the week it is? Have you left the house since your date with Jeff Goldblum on Friday?"

"It's Sunday," I said impatiently. "And yes, I'm still wearing the same outfit as whenever the last time it was I talked to you, since I know that's your next question. I've been working!"

"And you wonder . . . ," she started as the kettle began whistling. "What's that sound?"

"I'm boiling water for my French press," I said, taking the kettle off the stove and mixing the water in with the coffee grounds. "So anyhow, I created ten perfect men. At least perfect for me. And I cast them into the site to see which women would be interested in them," I said, making a fishing gesture with my press and accidentally splashing coffee everywhere.

"Okay . . . ," Hilary said.

"You're never going to believe this," I continued. "This morning, I had thirty-seven email messages! I think that LawMan2346 is actually the most popular," I said, scrolling through my inbox.

"Check this out," I said, reading from my screen. "Message from Elisa4u. She's blond, looks young, very pretty. She wrote: 'Hey. I read your profile and really like what u wrote in it. I majored in business too and also used to live in NYC. Want to talk more?'"

"Wow," Hilary said. "She sounds nothing like you at all."

"That's exactly my point," I replied, now clicking out of her profile and back onto the main page of JDate. "She's popular. She has an active profile, and apparently a bunch of men are interested in her. The kicker is that I would never, ever write a message like that. Or abbreviate *you* with the letter *u*. But obviously she's doing something right. And that's just one message. There are thirty-six more so far . . . Wait," I said, refreshing my screen. "Make that thirty-eight."

"It pains me to say this, but that's kind of genius," Hilary said.

"Kind of?" I shouted. "It's fucking brilliant! In a month, I'm going to have a pile of data collected that shows, definitively, not just who my competition is, but which kinds of profiles are most competitive. Then I'm going to take all of that information, analyze it, and make a super profile. An amalgam of the trends I observe, but using my own real-life data."

"Can you get in trouble for this?" she asked.

"I checked the terms of service, and I'm not doing anything that violates it," I said.

"Leave it to you to read all of the fine print and use it against someone."

"It's not like that . . . ," I started.

"You really should take a shower," Hilary said. "And one more thing . . ."

"Yeah?"

"You probably shouldn't tell anyone that you're doing this. Like, never ever."

I hung up with Hilary and put my credit cards back into my wallet. She was right, at least about the shower. I did need to clean up and to get out of that apartment, at least for a little while. I could do some laundry, get some actual food in me, maybe take a walk. The profiles were working, I had a system to collect data. I just needed to let a little time pass.

In the meantime, I had other projects at work to complete. My client list was growing much faster than I'd anticipated, and I started mapping out an organizational chart. In a month or two, if business kept pace with what I'd been seeing, I would need to hire an assistant and another consultant.

I was happy to have more work than I could handle, since it distracted me from my mom's condition. She was upbeat and positive, but this latest round of chemo had taken a severe toll on her strength. She was relying on a wheelchair more often now, which she hated, and she'd also developed thrush, a yeast infection of her tongue's mucous membrane. The stent pushing one of her tumors away from her bile duct needed to be replaced via an unpleasant outpatient procedure. I made plans to go home the following week.

By Friday, I was finally in a position to start answering the messages I'd received. The men I'd created turned out to be wildly popular, and each profile had a high level of activity.

Every time someone clicked on one of my profiles, I went back to the home page to see where that woman was listed, even if she didn't message me. If it looked like she was popular—posing competition to the real me—I'd start importing all of the information from her profile. I'd learn what kind of language she used, how she described herself, what she listed as her hobbies, whether she commented on her income, how much time it took her to respond to messages, and so on.

I knew I needed to wait a while longer before I could start to draw conclusions, but I was too excited about what I was seeing. I thought a quick visualization of vocabulary wouldn't hurt:

I knew that my data-geek friends would laugh at what I'd just made—a word cloud like this was so 1997—but it did serve a useful purpose.

I could clearly see that the best-performing profiles were those that read as easygoing and spontaneous. I'd never once referred to myself in writing as "fun" or even as a "girl," for that matter. I didn't use the word *love* unless it was meant for someone specific. But it was easy to understand now that I'd been too stuffy and professional in my profile, even without the bullet points. In real life, most people I knew wouldn't describe me as "a fun girl," but that didn't mean I wasn't fun to be around.

The profiles of these women were optimistic and aspirational. For fuck's sake, they'd managed to work in comments about "puppies" and "sunshine." And they used lots of positive descriptive language, like *pretty, colorful,* and *hilarious.*

I knew immediately that I'd inadvertently sabotaged my own profile. I'd foolishly assumed that these women were purposely not listing their accolades or talking about work in order to mask their ambitions—or maybe because they didn't have any at all. Instead, I started to understand that it's difficult to sound conversational and upbeat when talking about the minutiae of my job. Yes, *I'm* enthusiastic and excited and proud of what I've accomplished, but it was much easier to start a conversation with easier subjects, like summer concerts or your favorite breed of dog. Rather than impressing future dates, I was turning them off.

My cheeks grew red thinking about how horribly I'd presented myself on JDate. It would be so easy to just tweak my profile, and I desperately wanted to erase what I'd first written.

But my goal, I had to remind myself again, was radical change. This wasn't about subtracting a few sentences or using the word *fun* a certain number of times.

I had a lot more to learn. In order to create my super profile, I still needed more data. I didn't yet have answers to the bulk of the questions I'd asked at the beginning of this experiment. Sure, the word cloud I'd created was interesting, but it was too early to draw meaningful conclusions. Waiting another three weeks would allow me to collect more information, have more interactions, and make more observations.

I went back to my screen and replaced the word cloud I'd made with a different data set and printed out a new sign to hang above my whiteboards:

patience ^{endure}
· wait

You're a 5-Apatow, 5-Seinfeld

What the popular girls know.

Okay, everyone. Time for another quick break in my story. Before I move on to the next part, where I tell you about how I created my super profile, which cascaded into ultimately meeting my future husband, I need to explain what I learned.

I discovered some incredible trends and universal truths for successful online daters. And since I know that a few of you are probably reading this book because you're hoping to find 1,500-point husbands and wives of your own, I want to reveal what I found so that you can improve your own dating profile.

I thought about taking you through the actual process in narrative form, describing in gorgeous detail all of my late-night number-crunching benders. Like the moment I actually remembered how to calculate this beast:

$$\text{Correlation }(r) = \frac{n\Sigma xy - (\Sigma x)(\Sigma y)}{\sqrt{[n\Sigma x^2 - (\Sigma x)^2][n\Sigma y^2 - (\Sigma y)^2]}}$$

Or when, in the wee hours of the night, I made some truly stunning scatter plots. Though I know this all sounds glamorous and exciting to you, much of this work was just me, sitting at my kitchen table in a hoodie, playing with numbers.

In a few pages, I'm going to tell you about how most people don't like to talk about their jobs, because it reminds them of, well, working. I have a feeling the same is true about math. The more I describe how I arrived at my conclusions, the more your eyes are going to glaze over. Or worse, your mind might wander from this book to your high school algebra textbook, and you'll start resenting me for making you think about quadratic equations again. I get it.

Instead, allow me to fast-forward three weeks and get to the stuff you actually want to know. By then, I'd completed my data analysis and had unearthed a trove of insights.

During the experiment's run, I interacted with ninety-six women who lived in Philadelphia. I adhered strictly to my guidelines, never messaging a woman first. And I always capped our interactions at three. I anticipated that at least a few women would become angry after I told them I didn't want to pursue a relationship, but the entire process was wildly nondramatic. They'd typically say something like "thanks anyway" or "okay, best of luck," and that would be it.

At the beginning, I looked at these women and wanted to make fun of them. One of the first I interacted with was Jodi567, a thin and beautiful young woman. Her About Me section was generic, and she appeared so dull, so uninteresting. After the first email, Jodi567 seemed thin, beautiful . . . and super-nice. By email three I found her downright likable. She was a gorgeous, approachable girl next door who was up for adventure and ready to have fun.

It didn't take math to figure out why any man would clamor to date her, or why I found myself wanting to be her friend.

Cameron Diaz Syndrome! That affliction causing men to fall in love with the gorgeous but completely and totally fictional ready-for-anything girl next door. It was in full force with Jodi567, and I was finally experiencing it firsthand. It suddenly made sense why my male friends always fell for that type. They weren't just trying to get laid by some pretty bimbo. They could see themselves settling down with Jodi567, a carefree, spontaneous woman who's ready to be your best friend and looks hot in formal wear. I'd want to be in a relationship with someone like that. Who wouldn't?

I knew that in reality, though, Cameron Diaz secretly had flaws. She may seem perfect, but we all know that no one really is. We all have problems. Cameron Diaz was only an illusion, and I kept drawing unfair comparisons. Unfair, that is, to me.

The problem is that while I'd achieved a new self-awareness, my transformation to gorgeous, carefree Amy hadn't yet completed. I'd look at Jodi567 and then at my own profile—or worse, at myself in the mirror—and would want to throw my computer out the window. I saw woman after woman, and with each page refresh I lost a few more pixels of self-confidence. I had to remind myself that my JDate profile wasn't the real me and that I was still in the process of both digital and physical makeovers.

The more I looked, the worse I felt about myself. This process was supposed to be doing the opposite. So just a few days into my experiment, I vowed to stop looking at my own profile, and I would refuse to criticize myself anymore.

Now, as you remember, I created ten male profiles that were all very similar. Would you believe that even among my J-men, there was a mini popular crowd? All of the profiles gained traction, but it quickly became apparent which ones were the most desirable. JewishDoc1000 and Law-Man2346 emerged as the two most popular profiles, attracting the widest group of women. It seemed as though there was one primary characteristic that set them above everyone else: They had hair.

Here's a depressing piece of data: Even though JewishDoc1000 and LawMan2346 were attractive professionals with great family backgrounds, they had only a 50 percent chance of getting someone to email them more than once. A woman would reach out to Jewish-Doc1000, and he'd answer back with something innocuous like "Hi, [name]. Thanks so much for reaching out—tell me more about yourself." Then she'd never message back.

If JewishDoc1000 could get only a 50 percent return on investment, what did that mean for me? I had no way of knowing why messages stopped, but I imagined it was because someone like Jodi567 was interacting with a whole bunch of men at the same time. This taught me a valuable lesson early on—just because two profiles match doesn't mean that they match exclusively. Just as in the real world, someone may be casually dating a few people at once—and it was a hell of a lot easier to do that online.

This was unfamiliar territory for me, since I'd only ever really dated one man at a time. I could multitask at work, just not in relationships. In fact, the biggest problem I faced during those weeks was one I never anticipated: how to keep track of which male profile was talking to which woman. Though I had great systems for tracking content, I never came up with a good way to remember who was taking part in what conversation. More than once, I confused Ming850's job (tax attorney) with Ari1971's (accountant). I also kept forgetting that ProfAndy doesn't live in New York City anymore. It became especially confusing when one of the women decided to message two or more of my profiles. Did HorseTrainer23 tell Ming850 about her riding lessons, or was it JewishDoc1000?

Four weeks, 158 interactions, and ninety-six women later, I learned how to make my profile competitive and how to act in those critical important first few interactions. Although the conclusions I'm drawing stem from data that met specific parameters just for me, I uncovered what I now know is a universal truth that applies to everyone: The goal of online dating is to get offline as quickly as possible.

Online dating sites are catalogues meant for browsing. You simply need to look as good as you can, be relatable to the widest possible audience, and then throw in a memorable point or two that distinguishes you from the rest of the crowd. It's up to you to then apply the right filters using a list and a scoring system and to not screw up your timing, so that you can meet your mate. More on that in a bit.

Be a Fun Girl!

Because I'd already made a word cloud very early on to quickly analyze and show what kinds of descriptive language women were using on JDate, I had a basic sense of what I was going to find. As I expected, profiles using conversational, upbeat language did the best.

I evaluated the language used in written profiles—the About Me section, the extended descriptions—and also in emails and instant messages.

More than half of my ninety-six women referred to themselves as a "girl" or "fun girl." I often saw opening lines like "I'm a fun-loving girl that enjoys . . ." and "I'm a laid-back girl who wants . . ." Starting this way was immediately disarming. If someone said to you "I'm uncomplicated, generally in a happy mood, and I like to do stuff," you'd want to hang out with him or her, even if it wasn't romantic, right?

In contrast, I'd listed five things I do for a living while referring to myself in the third person:

> Yozora is an award-winning journalist, speaker, and future thinker, adapting current and emerging technologies for use in communications. She has spent twelve years working with digital media and now advises various start-ups, retailers, government agencies, and media organizations as well as our clients all over the world.

Yep, that's pretty bad. Even I wouldn't date me.
Popular women use positive, optimistic language, not buzzwords

like *future thinker*. Here's a visualization of the ten most often used words I found:

This positive sentiment set a nice conversational tone for the whole profile, unlike the marketing copy and bullet points I'd listed from my résumé. When I read some of these shorter, optimistic About Me sections in my head, they seemed juvenile. But aloud, they sounded exactly like what a normal person might actually say when introducing herself to someone new.

Instead of leading with my hobbies or activities, I went straight into a description about my job. That put me in a slim minority. Fewer than 10 percent of the women I interacted with mentioned their jobs in their opening lines or anywhere in their About Me sections. Instead, many stuck to a simple one- or two-sentence introduction more along the lines of:

> *I'm an outgoing, fun-loving person who finds enjoyment in mostly anything I try. I'm a great listener and an excellent friend. :-)*

It was an aspirational starter. Rather than describing my hopes and dreams, I listed my accomplishments.

> *Fluency in Japanese*
> *Conversational ability in Mandarin*

Fluency in HTML, CSS, JavaScript, and other web languages

And while we all know how ridiculous this looks now, the problem is that I usually mentioned these points at the beginning of an introductory conversation in the real world. The first question I typically asked someone, regardless of the situation, was "What do you do?" It's not that I'm trying to be competitive or to brag. It's that I identified work and my accomplishments as central to my being, and I didn't have any hobbies. Work is what defined me.

Do I have ambitions unrelated to my job? Of course. We all do. I also have a short list of places I'd like to travel, meals I'd like to eat, skills I'd like to learn. So do successful online daters. They don't list what they've done at work, but instead what they'd like to do with their future mates:

> *I currently love my job and where I'm at in my life. I want to travel out of the country, so I hope to meet someone who likes to travel as well. A big ambition of mine is to learn how to make the perfect Cosmopolitan. Maybe you can teach me?*

Yes, I was looking for someone smart and professional. And while I was optimistic and had a positive outlook on life, I didn't usually describe those qualities as important facets of my personality since I thought it should be assumed. Smart, professional men like women who are explicit about their happiness.

Desperate Women Write Too Much

It turns out that there's a direct correlation between profile length, especially in the opening section, and the likability of that person. "Easygoing girls" who "love to laugh" clock in at fewer than a hundred words. That works out to about three sentences for most of us. It's enough room to generically say you're adventurous and fun, but not to describe in detail what that means. Instead, good profiles mentioned characteristics that would probably be true for all of us:

> Popular Woman: *I want someone who will make me laugh.*
> Amy: *I'm looking for a young Larry David who knows what the correct cashew-raisin balance is.*

Unless you've seen that particular episode of *Curb Your Enthusiasm,* the joke won't mean anything. Worse, the other person may not get the reference and think you're being pretentious.

It is okay, however, to get specific about broad subjects: *I like going to the movies* or *I like to eat at new restaurants* seems to work fine, as long as there are no more details. Consider movies. I love *The English Patient.* I've seen it several dozen times and it's one of my all-time favorite movies. Lots of people hate it, though. *The English Patient* may be the only movie a potential date and I disagree on, but he might despise it so much he won't date me to begin with. Or maybe the day he saw *The English Patient,* his brother died. Now Ralph Fiennes and that movie—and by extension, me—are constant reminders of the person he's lost.

Either way, liking this movie or Ralph Fiennes or World War II period dramas in general was not listed in my first- or second-tier scoring attributes. Therefore, I should leave it off my profile. I learned that leaving off potential unknowns at the beginning would eventually help me get further into the dating process.

As I looked through profile after profile, I found that About Me sections with fewer than a hundred words tended to belong to Jodi567 types. I couldn't believe how generic they were—and yet these profiles were clearly popular. But I was learning that my goal on dating sites was to gain access to a man who scored 700 or more points. I just needed an introduction, and then I could unleash the rest of me.

Short profiles that express just enough information to pique someone's interest work best. At the five-hundred-word point, I found that a profile took a drastic turn in one of two directions. It was either from an accomplished woman with lots of education and usually some kind of license (doctor, lawyer) . . . or it belonged to a not-so-attractive woman who seemed horribly lonely and desperate to date.

Example A: Peony99, twenty-nine-year-old doctor

I'm an ophthalmologist and have recently moved to Philadelphia after living in Prague for the past year. I love seeing the world and taking on new challenges. My latest: I just got back from Ukraine and Russia, which was a truly fascinating trip. I got to use some of the Russian I've learned. Languages are a hobby!

I was a competitive swimmer all throughout my childhood and still try to get in at least 50 laps a day. I belong to a club and try to compete in regional meets when I'm in town on the weekends. I also grew up playing cricket and tennis with my family. We had a court in our backyard, so I was able to play daily and wish that I still could now. I have a very mean serve. Unfortunately, work has me really busy. I'm planning to open my own private practice in the next two years, so I'm constantly networking and building out my current patient base as I hunt for office spaces and surgical centers in the area.

I have a great family. They mean everything to me, and my three sisters are now living in Manhattan. They're all married and starting families, and they want me to join them! I'm there at least a few times a month to see them, so NYC feels like a second home. They'd describe me as smart, ambitious, and outgoing. We have just as good a time hanging out in their apartments as we do at the coolest bars. And that's a small bit about me. What about you?

Example B: HypotenuseYou, thirty-eight-year-old high school teacher

I'm a math geek working as a basic algebra teacher in a high school. It isn't my dream job, so I'm looking for something more challenging. I'm not surrounded by the best and the brightest, but the people I work with are very nice and mean well.

I thought I'd be married by now, but circumstances didn't turn out that way, so I'm still looking. Marriage is the primary reason I'm using online dating sites. I've never been very lucky meeting men at bars or clubs, since I'm too shy at first and don't dress to be ogled.

I have been engaged two times, once when I was in high school and another time after college. When those relationships didn't work out, I gave up for a few years and didn't date anyone. During that time I was really depressed, and I went through years of therapy. Sometimes I was lonely, but I couldn't get in the mood to meet new men. Now I'm ready to start dating again. I still have my cats and am looking for a husband to settle down very soon with and start a family.

I'm an avid collector of many things. I have a collection of Barbie dolls. Some are vintage dating back to the 1950s. I also collect American Girl dolls. I don't have a lot of time for other activities, but I try to get in exercise time during the week. I walk around my neighborhood when I can, but it's not every day. I'm someone who's more comfortable in sneakers than high heels. Would you like to go on a picnic with me? Please be in touch.

Would you date either of those women? The math teacher sounds horrible, of course. But the ophthalmologist reminded me of close friends. She was obviously smart, well traveled, and confident. In theory I should want to be friends with her and support her as a fellow smart, well-traveled woman dater. But on paper? She's too intimidating.

I knew now that my own profile was entirely too long. I'd written close to nine hundred words—a dissertation compared to what everyone else was doing. That put me in the bottom 8 percent of all profiles I looked at. The amount of text on my profile page was oppressive. If I was blathering on that much before even meeting someone, what would I be like on a first date?

This isn't to say that the details of my personality, tastes, and preferences aren't important, or that I should obscure the facets of who I am. For the purposes of attracting someone online, I learned that it's just better to roll them out slowly rather than all at once.

5-Apatow, 5-Seinfeld

Remember how earlier, I'd created five types originally and applied a rating scale of 1 to 10 to learn about how women used humor on JDate? Here's a quick refresher:

Dumb: Doesn't get the joke quickly, needs explanation, isn't able to be funny in her written profile. Also, someone who uses the word *silly* in the wrong context.

Apatow: Smart but also appreciates gross-out humor.

Sarcastic: Uses sarcasm in her written profile and messages but isn't mean.

Seinfeld: Makes sharp jokes and dry references in her profile, is quick to the punch line, seems a few steps ahead.

Bitchy: Makes fun of other people/places/things, tries to one-up others, is generally not a nice person.

Now, in real life, I'd rate myself as a 6-Apatow, 7-Sarcastic, and 9-Seinfeld. I actually knew that sarcasm doesn't translate well online, so I typically avoided using it.

Sarcasm definitely posed a problem for others on JDate. Without context, the real meaning didn't come through. Instead of seeming witty and clever, those women just sounded angry. One sent DrDNA a message that started "Oh gee, another Jewish doctor. How original." She continued with a few sentences about how she wanted to know more about the "DNA" in my username and if I worked in genetics, which she thought was interesting. But that opening sentence was so rude it made me think that if I ever did something wrong in our relationship, she'd rip me apart.

Some women went 10-Apatow way too soon, flirting in a clunky, cheesy way that would be endearing after a few dates, but not as a first email message. One woman told Jay12207 that the strangest thing she'd ever seen was a guy wearing a glow-in-the-dark condom that had a smiley face on it, and then he put on a puppet show for her. Next she asked Jay whether or not he was into glow-in-the-dark performance art.

Women like Jodi567 would say they "love to laugh," and they might reference a scene from a TV show or movie, or even something a friend did. But it was inoffensive, relatable, and meant as a tease for more to come.

Leave Work at Work

So if only 10 percent of the women I observed focused on their careers, what was everyone else doing?

JDate, like many dating sites, offered a drop-down box of choices. Most people selected something close to their career, like "business" or "education" and left it at that. They might write "career is important to me," but there would be no further description.

I'd forgotten that, given the chance, most people would rather do something besides working. For them, their job *is* actual work that doesn't pay well enough or offer acceptable benefits. To a lot of people, talking about work is tantamount to complaining, and smart women know that complaints have no place in a dating profile.

I loved my job. Since I started my own business, I determined how much money I made, how many days I could take off, and even what the dress code was in the office. I was working ninety hours a week by choice and making more money than I ever had working for someone else. I got to wear a hoodie and yoga pants during non-client-meeting days. My new career also allowed me to take on clients and projects that I absolutely loved. I was actually more excited to talk about work than anything else, so I'd attempted to describe what I do in my profile:

> *I'm the CEO of a consulting company that's not a traditional consulting company. We study disruptive technology and come up with hyper-creative, game-changing ideas that transform the companies we work with. That might be a mobile strategy, or a new way of engaging users, or looking at lots of data to spot new trends. Because we work with big corporations, governments, and others around the world, most of what we do is under strict nondisclosure agreements to protect our clients' privacy.*

Work made me happy. But it potentially reminded others of something they dread. (Quadratic equations, natch.) Making things worse, I didn't have a normal job. It took me a full paragraph to describe what I do—and even so, it wouldn't make that much sense to digital outsiders. I should have stuck with "consultant" and saved the details for the first or second date.

Popular Girls Are Short

I assumed that daters lied about their weight. I certainly did. You probably do too. So it didn't surprise me that just about everyone on JDate described themselves as "athletic/fit." There were other choices, of course, like "muscular," "curvy," and "thin." I would describe myself as "curvy," since I had a classic hourglass shape. But lately, that term connotes plus-size, which I wasn't.

What shocked me was how many women seemed to be lying about their height. All of the ninety-six women I interacted with listed their height as five-one to five-three, even though the average height of an American woman is five-four. Though it's not impossible that 100 percent of these women would have fallen below the average, it's statistically improbable. Plus, you could tell from photos that most of the women were taller than they described. The chairs, bar stools, and cars they were standing next to all tend to come in standard sizes.

I'm five-six without my shoes on, and in most circumstances, I'm close to eye level with most of the men in the room. I remember a photo of a woman wearing a dress and heels. She was sitting on an overstuffed couch, struggling to angle her legs to the side. I'd had the same problem—my legs would be slightly too long to sit with them in front of me, and if I attempted to cross them, I'd wind up accidentally kicking a passerby. That was either a miniature couch, or this woman was an extremely tall five foot two.

Show Some Skin

This should be obvious, but photos are critically important to an online dating profile. Profiles without photos get buried and ignored.

I looked at several hundred photos, trying to analyze each using a variety of data points. Rather than rating looks, which would have been totally subjective and somewhat unfair since we all have different tastes and preferences, I instead dissected elements of the photos, evaluating things like lighting, pose, activity shown, amount of skin shown.

My inclination to flash a big smile in a photo—it may be yours too—turns out not to be the best approach. Think about the last time someone took a photo of you. They probably said, "One, two, three, smile!" and you did, forcing a grin as you stood awkwardly, waiting for it to be over. Guess how we look in those staged photos?

Instead, photos where the woman seemed to have just finished laughing really hard while she made eye contact with the camera (and therefore, me, the viewer) appeared more authentic and natural. Flirty smiles worked, too. Women who were able to convey a truly happy mood or sexy attitude in their photos trumped the very pretty women who'd staged their smiles.

A solo shot of an average-looking woman laughing outperformed a very pretty woman shot in a group. That's because it's difficult to have good posture when someone has his arm around you. If you have long hair, it might get stuck or pulled as the photo is being taken. When taking group photos, we tend to focus our cameras on the tallest people. That means that women typically have to look up, which makes our faces appear fuller than they are.

Photos taken with pets always looked awkward. You may have the cutest English bulldog in your neighborhood, but you'll inevitably show unflattering slobber and pet hair in your picture. It's hard to look giddy and carefree when you've been clapping your hands and making cutesy sounds trying to get your dog to look at the camera. Plus, there's a whole group of people who try to figure out if pets look like their owners. Do you want JewishDoc1000 suddenly thinking that you look just like your Weimaraner?

Good lighting was also important. If it was too bright, a woman would look washed out, regardless of how much makeup she wore. Photos that were too dark or grainy made her appear less friendly and outgoing. Using a flash aged everyone, even the men, several years—suddenly, fine lines, wrinkles, and skin imperfections were highlighted.

It's an old, established rule, but "golden hour" lighting is ideal because the first and last hours of sunlight are diffuse and warm. For that reason, women with photos taken outside during those hours tended to look great.

Outdoor photos were better in general, particularly those taken during golden hour at an event. There was one fantastic shot of a woman standing on a beach at sunset, and that picture exuded backstory. She'd probably spent the day with her friends, laughing and relaxing, and was now suntanned and ready for an evening bonfire. She seemed to have a wonderful, fulfilled life into which a man could just insert himself. Photos weren't just another piece of data to explain who you are; they could act as inspiration agents for would-be suitors. A man could imagine himself touring the pyramids of Giza with you, or walking along a tree-lined river during the fall.

But mostly, a man wants to imagine his future wife with an incredibly hot body. Popular girls in the real world know this (otherwise what evolutionary advantage is there to wearing string-based underwear and letting it peek out of our jeans?) and post photos accordingly. All successful profiles show bare arms at a minimum. Most highlight a full, but not overbearing, cleavage. Some women had taken the extra step to wear a shimmery lotion to make their skin look dewy, glowing, and really healthy. It seemed like every gallery included at least one strapless dress and one deep V-neck shirt. These women also weren't afraid of color, which brightened their faces and made them seem more vibrant.

It's Okay—Make the First Move

I was always told by my parents and friends to let men contact me; otherwise, I'd seem too aggressive. I worried at the outset of my experiment that if I waited for women to make the first move, I might not have any data to collect at all. I was shocked to learn that the opposite was true.

Popular women didn't hesitate to reach out to my profiles. They sent casual messages that were just a line or two long. They would open with "Hey" or "Hi there" instead of "Hello [name]," and follow with "I like that you [detail from profile]. I'm interested in [detail] too."

There were no gimmicks or strange pickup lines. In great profiles, I didn't see any bad abbreviations, like "ur" or "luv." Most women just sent a friendly, noncommittal note with an average length of 542 characters, or about 98 words long.

Wait Approximately Twenty-Two to Twenty-Three Hours

There was a great scene from the movie *Swingers,* where the guys are sitting around a table debating how long to wait before calling a girl. A day? Two days? What's industry standard?

> *Mike: Well, how long are you guys gonna wait to call your babies?*
> *Trent, Sue: Six days.*

Six days is definitely too long in online dating. So was two. I found that online, the pace was pretty fast. Once I responded to an initial message, it took an average of twenty-two hours for a woman to get back to me. With so many forms of instant communication—Facebook, text messaging, IM—that twenty-two hours was enough time to make me wonder what she was doing but not enough time for me to lose interest.

Peak hours for sending a first email through the JDate system tended to be during work (eleven A.M. to four P.M.) and then just after dinner (seven P.M. to nine P.M.). I did have a few women send me a first message after eleven P.M. Those who did had an 82 percent chance of coming from a profile that had too many words.

Instant messaging seemed to follow the same pattern. More women used it during work hours and earlier in the evening, and they kept the conversation very short. I spent an average of twelve minutes on IM, with about ninety seconds between messages.

Flirt Using IM

While it was a disaster in profiles, on IM, light sarcasm worked well:

> *Woman: What did you do today?*
> *Me: Took a nice long walk.*
> *Woman: That's hot.*

One big difference between email and IM: 87 percent were more likely to flirt using instant messaging. Because of IM's conversational nature, it was much easier and more natural to flirt. Some women would ask what I was wearing. Others would tell me they were on their way out the door to meet up with friends and describe what they were wearing, which inevitably meant talking skin.

It also meant that I rarely got to end the conversation first. Most women would chat for just a bit, then say they suddenly had to go somewhere else. I could see how this would leave a man with a sense of urgency. It would definitely bait competitive men, who'd want to know the bigger, better deal she was off to see.

Ask Lots of Questions

All of the first interactions were casual, friendly, and inoffensive. Most of the women never mentioned an ex-boyfriend or even wanting to get married. They didn't complain about anything—not their jobs, friends, relatives—and kept messages pleasant.

They mainly asked a lot of questions. Did I like to go hiking? Had I seen a certain movie or eaten at a particular restaurant? They put the ball in my court and seemed very interested in learning more about me. The process was flattering rather than interrogative.

Don't Talk About Cancer

One piece of information I was hoping to learn was how quickly popular women share personal information. At some point, when my experiment was over and I was dating again, I'd need to explain that I was flying back to Chicago every other week to be with my mom, whose cancer was only growing worse. She was constantly on my mind, and a primary motivating factor in why I'd wanted to find a husband and settle down right away.

I wasn't socially inept enough to start a conversation with "By the way, my mom has terminal cancer and it's going to seriously mess up the next few years of my life. Are you in?" But the stress of my situation was causing insomnia and full-on panic attacks, where I'd fall over and black out. When was the right time to bring it up? Plus, I didn't want to be with someone who couldn't handle what we were going through. I realized that mentioning my family's issues too soon might scare off a perfectly decent guy before he had the chance to learn the good stuff about me.

Popular women never delved into their own personal details during those first few messages. I didn't get the idea that they were obscuring important facts, but they also didn't unload things like "Oh and by the way, my last boyfriend beat me up" or "I flunked out of medical school."

Once I crunched all the numbers and finished my analysis, I was able to build my own set of communication guidelines using this new information. I wiped one of my whiteboards clean and wrote out these rules, which I promised to observe going forward:

1. Only consider profiles that score at least 700 points.

2. I can send the first message, but if a guy doesn't respond, don't message him again. Also, stop clicking on his profile over and over hoping that will somehow change his mind.

3. Go forth with a 5-Apatow/5-Seinfeld and no sarcasm until the second round of instant messaging.

4. Let him IM me first. When messaging, keep the conversation very fast, light, flirty without being aggressive. Cap conversations at twelve minutes or less. Always say that I have to go meet friends or that I'm on my way to something fun.

5. Do not mention work until he asks me about it. Then be somewhat vague.

6. Spend at least a week exchanging messages until giving out my phone number. Then talk at least once before meeting in person.

7. Any in-person dates must score a minimum of 700 points based on a combination of his profile and initial conversations over email, instant message, or phone calls.

Once I'd nailed how to communicate with someone on JDate, my next step was to make myself over, both digitally and physically. That's what Chapter 11 is all about.

Before you turn the page, though, I want to offer one final note about all of these findings and word clouds and statistics. I've said "most women" and "the average women" a whole bunch of times to describe what I learned about online daters. Keep in mind that the data I collected probably doesn't jibe with JDate's own internal data or even what you might find on another dating site. That's because I built this whole experiment using details specific to me. I did, however, uncover some common threads and best practices for everyone else. Once you've finished reading the whole book (including the notes!), take a look in the appendix for more details.

I needed personalized data in order to learn how to become a popular, super-fun digital version of myself. My goal was to entice the right men to interact with me as they might Jodi567 or HottieDC or any of the other popular women online. Once we got past that crucial introduction, I could let my full personality shine.

Remember, you game a system by understanding it on a fundamental level so you can exploit its structure and gain a personal advantage.

In my case, that meant creating a JDate super profile.

11 | The Super Profile

Fun, outgoing breasts!

Sweat had soaked through the back of my racer-back tank top and most of the stretch capris I'd worn to the gym earlier. Now the air-conditioning was making it unbearable to sit comfortably with so little clothing. I reached behind me for my MIT hoodie and quickly pulled it over my head.

From my new vantage point at the kitchen table, I could see just beyond my laptop and past the trees to the sun bouncing off the art museum. I'd spent last night cleaning, moving the table away from the wall and back to the center of the room. I hung one of the whiteboards near the refrigerator and put the other one, along with all of my notebooks and folders, under my bed for storage. With the curtains opened and everything in its proper place, my shitty apartment finally looked more like a home and less like the dark lair of a sociopathic dating mastermind.

I took another bite of salad and looked at my screen, at the maroon Log In button and blue star logo that had become so familiar to me. A month ago I'd sat in the same place, flanked by a pack of cigarettes and a takeout container of General Tso's chicken. Now I was finishing a small Niçoise salad and my fourth bottle of water for the day.

Next to my plate was a file folder containing a single online dating profile. I'd arranged it neatly, just as I had the file folders for my experiment's ten men. It contained three fantastic photos, an interesting but not intimidating username, a chart showing dozens of innocuous details, and a schedule listing available times for sending instant messages and emails. At the top was a label I'd printed earlier: "Amy Webb—Super Profile."

The corners of my mouth turned up just a little as I glanced from the folder and back up to my screen, where a cursor was blinking in the log-in box. I started typing the required information:

You are a:
Woman seeking man

What kind of relationship am I looking for? And what's my current relationship status?
☐ Marriage
☐ Single

Username: TokyoGirl

As I clicked Enter and moved on to the About Me profile section, I stopped to consider just how much had changed during the past four weeks. Not only had my JDate competition taught me how to be popular digitally; they'd also shown me how to improve myself in the real world.

I'd joined a gym a few blocks up from my apartment and signed up for personal training. Without any data analysis or profile consideration, the gym matched me with a beefy ex–football player named Ronnie. At our first meeting, I violated all of the dating rules I'd created. I immediately launched into extremely personal details about myself and explained the rating scale, experiment, and super profile.

He was empathetic about my self-image issues in the wake of all the women I'd seen and wanted to start collecting data of his own. Ronnie forced me to step on a scale, pinched the back of my arm with a body-mass-index caliper, and gave me a food diary. Then he shot his hand into the air and shouted, "Let's get to work!"

This time, I voluntarily high-fived back.

If I was trying to land a permanent relationship with a 1,500-point man, I'd need to check in at the gym every morning by six A.M. Ronnie would meet me three days a week, and I'd be on my own to swim or hop on an elliptical machine three days a week. I was allowed one day away from the gym . . . as long as I promised to break a sweat somewhere else.

Two weeks into my new routine, I'd shed the six pounds I gained post-Henry. I'd also stopped smoking and hadn't even pined for a single cigarette. I created a new email template to use with my inner circle:

To: Friends & Family
From: Amy Webb

Subject: Week Two

Update: Ronnie spent 15 minutes this morning forcing me to alternate between plank pose and continuous sit-ups. He's 6'2" with a shaved head, blue eyes and amazing arms.

And I want to kill him.

Weight lost: 6.5 pounds
Panic attacks: 0
Units of coffee: averaging 6 oz a day
Sleep: finally averaging 5 hours a night!
High fives: 11

Just after I clicked Send, my phone rang.

"It's time to go shopping!" Hilary said.

I sighed as loudly as I could into the receiver.

"When was the last time you bought something new to wear?" another voice said.

"Mom?! Am I on a conference call?"

"You need our help," Hilary said.

"I'd love to see you in an outfit," my mom started. "Outfits"— matching pants and tops sold as a set—were her specialty.

"Mom, Amy's thirty, not sixty," Hilary protested. "She needs basic separates. A cute little black dress, a few tops that show off her waist, a decent pair of dress jeans . . ."

"You need a new bra," my mom added. "One that fits you. At Nordstrom's they'll do a fitting . . ."

"Why do I feel like I'm being ambushed? You guys know how much I fucking hate shopping," I said.

"Do you have to say that word?"

"Yeah," Hilary said. "You should stop using language like that now that you're dating again."

"Fine. I explicative hate shopping," I said. "But I agree that I need new clothes. What am I supposed to do?"

They dictated a list of what to buy and where to shop. I was supposed to go to Nordstrom and Banana Republic and buy a pair of dark-wash denim jeans, a pair of casual pants in a neutral color, two V-neck tops in bright colors, a lightweight jacket that was fitted at my waist, and a pair of casual heels that I could wear with anything.

"Don't forget to get fitted for a bra!" my mom reminded me. "Don't just buy something off the rack—make them measure you."

That weekend, I drove to the mall by myself. Since I'd be trying on lots of clothes, I threw on an old pair of jeans and a faded Monchichi T-shirt, which might have been hipster chic if hipsters weren't too young to recognize those cartoon monkeys.

Shopping list in hand, I started in the bra department at Nordstrom. My mom was right—there were plenty of salespeople ready to help. An elderly woman with a measuring tape around her neck led me back to a fitting room. She had me take off my shirt so she could examine my current situation. We stood facing each other, me peering a solid foot over her teased white hair while she reached her arms up to tug and squeeze.

"Stay put, honey," she rasped, walking out of my dressing room. "You need better lift! I'll be right back."

I pulled my mobile phone out of my jeans pocket and texted Hilary:

```
Old lady at Nordstrom just felt me up. It
was thrilling.
```

I was supposed to procure at least two bras, so after I found three I rode the escalator up two floors to the women's department. I took the list out of my pocket and reviewed all of the items I was supposed to buy. I'd shopped at big department stores before, of course, but always for something very specific, like a pair of black heels. I'd never gone in with a vague idea—a shirt—and had success.

The store seemed bigger now than I remembered. I looked across the floor, past the escalator bank, and past the baby grand piano to the other side, where two tiny heads were moving around a swirl of formal dresses. Even with my glasses on, I could barely make out their faces. I was surrounded by rack after rack of beautiful clothes and completely incapable of figuring out where to start.

I took out my phone again and started typing.

```
Got three bras. Too overwhelmed looking for
clothes here. Headed to Banana Republic.
```

As I walked into the next store, I immediately felt boxed in and confined. It was a space one-one-hundredth the size of Nordstrom's and yet seemed to have just as many clothes. Hot too. It suddenly felt unusually warm.

Was I supposed to buy a V-neck with or without sleeves? I found a dark blue silk top with short sleeves that had a tie in the back. I held it up to my neck and turned around to look at my reflection in the mirror. Yes, I'd lost a few pounds, but I had a feeling that tie would make me look pregnant. I pulled another shirt, this one a stretchy green cotton sleeveless V-neck, and held it up. Hilary had told me to find fabric that stretched, since it would supposedly highlight my cleavage while minimizing my waist. But next to my skin, that green made my complexion look pale and sickly. I found the same top in maroon instead.

I looked back at my list, suddenly unable to envision the clothes that Hilary and my mom had instructed me to buy. What did they mean by V-neck? Could I just buy a tank top? Was I allowed to let my arms show? Probably not. They probably wanted me to buy a V-neck with long sleeves. Why could I make sense of numbers and patterns but not colors and fabrics?

I peered over the racks of clothes and toward the front registers, hoping a salesperson would see that I needed help. Madonna was playing over the store's speakers—was someone in the back slowly turning up the volume? Why was it suddenly so loud? And hot? It was too fucking hot in that store.

I took the two V-neck shirts and walked over to another rack, trying to find the requisite pair of pants in a neutral color. Instead, I located an A-line light pink skirt, which had the same cut of the little black dress I was supposed to buy. The color probably doesn't matter that much, as long as the shirt and shoes match, I reasoned, and took everything back to try on in a dressing room.

I stripped down to my bra, underwear, and formerly white athletic ankle socks and stood in the stall by myself, just trying to get away from the noise and heat.

I slid the skirt off its hanger, folded it in half, and tried to fan my face and chest. It still felt as if my shoulders and back were on fire. I tilted my head up, wondering if the fluorescent lightbulbs above me were for some reason burning unusually hot.

I shimmied into the skirt, zipping it up in the back and fastening the tiny eyelet at the waistband. Then I tried on the maroon sleeveless V-neck, pulling its stretchy fabric over my head and breasts.

I turned back around to look at myself in the mirror. Hilary was absolutely right. The A-line did make my waist look tiny. But my pale legs against that pink color looked cadaverish, almost blue in that dressing room lighting. The shirt felt tight everywhere. Maybe I'd taken the wrong size? Yes, it brought out my hourglass figure, but that was only because it had shifted my breasts way up and over to each side. I know I was wearing a color-coordinated *outfit,* but all I could see were my enormous maroon breasts pointing awkwardly in the wrong directions.

I started laughing at my reflection in the mirror—I looked hilarious. Like Jessica Rabbit's demented Jewish cousin. I started dialing Hilary, wanting to describe this absolute fashion disaster. Then my cheeks grew warm and I felt a wave of nausea. I did look horrible. I looked *terrible.* It wasn't just this outfit; it was my frizzy hair, my mascara, my fucking misdirected boobs.

"Hello?" Hilary answered. As soon as I heard her voice, I felt a lump in my throat and watched my reflection blur in front of me.

"Hilly?" I said, now obviously fighting back tears.

"Oh my God," she said in a panic. "Is it Mom? It's Mom, isn't it? What happened? Where are you?"

"No, no, Mom's fine," I sobbed, collapsing on the bench and then sliding down to the floor.

"I'm . . . a . . . fucking . . . ," I wept, struggling to get the words out. "I did what you said. And I'm a fucking mess! I took the shopping list into Nordstrom and it was just too overwhelming, and now I look like a fucking pornographic Muppet! I told you I didn't want to go shopping."

"Okay, just calm down. Take a few deep breaths," she said.

"I don't fucking know what I'm supposed to fucking buy. Nobody will help me. And it's fucking hot in this store, and they keep playing Madonna . . ."

"Where are you? What store?" she asked.

"Banana Republic, like you said."

Hilary let out a deep sigh, just like I would have if she'd asked me yet again about how to connect to her wireless network. "Stay there," she said. "Don't move until I call you."

As I sat on the floor in those horrible clothes, I felt a thick stream of mucus sliding down my upper lip. My jeans and T-shirt were crumpled up on the bench along with my wallet and keys. I tried to control my breath but couldn't fight back another wave of tears. I threw my head back, bumping it against the wall, trying to redirect what was coming down my nose. I couldn't wipe it on the skirt.

As I whimpered more, I looked around for something to use. I gazed down to the mirror in front of me and to the bottoms of my feet. I'd still have shoes, I reasoned, and folded one bluish, cadaverish leg toward me. I slid off my sock and blew into it. Then I took the other sock and wiped it across my eyes and forehead.

My phone rang again, and at the same time, I heard a knock on my door.

"Amy?" everyone said in concert.

I stood up, snotty socks in hand.

"Okay, there should be some staff there to help you," Hilary said as I opened the door to three Banana Republic employees each holding several hangers of clothes, which looked nothing like the shirts and pants I'd chosen for myself. "I talked to the store manager and they're going to take care of everything. Just do me a favor and don't fight with them, okay? You can always return stuff later."

Back at home that night, I followed the rest of Hilary's instructions. I laid out the black dress, three tops, dress jeans, beige slacks, jacket, and heels on my bed and took photos of how to wear and accessorize each outfit. Then I printed each in color and taped the photos to the inside of my closet door, so I'd know exactly what to wear the next time I went on a date.

A few days later, I'd scheduled an early-morning haircut at a new salon that specialized in curly hair. I was told to block out three hours, since the stylist cut each curl individually. I walked into the salon and a receptionist with bright red curly hair greeted me with a triple kiss on the cheek. Afterward, she introduced me to a man I was supposed to address only as "Gregory" who was dressed in tight black leather pants and an oversized billowy pink top.

He led me to a chair in front of a gigantic storefront window, preening and lunging as he moved his scissors around my head. A young blonde walked by, and he stopped to knock on the glass. She waved, blowing kisses and motioning for him to call her later.

"Oh, Natasha," he whispered, smiling and blowing kisses back at her. "Gorgeous . . . fabulous . . . anorexic."

Gregory made two last snips, then handed me a mirror. "Voilà!"

As he spun my chair around slowly, I could see from every angle the value of a good haircut. He'd framed my face to minimize my high forehead, and the cascade of curls around my cheeks made me appear warmer, friendlier somehow. And every single curl was defined in a cohesive spiral. For the first time in my life, I was totally frizz-free.

However, I'd learned from my experiment that women with natural curls, even if they're styled really well, are at a disadvantage. Most men preferred women with long, shiny, straight hair. I'd thought about asking Gregory to straighten my hair once he was done cutting, but since I rarely straightened mine in real life, I let him work with my usual curls.

At last, Gregory turned and said, "You're gorgeous! Beautiful! I'll see you in three months." He air kissed each of my cheeks, then waved me toward the register, adding, "It's three hundred dollars, not including tip, and we only accept cash. There's an ATM right outside the door if you need it. Ciao!"

With my new hair ready, I walked a few blocks to a makeup store. This time, instead of meandering around by myself with a list, hoping some shopgirl might take pity on me and volunteer to help, I went straight to the counter.

"Hi there," I said to a young androgynous man wearing mascara and a fine layer of perfectly matched foundation.

"Good morning," he purred back.

"I need to buy all new makeup," I told him. "I have a whole bunch of money to spend and I'm free until two P.M. I'm also going to need a makeup lesson, and I'd like to leave here with a full face that's ready for photos."

"Let me get my brushes!" he squealed.

Several hours later, I reemerged from the store clutching a bag full of new creams, powders, and lipsticks. My hair and makeup ready, it was time to change clothes, slather on a glimmery lotion that would make my skin radiate, and take all new profile photos.

Back at my apartment, I had five outfits ready: the little black dress and a pair of black heels, dark jeans and a brown and green V-neck top, a black A-line skirt and a black and beige crossover shell, dark jeans and a deep red V-neck top, and the beige slacks with a white V-neck top. I'd also listened to my mother, finally, and now had three properly fitting bras. I popped in a pair of fresh contacts and left my glasses on the bathroom sink.

Following the rules I'd developed from my experiment, I knew I needed between three and five great shots of me both indoors and outside.

Juliet agreed to meet me at a nearby park just before golden hour. I started with the jeans and green-brown V-neck, which showed an ample portion of cleavage. I only had a small point-and-shoot digital camera, so posing by myself felt awkward initially, especially with lots of other people sitting on benches or walking their dogs, watching us. I forced myself to laugh as hard as I could. Thinking about how ridiculous we must have looked to everyone—my cute British friend saying "Okay, smile!" while I struggled to look "fun" and "casual"—made me laugh without trying.

I took the rest of the pictures indoors next to one of the windows in my apartment. I opened my MacBook and played a mix of the Postal Service and Coldplay. I knew it would be impossible for me to listen to "Such Great Heights" and "Kids" without hopping around—even by myself, in my crappy apartment—and dancing always lifted my mood. With the music on as loud as my speakers would allow and my face now flushed, I set my camera on top of my TV set, stood next to the window, and flipped my hair back, ready to look sexy-girl-next-door.

And now, with all that groundwork laid, here I was at last, in my sweaty gym clothes, looking through all of those photos on my computer. I took a final bite of my salad and pushed it to the end of the table as I started clicking through to select the three best shots for my new JDate profile. I was stunned at how seemingly insignificant changes like good makeup, hair, and lighting completely transformed me, bringing out my personality and making me seem more vibrant and tangible, even in two dimensions.

I was staring at the About Me section once again. Technically, I could use up to five hundred words to describe myself, but I now knew to write only three fantastic sentences. I needed precise language and details, while leaving certain elements out for later conversations:

> My friends would describe me as an outgoing and social world traveler, who's equally comfortable in blue jeans and little black dresses. I'd say they're right. I'm looking for a wickedly funny, insanely clever adventurer who's interested in making me laugh as we venture far off the beaten path together.

In the section asking about my physical appearance, I decided to be honest about my height: I answered five-six. Though I knew my chances were better if I also wrote that I was 115 pounds, the reality was that I weighed 160. I was still losing weight and was a respectable size 8, but I knew too much about my competition. Instead, I simply listed "Athletic/Fit" as my body type.

I selected three photos to use, two with glasses and one without, that featured a lot of skin, highlighted my breasts, and showcased a genuinely happy me.

I reached for my glass of water and rocked my chair back, examining my entire profile package. If I ever told anyone about all of the work I'd done, and then actually showed them my profile, they'd laugh at me. "You spend a month crunching numbers, and *that's* your amazing 'super profile'?" they'd no doubt ask.

The intricacies of keyword optimization, though, are much more complicated than it may first appear. This wasn't about me posting a handful of pretty pictures and using fewer generic words to describe myself. Anyone could do that.

I needed to crack the code, and to understand in detail what to say, as well as how to act during instant messaging. Dating services had far too many profiles for me to just search through for the perfect man on my own, and clearly they weren't matching me appropriately. This entire exercise was about learning exactly what I needed in a husband and then creating a user profile that would most likely attract that specific man while eviscerating my competition.

What I'd created represented me just as honestly as what I'd written originally. But in this version, I'd limited the information to share and purposely teased a few critical details.

Talking about a "little black dress" and then showing it in a photo exuded sexiness, and my writing "I'd say they're right" sounded confident, and even a tiny bit saucy. "Wickedly funny" allowed me to flirt more subtly than "that Big Vagina bit on *Curb Your Enthusiasm* was hilarious," and men would relate to my aspirational description of worldwide adventures.

At the end, I carefully selected a unique username. "TokyoGirl" would give someone a reason to ask me about Japan without my having to volunteer that information first, allowing him to lead the discussion by asking questions. That would enable me to talk about my work and accomplishments without coming off as a braggart. Plus, statistically I was better off using the word *girl* somewhere, since it evokes youth, happiness, and imagination.

At long last, I sounded exciting, spontaneous, and ready to have fun without having to sacrifice grammar or my own wit.

I clicked the maroon button to save and complete my profile. And though I wanted desperately to explore all the men on JDate, hunting for possibilities, instead I logged off the site. My super profile was complete, and I'd cast my net deep. Now I needed to let it soak for at least twenty-four hours, to see what it might attract.

I avoided looking at the time the rest of that night and even throughout the next day. After waking up, writing a client report, and realizing it wasn't even nine A.M., I decided to take off my watch and leave it facedown on the kitchen table. Instead, I distracted myself with my usual routine for as long as I could. I worked on some research, stayed at the gym for an extra two units, and made a slightly more elaborate salad than I'd had the night before. As I stood up from the table to clean up the kitchen, I finally glanced at my watch, hoping I'd made it to seven P.M.

It was 6:23 P.M.—close enough.

I left my dishes and silverware in the sink, refilled my glass with water, and propped open my MacBook. Suddenly, my stomach felt queasy. Had I eaten that salad too quickly, or was this just nerves?

To be fair, this next step was the most significant so far. I was dealing with my own material now. This time, if my inbox was empty, it meant a rejection of the best possible version of myself, not bullet points on my résumé.

I'd built a profile that I knew was optimized correctly with the right keywords, cadence, tone, and voice. I'd uploaded good photos of me, using what I'd learned from the popular girls. I needed to see not only a few clicks, but significant interest from 700+-point men; otherwise, it meant that something else—something I couldn't fix—was wrong. Since I refused to dumb myself down or drastically change my physical appearance, this super profile had to work.

I picked up my phone and hit the Redial key.

"Hey," Hilary answered.

"I'm about to log back in to JDate to see how my super profile did," I said. "I don't think I can do it alone. Where are you right now?"

"I'm at home, why?" she asked.

"Can you open up your laptop and go online?" I asked. Then I gave Hilary a URL and a password that would allow her to share my screen.

"Huh. That's pretty cool," she said. "Okay, I can see your computer. Now what?"

"Now wish me luck," I said, typing http://www.jdate.com and entering my account information. "Here we go . . ."

As the screen refreshed, I clicked onto the Communications tab, which would let me see which members had looked at my profile, who had favorited me, who'd sent me an email message, and who was using the Flirt tool. In the few seconds while the page loaded, my stomach cramped and sent a sharp pain up my right side.

Hilary spoke before I fully understood what had just happened. "Holy . . . shit . . . You have fourteen new email messages!"

"I have fourteen new messages!" I screamed back.

"Some of those guys are really cute," she said. "Scroll down so I can see more. Fourteen messages is a lot, right?"

I clicked my mouse around the screen, eager to see more statistics.

"Look at that!" I said, highlighting one of the numbers. "Sixty-eight guys have already viewed my profile since it went live last night! And look there," I said, highlighting another. "Three favorited me!"

"I cannot believe this actually worked," Hilary said. "You're . . . you're popular. Just like you weren't in high school. Now click over so I can see your profile."

I went back to my account and showed her the new page. "That's a million times better," she said. "I told you that dress looked good! And thank God you got a haircut."

"I fucking gamed the system!" I said. "I did it! I should date assholes and go on all-night benders more often. I think that weekend just changed my life."

"Speaking of dating, who are you going to go out with first?" she said.

"I don't know—we just logged in, remember?"

"Oh, right," she said. "What about Sammy810 on the third line down? He's gorgeous."

"I can't go out with anyone yet. Right? The rules?" I said.

"Wait, you're going to stick with those rules you made?" Hilary asked. "Amy, look at all these guys. You did it—you won. Now you can go out and have some fun."

"The super profile was only a part of this whole thing," I said. "I'm on phase three now, which means that I have to implement my scoring system. He has to reach seven hundred points or I can't go out with him at all."

"And . . . there's the Amy we all know and love," Hilary said.

"Listen, I've gotten this far, right?"

"So now that you finally look good in person and you have this wonderful super profile that's been optimized for whatever, you're going to refuse to date the men who find you attractive?"

"Yep. That's correct."

"Until you can test them?"

"Until they score seven hundred points."

"Well," she said. "You should at least tell Mom and Dad that a bunch of guys are interested in you. It'll make them happy."

"Okay, I'll call them tomorrow," I said.

"Hey, as long as I have you. I'm having problems with my email . . ."

As I hung up with Hilary, I looked back at my inbox. *Fourteen messages. I must be showing up on the home screen when men logged on too,* I thought.

It occurred to me that I could create a final male profile, in order to evaluate how I was faring against women like HottieDC and Jodi567. Were we all on the front page together? Were they getting more interest than me?

Then I realized I no longer needed to evaluate myself against these other women. My profile had bested theirs—obviously it was competitive, since I'd attracted so much attention.

I'd used math, logic, and a highly tailored data set to reverse-engineer an online dating algorithm so that it was personalized exactly for me. And now I had one of the most popular, active profiles on the site. I was more in demand in the digital world than I'd ever been in all of my thirty real-world years combined.

Most importantly, I knew that this finally put me in the right position. The mistake I'd made in creating my original profiles on JDate, Match.com, and eHarmony was exactly the same mistake made by so many other daters: because I didn't know exactly who I was looking for, and because I hadn't learned how to market myself to find that exact man, I was treading water in a vast, unending dating abyss. It should have been obvious to me the moment I first signed on to the sites. No business would launch a new product without first doggedly researching the market and then clearly identifying a target audience. Why wasn't I applying this same logic to my own online dating experience?

I had just solved the two key problems leading to perpetual singledom and unhappy marriages. First, we don't allow ourselves to dictate what we really want in a partner. I'm not just talking about a few key traits, like having the same views on religion or politics, but brainstorming a giant list like I initially made, and then scoring and ranking those characteristics. We're socialized to feel guilty for demanding certain immutable attributes, so we wind up not seeking out any at all.

For those people who do have a basic idea of what they want in a mate, they're not disciplined enough to evaluate those characteristics honestly. We're willing to rely on a dating site's secret algorithms to help us find true love. Why shouldn't we control the process ourselves and take an honest, quantitative look at the qualities that really matter to us individually?

It's unfortunate, but there's a direct correlation between self-confidence and our willingness to stick to our lists. People who have a poor image of themselves are more likely to take whoever comes along. There's an assumption that attractive people find love easily. But that's not always the case. A "normal" woman who's truly confident in her own skin and capable of marketing her assets will always fare better than a leggy blonde who may have perky breasts but lacks conviction.

Rather than agreeing to date everyone I met online, for fear of being left behind, I now had license to be highly selective and only contact a man who scored more than 700 points.

I wasn't sitting around, lonely and despondent, waiting for someone to ask me out when I least expected it. I was simply calculating my next move and evaluating all my options.

My last first date.

For three weeks I corresponded with more than two dozen men over email and instant message. I even agreed to talk on the phone with a few who seemed particularly interesting. But I wouldn't go out on any dates. I soon found myself under intense peer pressure, with Hilary and others continuing to question my motives. My mom, dad, grandmother, and extended relatives all pleaded with me to date anyone viable, at least once.

I had to remind everyone that my self-imposed isolation was no longer about me looking for love and hoping to find someone *mostly* compatible. If a potential suitor didn't score a minimum of 700 points on his profile, there would be no reason to email or IM him, no matter how much he talked about Larry David.

I already knew how to behave on a date, and how to get from date number one to a long-term relationship. I'd been down that path with Henry and a few others. This was about starting that journey with the perfect, 1,500-point man.

A few men came close, like Matt, the corporate lawyer. He was the oldest of three and extremely close with his family, who were all based in New York City. He graduated Columbia at the top of his class, traveled the same way I did, and had even spent two years living in China. He told me that while he was raised Jewish, he didn't feel a spiritual pull at all. Plus, he had thick, dark curly hair.

The problem with Matt was sports, a demanding and ubiquitous mistress who'd force me to share our bed at night with *SportsCenter* and who would claim all future sunny afternoons. Matt was a season ticket holder for teams in both Philadelphia and New York City, and he went to every game. When he wasn't sitting courtside at the Knicks game, he was on the fifty-yard line at Lincoln Financial Field watching the Eagles. On nongame days, he golfed near his home.

I supposed I might learn how to golf—Matt said that he'd teach me and that I'd enjoy it—but hanging around outside, drinking beer, and waiting for groups of people to sink a one-and-a-half-inch ball into a similarly tiny hole hundreds of feet away wasn't my idea of fun. Sports were a significant part of his lifestyle, and something that we'd never share together. I'd grow to resent him for preferencing five men and a basketball over just one me. Matt scored 750 right away, but once he divulged his affinity for sports and his dislike of some of my activities (cooking, touring historic homes), he dropped down to 600. That missed the threshold for a first date.

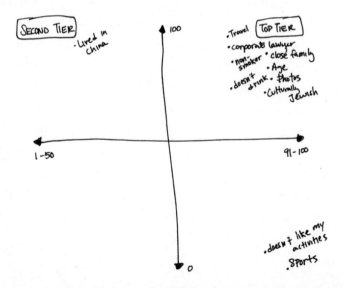

Ben also looked promising. He was a Realtor specializing in high-end properties. Ben's sense of humor was incredibly fast and witty, and he seemed to already know my response before I started typing in IM.

He thrived on luring in customers and then closing the deal. He seemed to be masterful at selling without actually selling, which I found fascinating. I wondered more than once if he was using those techniques on me, just as I was using my scoring system and super profile on him. We shared a natural competitive spirit, but ultimately, our similar intense drive is what made me realize that we were incompatible.

Ben had recently left a big firm where he'd worked for ten years in order to start his own commercial real estate company. As a new business owner, he'd need to work very long hours, nights, and weekends for the next several years. I had intimate knowledge of what that lifestyle meant, since I was already in the first year of my own nascent business. If we wanted to start a family soon, we couldn't both work ninety to a hundred hours a week. Ben was handsome, funny, and very smart, and on paper he initially scored 800. But he quickly lost points for not meeting my "career must be important but not all consuming" criteria.

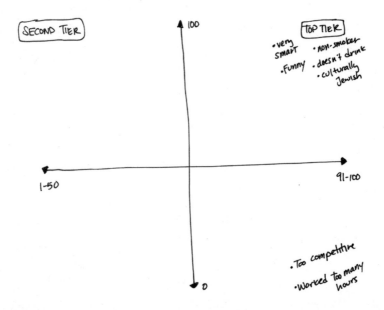

"I admire what you're trying to do," my dad would say when I called home. "But at some point, can't you just go out with one of them?"

"You're rushing to judge," my mom would add. "What if one of these guys is really great, but he's not representing himself well on JDate? You might be overlooking Mr. Right."

I knew that was a possibility, and to be fair, I was getting antsy. It had been nearly a month without any dates at all, and while I knew deep down that my method would eventually work—because it had to work—I found myself questioning the harm in casually going out with a few men.

Then again, a few casual dates might inadvertently evolve into some kind of relationship, one that my math proved wasn't sustainable in the long run. It would be a waste of my time, and eventually I'd need to start over again. To all those who would listen, I'd argue that I'd already used conventional methods to meet men. I'd done the bar scene, I'd gone out on blind dates, and I'd followed the basic protocol on dating sites. Yes, there were men to date. But they weren't the right men for me.

"I just want you to be happy," my mom would say over and over. "I don't want you to be alone."

Loneliness was, of course, a constant threat in our family. While I was running my experiment and getting back into shape, my mom seemed to have rounded a corner. She'd completed her third full series of chemo, and within a week she'd gained significant strength back and was able to walk unassisted, though slowly. The wheelchair she was embarrassed to use now spent most of its time folded up against the wall. Her hair had grown back thick, black, and shiny, just as it had always been. Though most everything still tasted metallic to her, she was willing to start eating again. She gained a bit of weight and started fitting back into some of her pants and tops.

Everyone around us was excited with her progress. She talked about a family spring vacation to Disney World and possibly another trip to Ireland in the summer. Some people, meeting her for the first time, had no idea she was sick. She'd been overweight and exercise averse her entire life before cancer, but ironically this was the best my mom had looked since she was a teenager.

I had to remind myself that my mom was the ultimate saleswoman, unintentionally pitching each time she spoke, convincing others to believe in her every idea. Even if that idea was the false premise that she'd beaten a disease that was quietly and quickly killing her. My mom's seemingly improved health was only a mirage, one her doctors said was a temporary rebound.

Her warnings about not waiting too long played in a constant loop, and they were the reason I was so driven to find the right man to marry. I wanted her to stop worrying about me. And I wanted to feel secure knowing that should something ever happen, I'd have someone to care for and support me just as my dad had done, unconditionally and with great sacrifice, for my mom.

As I continued to look through JDate and interact with the various men on the site, I soon encountered a problem I hadn't anticipated. I was now seeing Matt, Ben, and a handful of the same almost-dateworthy men again and again. I knew that JDate, like all online dating sites, offered efficiency but that ultimately it was a finite resource. I was shown profiles based on geographic proximity, and within a matter of weeks, I'd depleted all of Philadelphia's options.

But a worse thought occurred to me: What if JDate didn't have any 1,500-point men? What if he didn't exist?

I was explaining this to a group of friends one night after work. I'd met up with Juliet and Ben in a private room at a local bar. Ben was wrapping up his first solo film project, a feature about two old friends who mysteriously awoke trapped in a stranger's basement, with nothing besides a pantry full of canned food and a gun with one bullet. Ben was screening a mostly final cut for us and talking about music and edits, when the conversation drifted to my experiment.

"Amy's story should totally be your next movie, Ben," one of Juliet's friends said. "Girl meets boy, boy is an asshole, girl goes crazy one night and hacks into JDate . . ."

"I didn't hack into anything," I protested. "Not even close!"

"Fine," she said, holding up her fingers to frame my face, the way filmmakers used to in the old days. "Girl goes crazy one night and studies women like a mad scientist, cue 'Jump (for My Love)' by the Pointer Sisters."

"Except that she's still single," said another friend of Juliet's. "Romcoms need happy endings. Ben, give this woman a happy ending!" she said, raising her beer bottle up for a toast, as everyone laughed.

"Ha-ha," I responded, as dryly as I could. "I'm only single because I've run out of men. I keep seeing the same profiles. I just have to wait for some new people to join the site."

"Or move to London," Juliet said.

"I cannot move to yet another city," I said, taking a drink of my water. "This is getting ridiculous . . . ," I trailed off, suddenly realizing that actually, there was a very easy, obvious solution to my problem. I pushed my stool back, grabbed my bag, and apologized for leaving early. "I have an idea . . . gotta go. Talk to you tomorrow," I said, walking toward the door. "The movie is amazing, Ben!" I shouted over my shoulder.

As soon as I got home, I threw my bag on the kitchen table, poured myself a big glass of ice water, and opened my MacBook. I had a good, exciting feeling about tonight, like I was waiting to go out on stage and rock a massive stadium. I clicked into iTunes and hit Play on the quintessentially upbeat George Michael pickup song "I'm Your Man." It was part of my power mix, the list of songs I listened to when I needed to get pumped up for a meeting or a speech or some other event.

As he sang, "So why waste time with the other guys? I ain't askin' for no sacrifice," I couldn't help but smile to myself, thinking I should have played this song the night I first logged in to JDate as Jewish-Doc1000.

I opened my laptop and signed in to my account. I clicked around, looking for a very specific button. There, at the top, was the distance setting that I'd forgotten I could change. Originally, I told JDate that I'd be willing to date men whose zip codes were within 15 miles of mine. But I owned a car, and I could certainly drive farther—20 miles, maybe even 50.

I also lived near a major Amtrak train station. I opened a new tab on my browser and went to Google maps. What surrounding cities might be an option? Wilmington, Delaware, was thirty-two miles away, or about forty-five minutes by car without traffic. What about farther north? Newark, New Jersey, was eighty miles. New York City was ninety-two. I could easily take the train to either one of those.

How far was too far away? Should I try twenty miles? Fifty? There was nothing really shackling me to Philadelphia. Why not see who else was out there?

I moused over the distance box, changed the setting from fifteen miles to one hundred, and hit Enter.

When my screen refreshed, there were twenty new faces I didn't recognize. Immediately, I felt a simultaneous sense of relief and excitement. I sat back in my chair and gulped my water, staring at my screen. On the fourth row down, in the middle, was Robert22 from Princeton, New Jersey, very religious, and had two kids. On the third page in, I found Nice2MeetU, an observant Jew from Brooklyn who was a five-foot-three banker.

Great, I thought. Expanding my geographic radius only diluted my probable dating pool with a bunch of men I'd never consider.

Still, there were plenty of new options, I assured myself. Rather than clicking randomly through the site, I decided to move through it methodically and to start with the profile at the very top left and to work my way down the list.

His username was Thevenin, and while I didn't recognize that name, it certainly didn't seem desperate or dumb. His profile photo transfixed me. It seemed as though he was looking directly at me, not smiling blankly into someone's camera. He was bald and fair complected and had remarkably smooth skin for a man. Though he was wearing modern horn-rimmed glasses, I could easily see that he had deep greenish blue eyes. I clicked through.

I started with his photo gallery. Two of his pictures were taken in remote places I knew quite well. In one, he was on top of Victoria Peak in Hong Kong, and from where he was standing, I could see down to where I used to live in Mid-Levels, a famous neighborhood marked by escalators to help residents move up and down the mountain. Judging by the architecture, it seemed like the photo was maybe a year or two old. Had we already crossed paths halfway around the world?

In the next photo, he seemed to be standing just outside of Toshogu Shrine in Nikko, Japan. Toshogu is a lavish, colorful complex in the middle of a deep forest, and it's lined with more than a dozen Buddhist and Shinto buildings and shrines. Toshogu is a famous spot among Japanese but a bit off the beaten path for foreigners. *Why did he visit? How'd he get there?* I wondered. On the regional train? I'd been just once, but it was one of the most peaceful spots I'd experienced in Japan.

In the next photo, he was sitting outside at a restaurant, wearing a dark suit. His arm was draped over the chair next to him, but there was no one sitting in it. He had a small tumbler in the other hand, which now only had one large ice cube left. Again he was smiling and seeming to look directly at me, confident and at ease with himself.

I looked at his profile data. He said he was six feet tall, a nonsmoker, and "culturally Jewish." Next to job, he listed "Arctic Baby Seal Hunter."

As the synthesizer glissando ushered in the next song and George started singing, "Hey, you're just too funky for me," I found myself wondering who this guy really was. His photos piqued my curiosity, but now his profile had captured my full attention.

About Me:

Work is important to me, obviously. There aren't many of us out there who can do the job of hunting baby seals in the Arctic. For one thing, there are a serious lack of direct non-stops from Baltimore. Because of my work, I'm able to travel. I've been through Asia and Europe more than once. I'm a good cook, and a better eater. I know which knife and fork to use when. I'm looking for someone who has a sardonic sense of humor, who's independent and who's very smart. Only carnivores need apply.

"I like this guy," I said aloud, biting my lower lip. I started a new matrix.

I hadn't written anything below the horizontal line. Was it possible I'd found someone with enough points? Just to be sure, I pulled out my list and tallied his score:

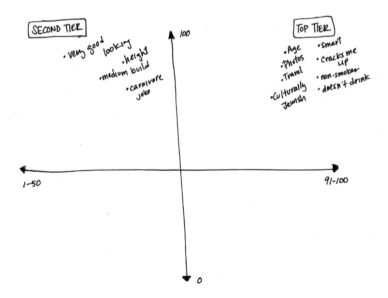

To be fair, I couldn't accurately assess many of the categories, and if we ever met in person, his score might change. But for now, at least on paper, he was a 760. At last, I'd found someone who crossed the minimum point threshold!

THEVENIN: TOP-TIER TRAITS	SCORE
Smart	100
Be very good with money. Understand how it works. Make it work for us.	?
Be very, very, very good in bed. So good that I'll feel sheepish talking about him.	?
Jew . . . ish	97
Career must be important, but not all consuming (like me).	?
Wants to have two kids with me.	?
Challenges and stimulates me.	94
Is genuinely able to crack me up.	93
Genuinely like and appreciate my giant, loud Jewish family.	?
No history of cheating. No smoking. No drugs. At least the smoking and drugs, as far as I can tell. I'll call it a temporary 91.	91
THEVENIN: SECOND-TIER TRAITS	SCORE
Never married before. No crazed ex-girlfriends either. No children. No insane mother or mother issues.	?
Must not be in debt of any kind.	?
Must have an actual career. Cannot be an aspiring writer/ chef/ artist/ whatever. And if he says he's a doctor, he needs to produce actual ID on the spot.	?
Feel compelled to woo me.	?
Has a positive outlook on life.	45
Likes computers and gadgets, like me.	?
Appreciates the beauty of a well-crafted spreadsheet.	?
Adventurous. Doesn't want to sit still.	20
Loves to *really* travel. Not cruise-ship travel. Travel to Petra, Jordan, and walk through the ruins. Travel to northern Japan to visit my friends. Wander around the souks in Cairo.	50
I have to think he's smart enough and savvy enough to take his advice. He should be right most of the time. (But he shouldn't necessarily know it.)	?
Be of medium build. Not fat, not skinny.	30

Dress well, in a way that I can appreciate.	20
Is willing to participate in or try some of my activities: cooking, going to museums, seeing new places, etc.	20
Between 5'10" and 6'2". Any shorter and I won't be able to wear heels. Any taller and we won't be able to snuggle in bed.	50
Head Hair: Curly and dark or balding on the top. Stylish balding. No male pattern balding in the back.	50

I clicked to open a new message window and typed:

To: Thevenin

From: TokyoGirl

Subject: Does it taste like chicken?

Message: Okay, I'm intrigued. Does baby seal taste like chicken? You'll find the basics about me in my profile, but what it doesn't say is that I know where those two Asia photos were taken. In fact, from where you were standing on Victoria's Peak, you can kind of see where I used to live. We should talk more.

I read over my message a few times, considering what I'd written and whether or not I should tweak anything. The subject line was strong. Funny, a little strange, definitely attention grabbing. But did the rest of the message sound pretentious? Should I not mention that I'd lived in Hong Kong? Did I accidentally sound know-it-all-ish, saying that I knew where the photos were taken?

I moved my cursor to the end of the paragraph and started deleting. I got the Arctic baby seal joke, so maybe my sardonic sense of humor would work on him right off the bat?

Funny, because I just bought glacier-front property up there . . .

"That's not funny," I murmured to myself, deleting the sentence. "Too much fucking pressure."

I tapped my fingers on the keys, trying to figure out what to do. I've followed the rules. I have the requisite five-line email written, and it's not too long or too short. The more I tweak and edit, the worse this message is going to sound. I should just use my initial instincts and my framework and . . .

Send.

I clicked back to the home screen and started looking through the next profile. HebrewHammer was an investment banker living in Manhattan, five foot ten, and very good-looking. As I started to read his About Me section, I saw that I had a new message notification. I went to my inbox and started reading.

> *To: TokyoGirl*
> *From: Thevenin*
>
> *Subject: Re: Does it taste like chicken?*
>
> *Message: We should compare travel notes. I'm an aisle man, and always on the left side of the plane. Flight attendants start by serving to the left, and I like to have first pick at their delicious, stale snacks. You can email me back at thevenin23 @yahoo.com.*
>
> *PS: Yes, yes it does.*

I took a screenshot and printed out his message. Once the printer stopped, I picked up the paper and rushed into the bathroom. All that water was finally going through me.

Sitting on the toilet, looking at his message, I couldn't help but fantasize about what he must be like in real life. This six-foot-tall Jew . . . ish guy with a great sense of style and bizarre sense of humor was probably a lightning-fast thinker. What did Thevenin mean? Could it be part of his name?

I pulled my mobile out of my jeans pocket and looked it up on Google. "Léon Charles Thévenin was a French engineer who developed a way to simplify complex circuits." Was this guy an engineer? Or some kind of mathematician?

I stood up and flushed, and as I washed my hands, I looked into the mirror. This time, I didn't see a schlubby Aunt Esther standing before me. Instead, I'd become a damn good version of myself. I'd dropped a dress size, my hair was frizz-free, and I was wearing comfortable—but stylish—yoga pants that were also being used at the gym.

I reread his message and felt a desperate pull to sit down at the table and write something back. I went back to my laptop, opened my email client, and started typing a new message:

To: thevenin23@yahoo.com
From: tokyogirl74@hotmail.com

Subject: Seals, chicken & JDate

Message: Funny, I prefer the window. But I'm with you—left side, as far front as possible. On Southwest flights, I always put my bag in the center seat and pretend like I have a cold to discourage people from sitting there. I like having two-tray access.

Any interesting plans for Halloween weekend? I'm going to a big, elaborate costume party, wearing an old getup from Japan. What do Arctic Baby Seal Hunters wear on the job? Is there an official uniform?

If you want, I'm on IM. My username is Tokyogirl74 on AIM, Adium, or iChat.

Amy

As I went to hit Send, my eyes were drawn to the whiteboard I still had hanging in my kitchen, near the table. I'd listed the rules I needed to follow, now that I was using the framework I'd developed. Whether or not he was online, and regardless of how much he might like me so far, I couldn't send the message. Right there, in the number three position, was an edict on how long to wait before replying to email: between five and twenty-three hours.

I saved the message and configured it so that my computer would automatically send my message the next morning. Until then, I'd have to occupy myself with something else.

I had a difficult time relaxing that night, too excited about Thevenin to sleep. My computer sent my reply message around nine A.M., and within an hour he'd already emailed me back:

> To: tokyogirl74@hotmail.com
> From: thevenin23@yahoo.com
>
> Subject: Re: Seals, chicken & JDate
>
> Message: I'm so old fashioned that I still use Yahoo and ICQ. (Not much, too many Nigerians looking for help with some inheritance or government finances they can't seem to claim).
>
> I'm going to a costume party, too. Dressing up as a cowboy, with a hat and spurs and chaps and everything. Arctic costume too hot for the Mid-Atlantic this time of year.
>
> Want to try IM tonight? What handle should I use? But I don't want to interrupt your preparations for what I'm sure is a killer costume blowout. If I remember it can take hours to properly put on a Kimono. Or was that the tea ceremony?
>
> Brian

I set another timer for five hours and crafted a response:

To: thevenin23@yahoo.com
From: tokyogirl74@hotmail.com

Subject: Re: Seals, chicken & JDate

Message: Sadly, I'm busy tonight. But we can IM tomorrow if you're around. I can use whatever client or service you'd like. Add Yozora to your address book and I'll look for you. You know, you can really screw with the Nigerians by telling them you've just come into an inheritance and that you need assistance wiring money. You should instant message them in Baltimorian. That's a bona fide language, right?

I'm actually going to wear a yukata rather than a kimono— less prep time, fewer layers, less binding, easier to get out of quickly.

Amy

Again, I waited as patiently as I could for Brian to respond. As far as he was concerned, I was out enjoying my fabulous social life and a string of boyfriends. In reality, of course, all I could think about was him. Within minutes of my computer's sending the message, he wrote me back:

To: tokyogirl74@hotmail.com
From: thevenin23@yahoo.com

Subject: Re: Seals, chicken & JDate

Message: Even though I'm very well traveled and highly cultured I don't know the difference between a Yukata and a

Kimono, but I want credit for knowing it takes a long time to correctly dress in one. I bet I'd be surprisingly fast at getting one off, though.

Brian

My face grew hot reading that last sentence. He's flirting with me. That was definite flirting.

I woke up early the next morning without having to set an alarm. It was Saturday, the start to a new weekend and, possibly, hopefully an interesting new something or other with Brian. I ran errands, going to the grocery store and to the gym in order to distract myself from my computer. Finally, just after two P.M., I opened my laptop and turned on my instant message client.

Almost immediately, I heard a *ping* and nearly jumped out of my chair. It was Brian! He wanted to talk! I opened the new message pop-up on my screen:

CHITOWNALEX: Hey—long time. How've you been?

"Ugh," I said audibly. "Not now." It was an old friend from high school. My heart sank, but it was still very early. Brian had an entire day left to IM me.

YOZORA: Hey there. Now isn't a good time. Catch up with you later?

I opened iTunes and looked through my playlists. I found a Motown collection I hadn't listened to in a few months. Sam and Dave, Otis, Ray, Aretha. I played "Try a Little Tenderness" and decided to answer email while I waited. Just as Otis finished his big crescendo, I heard another *ping*.

THEVENIN: Hello! It's Brian.

Finally! It was him . . .

TOKYOGIRL74: Hey. You figured it out. Welcome!

THEVENIN: I used to use ICQ. This seems better though.

TOKYOGIRL74: So I have to ask, what do you really do?

THEVENIN: I hunt seals.

TOKYOGIRL74: Come on. What's your day job?

THEVENIN: Optometrist.

TOKYOGIRL74: I've had a long history with optometrists. Glasses since I was eight. So how long have you been doing the eye thing?

THEVENIN: Years. My grandfather was an optometrist as was my father. So of course I wanted to be an engineer.

TOKYOGIRL74: That explains your username.

THEVENIN: You know who Thevenin is?

TOKYOGIRL74: I'm very worldly.

THEVENIN: Nice. Yes. I'm an eye doctor. Graduated from OD school in 1999.

TOKYOGIRL74: Wait . . . we're the same age, right?

THEVENIN: But I worked in the office for years before that.

TOKYOGIRL74: Did you graduate really, really early from high school?

THEVENIN: No I'm just really smart and I spent all of my time in America vs playing on the Pacific Rim.

TOKYOGIRL74: Ha ha ha

THEVENIN: I'm 26. How old are you?

TOKYOGIRL74: 25, so I beat you.

THEVENIN: I lied. I'm 24. Grandma.

TOKYOGIRL74: Can I change the subject? What kind of stuff do you read?

THEVENIN: Mostly magazines and trade articles.

TOKYOGIRL74: Which mags?

THEVENIN: *Discover, Air & Space, Martha Stewart.* Some cooking stuff that comes in that you've probably not heard of.

TOKYOGIRL74: I read the *New Yorker, Atlantic Monthly.* I think one of the best stories I've ever read was about the crash of EgyptAir 990 in the Atlantic. Here's the link: http://www .theatlantic.com/magazine/archive/2001/11/the-crash-of -egyptair-990/2332/. You should read it.

THEVENIN: I can't believe I'm getting homework from you.

TOKYOGIRL74: Not homework, just a great story.

THEVENIN: Fine. I'll read it, but it better have a lot of pictures.

TOKYOGIRL74: *Popular Science* had a really great spread on the future of NASA a few months back.

THEVENIN: I read that. It was fantastic. Have you been to the National Air and Space Museum down here?

TOKYOGIRL74: Udvar-Hazy? Haven't yet, but I'd love to go. It's on my list.

THEVENIN: Then I'll put it on mine too.

I suddenly realized that James Brown was singing "Sex Machine" in the background, which meant that I was more than halfway through my playlist and that we'd definitely been chatting too long. My rules dictated that the first few IM conversations could last only fifteen minutes or less, and that I needed to try to hang up first. Even when I really, truly didn't want to.

TOKYOGIRL74: Hey, my battery is about out of juice.

THEVENIN: Can't you plug in your laptop?

TOKYOGIRL74: I leave my power supply at work on purpose. Work–life balance. Etc.

THEVENIN: What are you doing next, after you leave me?

I thought for a moment about how to respond. I'd already accidentally mentioned work, which I knew was verboten at this stage. The honest answer was that I needed to finish up a client report. But I needed to come up with a compelling, enticing reason to end the chat session. Less work. More flirt.

TOKYOGIRL74: Taking a bath.

THEVENIN: Sitz or bubbles?

TOKYOGIRL74: Japanese bath salts.

THEVENIN: That sounds nice. Try not to let your mind wander too much.

Okay, *that* was definitely Brian flirting with me. No question. Do I acknowledge it? Flirt back? According to the rules, I can't yet. Seemingly unintentional flirting only for now.

> TOKYOGIRL74: Have a good rest of the day—talk to you soon.

Though I desperately wanted to keep the conversation going, I logged off my IM client and shut down the application so Brian wouldn't know I was still online.

The next day, and for many days after that, I started going to bed with my MacBook. I'd put it on my nightstand and leave myself logged in to IM while I did something else, like reading or answering email. Usually, just before eleven P.M., I'd hear a familiar *ping* and see that Brian was waiting to chat.

> THEVENIN: Is it bath time yet?
>
> TOKYOGIRL74: Good evening, doc.
>
> THEVENIN: I'm imagining you had a fantastic night out and now you're relaxing?
>
> TOKYOGIRL74: You have a very active imagination.
>
> THEVENIN: I do. I do.
>
> TOKYOGIRL74: I have to ask you a question . . .
>
> THEVENIN: Ok
>
> TOKYOGIRL74: What's your position on bread pudding?
>
> THEVENIN: Bread pudding combines two amazing things. One, bread. Two, custard. It's a carbo bomb dream. Why do you ask?

TOKYOGIRL74: I just tried it for the first time tonight.

THEVENIN: How is that possible? Now that you're back in America, are you mostly eating hamburgers and French fries?

TOKYOGIRL74: Actually, I'm not a French fry fan. Greasy food does bad things to my stomach.

THEVENIN: They're only greasy if they're cooked improperly. Sea urchin. Now that's bad to the stomach.

TOKYOGIRL74: Only if it's prepared improperly.

TOKYOGIRL74: When I lived up north in Japan, I used to drive out to the ocean every summer with my friends . . .

TOKYOGIRL74: . . . and we'd go diving for fish. Uni, awabi, and we'd crack them open on a big rock out in the bay and have sushi right there.

THEVENIN: Clothing optional sushi. Interesting. Go on.

TOKYOGIRL74: We wore clothes.

THEVENIN: Not in my version. Anyhow, go on. How did you catch fish while swimming naked?

TOKYOGIRL74: Dove three meters wearing gloves, grabbed them and then swam back up.

THEVENIN: Grabbed swimming fish?

TOKYOGIRL74: No, the uni (sea urchin) just sort of float.

THEVENIN: Uni isn't kosher, you know. What kind of Jew are you?

TOKYOGIRL74: A bad one.

THEVENIN: Very bad. Naked swimming for traif fish.

THEVENIN: Gefilte. That's what you should be eating.

TOKYOGIRL74: Ugh. Hate it.

THEVENIN: I've made it from scratch. It's much better than that crap out of the jar.

THEVENIN: Oops. Did I say "crap"? Should've been carp.

TOKYOGIRL74: Funny.

THEVENIN: Very.

TOKYOGIRL74: You're kidding me—that's insanely ambitious.

THEVENIN: I'm ambitious, but not insane.

TOKYOGIRL74: I've been dying for a decent bagel and lox since moving here. The best are up in Manhattan.

THEVENIN: There's got to be a good place somewhere in Philly. Hell, they invented cream cheese.

TOKYOGIRL74: Speaking of cream cheese and bagels . . . I have to get up to go to the gym in like six hours . . .

THEVENIN: Late again, I know. Sorry.

TOKYOGIRL74: I don't mind. I look forward to our IMs.

THEVENIN: Oh well. Maybe IM tomorrow night?

TOKYOGIRL74: We'll see . . . 'Night doc.

Ping!

THEVENIN: Anyone home?

TOKYOGIRL74: Hey.

THEVENIN: So how long have you been single?

TOKYOGIRL74: A few months. You?

THEVENIN: Since 12:17 am

TOKYOGIRL74: Tonight?

THEVENIN: 1982

TOKYOGIRL74: Come on. I told you.

THEVENIN: I broke up with the last girl I was seeing about two months ago, give or take the lingering at the end of the relationship before we took it off life support.

TOKYOGIRL74: How long were you together?

THEVENIN: Almost a year.

TOKYOGIRL74: I'm sort of surprised that you're available.

THEVENIN: Funny, that's similar to something she said. Having a private deja-vu thing happening here.

TOKYOGIRL74: Should I leave you alone?

THEVENIN: Ok. It's passed.

THEVENIN: The last thing I want you to do is to leave me alone.

TOKYOGIRL74: How was your party? Did the cowboy outfit go over well?

THEVENIN: Me? Yes. But I was only one of five people that actually dressed up.

TOKYOGIRL74: What did the other four people come as?

THEVENIN: Um, let's see.

THEVENIN: Hugh Heffner and a very haggard Playboy bunny, stuffed like a sausage into her costume.

TOKYOGIRL74: That's hot.

THEVENIN: The evil witch from Snow White, and an attempt at Britney Spears in red spandex

TOKYOGIRL74: Nice!

THEVENIN: Except that Britney was a man.

THEVENIN: That was about it, I think.

TOKYOGIRL74: Did you bring along your keratometer and that horrible bright light?

THEVENIN: Most cowboys don't do refractions. Have you ever seen a cow wearing glasses?

TOKYOGIRL74: Well, I had a blast at my party.

THEVENIN: I'm sure you looked fantastic. Photo?

TOKYOGIRL74: Sorry. Didn't take one. What about you?

THEVENIN: Cameras were banned to protect the innocent.

TOKYOGIRL74: What the hell kind of party was it?

THEVENIN: One that would have been better if you were there. What are you doing tomorrow?

TOKYOGIRL74: Brunch with friends.

THEVENIN: Can I call you after? I think it's time I heard your voice.

TOKYOGIRL74: Working on a Saturday? Maybe I'll have an eye emergency.

THEVENIN: How about 4pm or so?

TOKYOGIRL74: It's a date.

I saved our chat transcript, turned off the IM client, and lay down. Staring at my bedroom ceiling, I was suddenly very nervous about talking to Brian on the phone. He seemed so great so far. What if he had a terribly high-pitched, squeaky voice? Glen and Jim had used old, misleading photos. What if there was something really wrong with Brian that I'd suddenly learn when we talked in real life? Or what if we were great digitally but there was no chemistry in person?

I turned my head to look back at the screen, and the pillow jammed the hard plastic frame of my glasses into the side of my nose. I thought briefly about taking them off, but then I wouldn't be able to see anything clearly.

I reread our chat and started thinking about how, eventually, I'd describe Brian to my parents and to Hilary, who'd no doubt be skeptical of the one man who'd survived my system. They'd therefore have unrealistically high expectations of him—and of us as a couple.

It was close to eleven thirty P.M., and I let my eyes close for just a few minutes as I imagined the scene. I'd email everyone using the old template . . . no, Brian deserved better than that. I could wait until I saw my family in person next month, and bring a few pictures of him with me . . .

My leg jerked violently, and as I twisted my neck to look around, I suddenly forgot where I was. I must have dozed off for a moment. That sometimes happened in the middle of solving a problem, especially when I was just on the verge of an answer.

I stared back up at the ceiling, thinking. I couldn't use an email template. Maybe a call? I blinked slowly and finally let my eyes close. If I went silent about dating for another four weeks, my family would suspect that something had changed. A conference call? I could say: "So

I don't want everyone to get excited just yet, but I've met this guy, Brian. He's Jewish, an eye doctor, really funny, really good-looking . . ."

"He sounds lovely," said my mom. Her newly grown black hair seemed more like feathers now. Why did she look so much like a bird?

"Will this Brian take care of you?" said a bird next to her. I could see now that they were both perched on my laptop.

"Dad?" I said, rubbing my eyes. "Is that you? Why are you a bird?"

"I told her to wear contacts," chirped another bird, though this one was bright blue with pretty orange feathers. "Brian likes girls in contacts. Get a decent pair," she said. "From Banana Republic. I'll talk to the manager for you."

"She looks very nice in her glasses," my mom said.

"Smarter," my dad said. "You don't want to give Brian the wrong impression. Keep the glasses."

"But, Dad!" Hilary chirp-whined. "They don't match her outfit!"

"Let's not pressure her," my mom said, as the three of them erupted into a chorus of noise.

"Stop! Can everyone please stop?" I said, shooing them with my hand. "Get off my computer. I don't want your poop and feathers everywhere . . ."

"Don't talk to your mother that way!" my dad said, pecking at my hand.

"Hey . . . that hurts!" I shouted. "That really hurts . . ."

I blinked my eyes open and noticed that my glasses were still on, though crooked. I opened and shut my eyes a few times more, trying to focus enough to see clearly, but everything looked skewed. Then I noticed a shiny piece of plastic jutting into my right hand. I glanced at my clock. It was 5:23 A.M.

"Fucking birds!" I shouted, seeing now that because I'd fallen asleep with my glasses on again, the lens had popped out of the frame. Why are those fucking birds outside of my fucking apartment so fucking loud?! What could they possibly be saying to each other?

I sat up in my bed and tried to pop the lens back in, but because I'd bought a specialty frame in Japan that was rimless on the bottom half, I couldn't do it myself. I lay back down, shut my eyes, and tried to fall back asleep.

Later that afternoon, I called a few stores in the mall to see if anyone was able to fix my glasses. The consensus was that it would take about an hour and a half, which meant there wasn't enough time to drive there and back in time for my call with Brian. Without a choice, I decided to talk to him from my car while I waited.

I moved the seat back for more legroom and maneuvered to find a position that was as relaxed and comfortable as possible. It was 3:54 P.M., and I could feel my heart pounding through my shirt.

I reached into my bag for a small makeup case, which I now carried with me regularly. I moved the rearview mirror down so that I could see to apply a fresh coat of lip gloss.

"It's a fucking phone call," I said, rolling my eyes at myself. "He can't see my face." I wasn't thinking clearly.

I turned on the stereo and shuffled through my music to find a song I could sing to, one that would keep my mind off the time and my stomach, which now felt queasy. Then I turned up the volume as high as it would go.

> *What you gon' do with all that junk?*
> *All that junk inside that trunk?*

I shouted along to the music, nodding my head along to the beat. As a family of five walked past my car, a little girl in a stroller pointed and laughed. Her mother glared at me and dramatically gestured at her ears.

> *What you gon' do with all that ass?*
> *All that ass inside them jeans?*

My hand vibrated. I looked down to where I was clutching my mobile phone and saw a 410 phone number illuminated on the screen; 410 was Baltimore's area code. It was him.

I scrambled to turn off the music, then took a deep breath.

"Hello?"

"Hey. It's Brian," he said. No screeching or whining detected. He had a warm voice, masculine but friendly. It sounded like he was speaking through a wide grin.

"Hey there," I said and paused, trying to hide my nerves. I glanced up at the mirror and saw that my neck was covered in giant red splotches.

"Hey there," he said back.

Fucking say something, Amy!

I took another silent, deep breath. "So you'll never believe what happened to me last night . . . ," I started, telling him about how I'd fallen asleep with my glasses on, about the insanely loud birds outside my windows, about how eyeglass stores in the mall seemed to take forever.

Brian laughed as I described the parts of my dream that didn't include him, saying my bird family sounded a lot like his. We talked about his parents and older brother, who made commercials and films and was now living in Texas. I told him about my younger sister living in North Carolina, and we joked about how our siblings could possibly survive in the South without any decent deli options.

"You know, I could've fixed your glasses for you," Brian said, explaining a simple restringing procedure that would snap my lens back into the frame. He was so confident and at ease telling me about his work that an otherwise incredibly boring technical description became fascinating. He sounded smart and trustworthy.

"Why don't I take a look in person?" he asked finally.

"But . . . I'm already getting them fixed . . . ," I said.

"You're not so good at subtlety," he said. "I'm asking you out on a date. Would you like to see me this weekend?"

The red splotches spread up to my face.

"Uh . . . yeah. I mean, yes. Sure," I stammered.

"How about up in Philly?" he said. "I haven't been there in a couple of years."

"That'd be great," I said, stomping my feet excitedly on the floor. "There's this *Body Worlds* exhibit at the Franklin Institute, where they . . ."

". . . have those plasticized bodies so you can see anatomy and stuff, right? I'd love to go," he said. "Meet you at noon?"

On the drive home, I couldn't wait to tell Hilary everything. I dialed and waited for her to pick up. It rang and rang and then finally went into voice mail.

"Where are you? I wish you'd pick up. Okay, so don't tell anyone, but I'm going on a date tomorrow. It's a guy from JDate. Seven hundred and sixty points! Lives in Baltimore. Doctor. He's . . . he's really . . . ," I said, suddenly realizing I shouldn't divulge too much. I really liked Brian, and I knew that the more I talked about him, the more I'd get excited, and the less I'd be able to pull off "fun, nonchalant girl next door" when we met in person. Plus, if things didn't work out, I didn't want anyone asking questions or asserting that my system wasn't working.

"Anyhow," I said, "I'm going out with him this weekend. Just . . . let's just not talk about it again. Never mind. Don't tell anyone anything, okay?"

Later that night, I looked through the choices in my closet. I wanted to look sexy but approachable, and I needed a shirt that cinched my waist. I decided on my new jeans, the brown-green V-neck top, and a brown jacket. I'd wear one of the push-up bras I'd bought and my new pair of brown heels that matched the outfit. I laid the clothes out on my bed, thinking about what jewelry to put with it.

Since I lived so close to the Franklin Institute, I wanted to walk there tomorrow—it'd calm me down a bit and I wouldn't have to worry about parking. With my laptop still open, I checked the weather report. It was going to be much warmer than usual for early November, chilly in the morning but close to eighty degrees by late afternoon. The jacket might get a little hot, but it completed the look, I thought. I rifled through my underwear drawer, trying to find one of the handkerchiefs I used to rely on during Tokyo's muggy, hot summers. I could hide that in my bag in case I needed it.

As I considered which handkerchief to pack, my phone buzzed. It was my uncle Todd, my mom's younger brother and a stunningly proficient practical joker who'd always treated Hilary and me more as siblings than nieces. It seemed unusual for him to be calling, and especially this late at night.

"Helloooo!" he shouted, imitating the famous belly-button voice on *Seinfeld*.

"Helloooo!" his wife, Mary, chimed in behind him.

"What's his name?" Todd asked me.

"I'm pretty sure that was Seinfeld's girlfriend on the show," I said. "Not a guy."

"No, the *doc-tah* you're going out with. Who is he?"

"*Doc-tah!*" Mary repeated.

I suddenly realized the implications of the voice mail I'd left earlier.

"Please tell me you heard this from Hilary," I said, feeling my stomach drop. "Please tell me you called to see how she was doing, and she accidentally mentioned it to you?"

"Oh no, it's much worse than that," Todd said, laughing. "Your grandmother called to tell me."

"Fuck!" I shouted. "Grandma has nothing to do all day except for reading obits and calling people to see who else is sick. In three hours she's probably canvassed half the state! I bet the entire Jewish population of Chicago knows."

"She's very excited for you," Mary said.

"So you're serious with the Jewish *doc-tah* already?" Todd asked. "Seems fast. What's his name?" Todd asked again.

"I don't really want to talk about it," I said.

"Then I shall name him . . . ," Todd started, making a snare drum sound against the phone's receiver. "Bobo!"

"From this point forward, we shall call him Bobo!" Mary said.

"All hail Bobo!" Todd shouted.

No! No, no, no . . . this isn't happening, I thought. *This is going to ruin everything!*

"What's his phone number? I want to call and give him a few pointers," Todd said.

"I've gotta go," I said. "Good night."

"Amy and Bobo, sitting in a tree . . . ," Todd sang. "Mary, sing it with me. Mary!"

"I'm tired, honey," she said back. "Let's sing to her tomorrow."

"Good night!" I said, hanging up.

I may not believe in God, but I did harbor some intense, wildly illogical superstitions. If everyone started talking about Brian and me as a couple before it was time, it might jinx the entire thing. We couldn't make a big deal out of him or the date—it was much too early. And for fuck's sake, I couldn't have people calling him Bobo!

I'd just ignore everyone until tomorrow. No emails, no phone calls from family members.

I set my phone down on my bed again and went back to jewelry selection. Then there was another buzz.

"Mom," the screen read.

"I'm ignoring you . . . ," I said, considering two necklaces. Still, out of the corner of my eye, I could see the screen flashing. I knew she just wanted to ask me about the date, since I hadn't called home. Eventually, it went to voice mail.

No necklace, I thought. *It's overkill.* Then my phone buzzed again.

"Mom," the screen read.

I could let it go to voice mail and turn off my phone for the rest of the night. But what if it was something important? What if there was something wrong? Fucking guilt!

"Hello?" I answered with trepidation.

"Will you tell us his name, or do we all have to call him Bobo from now on?" my mom said.

"Damn it, Mom, not you too!"

"Sorry, Aim . . . ," Hilary said. "I only told Grandma, and she promised not to say anything."

"You were the one who told Grandma?" I shouted in disbelief. "What part of 'don't tell anybody' did you not understand?"

"And he's a doctor?" my dad said.

"Yes," I answered. "Is anyone else on this call I should know about? Maybe a reporter from the *Chicago Tribune*?"

"He's driving up to see you this weekend?" Hilary asked. "What are you going to wear?"

"Listen, don't worry," I said. "I have everything under control. I don't want to talk about it. And please stop telling people!"

"I have a feeling," my mom said. "I have a very good feeling."

13 | The Train Home

Subtlety wasn't my strong suit.

Sunday late morning, I stepped out of my apartment and into a gorgeous day in Philadelphia. The sun was peaking through fast-moving, fluffy white clouds, and it seemed like the population of my little block had quadrupled overnight. Couples were sitting on their steps having coffee and reading the newspaper, and kids were hopping along the sidewalk. We'd been given one last, glorious day of warm weather ahead of the winter season, and everyone was attempting to exploit it.

I put in my headphones and made one final purse check. I'd packed my mobile phone, makeup bag, wallet, handkerchief, iPod, and tin of breath mints. Now all I needed to do was walk slowly, without tripping or falling down in my new heels, for the next twenty minutes.

This was an important, potentially life-altering moment, one that called for my all-time, number one battle anthem. I scrolled through my George Michael playlist looking for the 1991 live version of *Freedom,* which he'd performed acoustically and with a full gospel choir. As the music started, I smiled broadly at no one in particular. I was so excited, so happy—I felt like even though I might topple over at any moment from nervous energy and the strange imbalance of these new shoes, I could take off running.

As the music crescendoed, I found myself walking faster and faster. If Brian was just interested in easy sex or a quick night out, he could have found that in Baltimore. It was finally happening. This gorgeous, funny, 760-point *doc-tah* had just driven two hours north to spend time with me.

At last, I reached the building. I just needed to turn the corner and walk up three flights of pink granite stairs to the entrance, where he'd be waiting for me. I stopped to catch my breath, put away my iPod, and chew on a few mints. As I reached into my bag, I suddenly noticed how warm it was. My neck felt wet, as did the small of my back. I located my handkerchief and dabbed at the sweat, only to find droplets streaking down my forehead and the sides of my face.

Why was it so hot outside? What was this jacket made of, some kind of wool blend? I looked around to see if others were sweating as much as me.

"Calm down," I said aloud. I was probably just overheated from walking here so quickly. I took three very deep breaths and then counted to ten. I tossed a few mints into my mouth, slicked on a fresh coat of lip gloss, and closed my eyes. "Here we go."

I went past the side of the building and over to the steps. I could see Brian standing at the top, leaning against one of the granite pillars, wearing jeans, a blue dress shirt, and funky blue-and-tan sneakers. He looked exactly like his photos. He was the right height, the right amount of bald, and the same amount of sexy I'd seen online. He saw me immediately and smiled. As I started up the steps, my heel either got caught in my pant leg or I misjudged the distance, and I started to fall forward.

"I'm okay!" I said under my breath, smiling at him. But I wasn't okay. Sweat was now pouring down, inexplicably, from the crown of my head, and my chest was itchy. I could literally feel red splotches sprouting on my neck.

At last, I reached the top of the steps. He reached his hand out to help me with the last two.

"You made it," I said.

"Of course I made it," he said, looking directly in my eyes. "I've been looking forward to this since you first emailed me."

As Brian opened the door to the museum for me, a wave of heat spilled outside. How could it possibly be hotter in the building? I knew it was freakishly warm, and the rest of the week was supposed to be cold as usual, but wouldn't they try to keep the building from cooking its visitors? At least on this one day?

We stood in line to buy tickets, and my sweating only intensified. Moisture was now soaking through my armpits and the tops of my thighs. The soles of my feet felt wet too, and I slid a little in my shoes as we moved up to the next position.

"Warm in here today," I said apologetically, dabbing my handkerchief behind my ears and neck. I started feeling my tongue relaxing into the back of my throat as the noise around me dampened almost to a whisper.

Fuck. *Fuck!* Not now. Get it together, Amy. This is not the time for a panic attack.

I pushed my fingernails as hard and deep as I could into the back of my neck in a desperate attempt to divert my overactive neurotransmitters to a less sensitive part of my brain.

Numbers. Stare at the numbers on the ticket board. Adults are $16.50. Children are $12.50. A family of two parents and six children costs . . . $108. That makes the average cost of a ticket for that family . . .

"Really warm," Brian said, smiling at me. "I should've brought one of those. Speaking of . . . where'd you find a handkerchief? Do they even make those anymore?"

"I know you don't see them in the U.S.," I said, coming out of it. "We used to use them in Japan. It was so muggy there."

We walked into the exhibit hall, through the first set of doors. I felt my bag vibrating and tried to discreetly look inside. It was my mom. I'd missed two calls. I could answer the phone and potentially hear terrible news, or it might just be my family checking in on me. Either way, one hour wouldn't make that big a difference, I reasoned. I could be taking a bath right now, or drying my hair, and I wouldn't hear the phone, I rationalized. An hour won't hurt.

Once through the doors, we stopped at the first specimen. Brian and I stood side by side, looking at a human body, stripped of its skin to reveal deep red muscles, whitish-gray tendons and ligaments, and also pieces of bone. It was a man, eyeballs and lips intact, suspended in motion via a heavy metal pole, kicking a soccer ball. His genitalia were exposed and all cut open, and his balls splayed out to show how they functioned while in motion.

"So I thought you could tell me what I'm looking at," I said. "I never took an anatomy class in school," I said, continuing.

But Brian didn't say anything back.

"What is this, anyway? Is it supposed to be art? It's kind of gruesome," I said.

Again there was silence.

I turned to look at Brian, unsure of whether he might have a hearing problem or if maybe he was checking his phone. It was neither. Brian had lost all color in his face and even his lips, and he didn't seem to be breathing very well.

"Hey . . . ," I said, clutching his arm. "Are you okay? Do you need to sit down?"

He smiled weakly and nodded. I spotted a bench in a small hallway, next to an elevator and emergency exit. I led him over to it, which was already occupied by an elderly woman resting her head on her walker and a morbidly obese woman wearing a floor-length muumuu and breathing from a portable oxygen tank. Brian squeezed into the middle of the bench and put his head between his legs.

"I just need to sit down for a minute," he said.

"Can I get you some water? Or juice? Are you diabetic?" I asked.

"I'm having a vasovagal response," he said. "It's a hundred degrees in here, and his balls were . . . they were all torn open . . ."

"A vaso . . . ?"

"It's a nervous system thing," he said. "Just give me a sec."

Morbidly obese lady looked over at us and jerked her arm so it no longer touched his, as if we were somehow invading her private space. I shot her the shittiest, angriest look I could muster and put my hand on Brian's shoulder, trying to comfort him.

He looked up at me and laughed a bit. "This is embarrassing," he said.

"It's okay," I said. "I'm pretty sure I've sweated through my shirt and also my underwear. I have hives all over my neck, right?"

"But you still look really good," he said, smiling. "So we have a pretty fantastic first-date story. You had a panic attack and I almost passed out."

"Want to get out of here?" I asked.

"Desperately!" he replied.

We couldn't leave the building fast enough. It now seemed pleasant and downright balmy outside. We walked along the Parkway, talking about everything without ever running out of things to say. We sat down on a few benches during the day, and eventually, we wound up back at his car. He looked down at his watch.

"Can you believe it's been four hours?" Brian asked. "Wait a minute, let me get something." He pushed a button on his key fob and the trunk opened automatically. Inside was a jacket, a briefcase, and a small wrapped package. "I thought you might like this," he said.

I made a small rip in the nondescript blue paper and pulled back a tiny piece. I recognized the package immediately.

"Where did you find Pockey?" I asked, obviously shocked that he'd found the chocolate-dipped cookie sticks that were so popular throughout Japan.

"There's an Asian market sort of near my office, and I thought you might want a little taste of your old home," he said. "Want to find a nice spot for dinner, and we'll share these for dessert?"

We found a table at a gourmet pizza shop a few blocks away. After the maître d' seated us, I excused myself and went to the bathroom. Once in the stall, I opened my unusually small bag—no room for a laptop!—to retrieve my phone. I had six missed calls, all from my mom. I dialed her back, stomach in knots.

"Hello?" she answered, sounding perfectly fine.

"Are you okay? Did something happen?"

"I'm fine. Wait . . . ," she said, audibly brushing her hand over the receiver. "Don! Pick up the phone!"

I heard a click, then my dad's voice. "What is it, honey?"

"I finally got ahold of Amy."

"How come you didn't call us after the date?" my dad asked. "We've been worried sick!"

"*MAYBE BECAUSE I'M STILL ON THE DATE?*" I shouted. "I can't believe you've been speed dialing me all afternoon. I'm a grown-up! This isn't my first date!"

"But it's your first date with Bobo," my mom said. "What's he like? Does he look like his pictures?"

"I take it things are going well if you're still with him?" my dad asked. "What are you doing right now?"

I sighed loudly into the phone. "Listen, I'll call you guys tomorrow. Okay? I'm fine. We're fine. Everything's fine."

I went back to the table and sat down. Brian was already looking through the menu and had made a few choices, but he wanted to get my opinion first. It seemed like in the five minutes I was gone, he'd made best friends with our waiter, who was now bringing us some new appetizer the chef was testing back in the kitchen.

"Everything okay?" Brian asked. "You were back there a while."

I knew that at some point I would need to tell him about my mom's cancer and about the experiment that had helped me find him, but for now I just wanted to enjoy his company. The day with Brian had been oddly perfect.

As we left the restaurant, Brian reached down to hold my hand. "Would you believe it's exactly 99.3 miles from my door to yours?" he said, looking at me. "If you'd have lived just a few blocks over we never would have met." Then he put his hand behind my back, drew me in, and kissed me.

He opened his eyes and while still holding me close smiled broadly at me. My neck was bright red, my cheeks were flushed, and I felt a sudden wave of bliss. I stared right back at him, saying nothing.

What do I do? That was the best first kiss ever and this is totally the best first date ever. I really like this guy. He's so good-looking too . . . Shit. I'm just staring at him. He's going to think there's something wrong with me. Say something, Amy!

"Now, that was a damn good first kiss, wouldn't you say?" he said, breaking our silence. "I mean, we showed a solid technical proficiency. The East German judge might knock us for . . ."

I finally reached my hands behind his neck and kissed him right back, in the middle of his sentence.

At home that night, I took out my list and read through it again. Now that I knew Brian a little better, I should review, and—as objectively as possible—score him again. In fact, if we kept dating, I should probably do that once every few weeks. My list had two purposes: to help me find the right man to date, and to keep me grounded once we started seeing each other. A future husband's score had to continue moving up as I got to know him.

THEVENIN: TOP-TIER TRAITS	INITIAL SCORE	AFTER DATE #1
Smart	100	100
Be very good with money. Understand how it works. Make it work for us.	?	?
Be very, very, very good in bed. So good that I'll feel sheepish talking about him.	?	?
Jew . . . ish	97	97
Career must be important, but not all consuming (like me).	?	96
Wants to have two kids with me.	?	?
Challenges and stimulates me.	94	94
Is genuinely able to crack me up.	93	93
Genuinely like and appreciate my giant, loud Jewish family.	?	?
No history of cheating. No smoking. No drugs. Looks like he gets the full score.	91	91

THEVENIN: SECOND-TIER TRAITS	INITIAL SCORE	AFTER DATE #1
Never married before. No crazed ex-girlfriends either. No children. No insane mother or mother issues.	?	50
Must not be in debt of any kind.	?	?
Must have an actual career. Cannot be an aspiring writer/ chef/ artist/ whatever. And if he says he's a doctor, he needs to produce actual ID on the spot.	?	50
Feel compelled to woo me.	?	50
Has a positive outlook on life.	45	45
Likes computers and gadgets, like me.	?	30
Appreciates the beauty of a well-crafted spreadsheet.	?	?
Adventurous. Doesn't want to sit still.	20	20
Loves to *really* travel. Not cruise-ship travel. Travel to Petra, Jordan, and walk through the ruins. Travel to northern Japan to visit my friends. Wander around the souks in Cairo.	50	50
I have to think he's smart enough and savvy enough to take his advice. He should be right most of the time. (But he shouldn't necessarily know it.)	?	?
Be of medium build. Not fat, not skinny.	30	30
Dress well, in a way that I can appreciate.	20	20
Is willing to participate in or try some of my activities: cooking, going to museums, seeing new places, etc.	20	20
Between 5'10" and 6'2". Any shorter and I won't be able to wear heels. Any taller and we won't be able to snuggle in bed.	50	50
Head Hair: Curly and dark or balding on the top. Stylish balding. No male pattern balding in the back.	50	50

We went out on marathon dates the following two weekends. Brian asked me to visit the Udvar-Hazy Center with him next. We spent hours looking at all the planes and spacecraft, and then we went out for a delicious dinner. On our third date, Brian told me to dress comfortably and to meet him at his house. He'd planned an elaborate day of events, which culminated in him taking me to shoot guns at a range, something I'd mentioned that I'd always wanted to try. Every day was special and amazing, but it never ended with one of us spending the night. He was a great kisser, but I was ready to see how many points he'd score on item number three of my top-tier scorecard.

On our fourth date, we decided to meet on an Amtrak train—he'd leave from Baltimore, and I'd join him in Philadelphia—to spend the day in Manhattan. Since I used to live there and was now in the city often for work, we decided that I'd plan our date. I took us to eat ramen at one of my favorite Japanese restaurants, then to the Museum of Modern Art, then down to Bryant Park.

About a half hour before our return train was set to depart, we waited in Penn Station for an announcement of our track. I pulled out my ticket to find our train number as Brian rifled through his pockets and wallet looking for his.

"I think I lost my ticket," he said.

"Ooh . . . that's not good," I said. "Amtrak tickets are like cash. It's not like an airline where they can just print you another one. That sucks . . ."

"It's not a big deal," he said without losing his cool or temper. "I'll be right back." He walked over to the automated teller machines and pulled out his credit card.

As we boarded a very crowded train, I worried that without reserved seats, we might not be able to sit next to each other. I got off in Philadelphia, which was several stops before his in Baltimore. That gave us just over an hour to be together, and I couldn't bear waiting another week to see him again.

We found seats together, toward the back vestibule. The conductor was already taking tickets on the other end of the car. Brian sat on the aisle seat and put his ticket, facedown, on his right knee. He reached over for my hand.

"So what was your favorite part of the day?" he asked, nudging me with his shoulder.

"I don't know," I said as the conductor reached our seats.

"Tickets?" he said, looking at us.

"I really enjoyed showing you my version of New York," I said, handing the conductor my ticket. "The ramen place, that table in the park, even the subway, which I know wasn't that exciting . . . I don't know, all of it? What about you? What was your favorite part of the day?"

"When you noticed," Brian said, bringing my hand up to his mouth and kissing it lightly.

The conductor punched our tickets and handed them back to Brian. "It's about an hour for you both to Philadelphia."

I turned my head to look at him. "Your favorite part of the day was when I noticed the conductor punching our tickets?"

"Look down," Brian said. There, on both ticket stubs, was PHILA-DELPHIA printed in all caps. "Subtlety's not your strong suit. Don't worry," he said. "That's not on my list."

Epilogue

What happened next, and the other side of my story.

B rian was the only person who scored enough points in my system. He was the first and last man I dated after running my experiment. For date number five, Brian had planned another fantastically romantic series of events and activities in Baltimore. This time, I brought an overnight bag packed with two solid outfits, a sexy new nightgown, and a file folder. It was a dossier labeled with his name, and the folder included a copy of my original list and his scorecard.

After our first night together in Philadelphia, Brian had surpassed 1,000 points. It was time to reveal my experiment and my spreadsheets. And to tell him about my mom's cancer.

Looking back at that conversation nearly eight years later, I'm absolutely not surprised at his reaction. Brian responded in a way that was . . . Actually, thinking about it now, I think it makes more sense for him to tell that part of the story:

We had gone on about a half-dozen dates when Amy explained her experiment and all of her lists. My first reaction was "Hey, that's a pretty good idea." I've always been a big fan of outthinking a problem. For example, in my freshman year of college, we had terrible TV reception on our side of the dorm. We tried to get facilities to fix it, and we were told, "Sorry, that's just the way it is." So instead, I rewired the antenna system, running a circuit through the building so no one would see it. Problem solved.

I felt Amy's experiment was another example of not standing for things as they are, and instead using your brains to reshape the world into what you want.

I have to admit that reading through her seventy-two-point wish list was a little creepy, but not in the way you might think. Her list described me so perfectly, it was almost psychic. She'd listed so many intimate details, and they were so spot on that I got a strange feeling she'd somehow conjured me up just to match this list. The night she showed me those sheets of paper for the first time, I made sure to earn an extra star next to number sixty-six on her list.

You see, what Amy doesn't mention in this whole book is that while she searched far and wide for the perfect man, an amazing thing happened when she finally found him. She made me realize that I'd been looking for someone just like her, even though I didn't have an official list. I never realized that I'd had a missing piece in me that she, somehow perfectly, fit.

When Amy told me about her mom's cancer, I didn't say anything at first. I didn't use a simple platitude like "I'm so sorry." Instead I told her that her situation was terrible, but at least she didn't have to go through it alone. I'd be here for her, and for her family.

I decided to prove to Amy and her family that she'd been right all along. I took it as my responsibility to show everyone that even though she'd set these ridiculous expectations, I'd exceed all of them. I planned exotic dates, learned how to cook her favorite dishes, and tried to sweep her off her feet all over the world. That included a surprise forty-six-hour weekend trip to Paris. I wanted Amy to be able to brag about how her system really had worked.

When Amy finally introduced me to her mom and dad in person, I think they were more nervous to meet me than I was to meet them. That night, I presented them with a bound book of all the photos I'd taken of their daughter having a great time on our many dates and adventures. I wanted to show them how happy she was and how successful she'd been on her search, and that all the waiting and nervous nights had all been worth it.

And because I'm sure you're wondering, yes. I did appreciate the beauty of her perfect spreadsheets. Now I'll let Amy tell you how our story ends.

On one of our far-flung adventures around the world, Brian took me hiking through Petra, Jordan, with a Bedouin guide. After some mint tea, he walked me over to the famed Al-Khazneh, got down on one knee, and asked me to marry him. A photographer who was there working on another assignment just happened to see us and, as Brian reached into his pocket to get the ring, started snapping photos. Within hours, he'd emailed us shots of that moment.

We called my parents just after, and my mom burst into tears. It had been a rough week. She'd started another round of chemo and had lost all her strength. Now confined to a wheelchair, she was depressed and hadn't been eating with any regularity. When she heard the news, it was the first time she'd smiled in a long while.

I flew out to see her as soon as we returned, and my mom and I spent the next few weeks planning our wedding. She insisted on a venue I didn't like and wanted to include extended relatives whose names I didn't know.

We bickered just like any normal mother and bride. But ultimately, I relented. We both knew that she wouldn't be there to walk me down the aisle.

My mom entered home-based hospice very soon after. Brian and I were at her side, along with my sister and dad, for her last few days. She often held Brian's hand while lying in bed, smiling at both of us.

A year later, my dad stood outside with me in a grand hallway, while all of our friends and family, dressed in tuxedos and fancy gowns, waited inside a large, wood-paneled ballroom. I held a bouquet of deep red peonies, which were fastened together with a locket bearing my mom's photo. My dad held my hand and took a deep breath.

"Your mother would have been so proud of you today," he said as a heavy set of double doors opened. He walked me down the aisle to where Brian was waiting for me under a white chuppah. "Take good care of my little girl," my dad told him.

Two years and one day later, our daughter, Petra, was born. We gave her a special middle name after the school where my mom spent her entire career—that would remind her of my mom's strength, work ethic, and courage. Looking at her for the first time, I knew that someday, I'd share a great story with her, one about a smart, high-tech heroine in search of true love who believed in happy endings.

Notes

Answers to everything you were wondering.
(And a diatribe on the musical genius of George Michael.)

Now that you've finished the epilogue, I'd like to offer you a behind-the-story read of this book. If you're a page skipper and have for some reason found yourself here before getting to the end of the story, turn back now! There are spoilers below, and I don't want to ruin all the surprises for you.

For everyone else, I'd like to leave you with some answers to what I'm sure are a few lingering questions you have about some key details. (Also, I need to cite my sources and facts.) For example, did you wonder how I know some of the inside workings of dating sites, or why I chose to use certain math equations? I'm sure at least one geek out there took issue with my explanation of an algorithm. And a few of you just might want to know about why George Michael is my go-to power music.

You should find most of what you're looking for in this section. But if not, let me know. Email me at question@datalovestory.com and we can have a short conversation about what's on your mind.

And in case you're wondering, the answer is yes. I will be recording and charting your email data.

1: Missed Connections

I've changed the names throughout this book for obvious reasons. Henry's real name isn't Henry, and none of the usernames belong to actual people. I did, however, use real names for my family members, Ben, Juliet, and Brian, with their permission. The "Bad Algorithms" chapter, where I explain the origins of online dating, uses real names and places too.

It's possible that I've accidentally created a username for the purposes of this book that's already being used elsewhere, and I want you to know that any likenesses are purely coincidental and unintentional.

Speaking of names, I never really offered a thorough explanation of mine. I'm usually asked two questions about my last name that go something like this:

Your last name is Webb and you work on the web—is that your real name?
You're Jewish with Webb as a last name—did it get shortened from something?

The answer to the first question is: give me a fucking break.

The answer to the second question is a little more complicated. Hilary and I gained access to the J-club on a technicality: since our mother was Jewish, we are too, automatically, even if our last name doesn't sound that way. My dad's family is devoutly Christian, but my parents agreed to raise us as Jews. Just like everyone else, we didn't eat pork, we languished for many years in Hebrew school, and we grew to tolerate the taste and texture of matzo balls. We spent the bulk of our time with my mom's side of the family, surrounded by older relatives gossiping in Yiddish.

Some of the people mentioned in this book are no longer with me, so you may be wondering how I managed to quote them. I treated this story as I would any reported story, doing as much research as possible using primary sources.

I always imagined that I'd write at least one book someday, but it never occurred to me that eighty thousand words about how Brian and I met would be my starting horse out of the gate. As luck would have it, I'm a digital pack rat. I have a case of external hard drives and several old computers where I stored everything, from recorded conversations to digital scans of old journals and notebooks to chat transcripts and old email messages. I was lucky enough to have that material to form the basis of my outline. Then I went back to my sister and dad and various other friends and family members, asking them to help me remember certain details. There were times when we even set up scenes in order to re-create the conversations we'd had many years ago.

While I was doing all that research, I unearthed a journal entry from the summer after my freshman year of high school. You see, my Mr. Mary Poppins list wasn't a first attempt at planning for my future. I've been a life-long list maker.

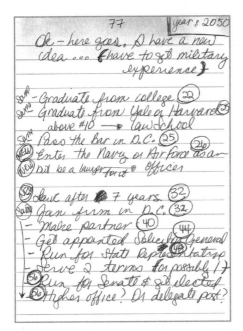

I'd apparently made some early decisions about my career, which included a stint as solicitor general. It's a lower-profile appointed cabinet post, but one that's incredibly powerful. The solicitor general determines what legal position the United States will take in the Supreme Court, by filing briefs and often by arguing before the Supreme Court justices in person. It may seem like a strange career choice for a fifteen-year-old, but then again, I was kind of a strange kid.

Also in this chapter, Henry references a story I'd written in *Newsweek*. In case you want to read it, so that someday you can quote me back to me too, head over to your library (online or off) and look for the September 16–September 23, 2002, double issue. The story is DANGEROUS LIAISONS: JAPAN'S CASUAL "SEX FRIENDS" RISK MORE THAN BROKEN HEARTS.

As long as we're on the topic of journalism, Juliet is Juliet Fletcher, an exceptionally talented, award-winning journalist who also graduated from the Columbia University Graduate School of Journalism and has spent the past decade covering state and local politics for *The Record* (Bergen County, New Jersey), *The Press of Atlantic City*, and elsewhere. I know few people on the planet who work harder than Juliet at digging through records, surfacing vital information, and doing quality journalism that's in the public interest. Her husband, Ben Hickernell, is an acclaimed filmmaker who directed *Backwards* (starring James Van Der Beek) and also wrote and directed *Lebanon, Pa.* (starring Josh Hopkins and Samantha Mathis). He's creative and bright and a damn good storyteller. Look him up on IMDB.

2: Single in the City

My cousin was only trying to help, I know, but my date with the man who may or may not have been a famous talk show host's lawyer was just terrible. I never actually learned his last name, and I never saw a business card, so it's possible he was a lawyer—and it's also possible he was an assistant alpaca shearer at some nearby farm. Thankfully, I never heard from him again.

In this chapter, we all learn that my mom has been diagnosed with terminal neuroendocrine cancer, and I wanted to explain just a bit more about that disease.

There are two cancers in this category, one that affects the pancreas and another that affects the lungs. As the name suggests, these cancerous cells latch on to the nervous and endocrine systems, which is what makes this disease particularly dangerous. We have nerves and hormones throughout our bodies, and while tumors often show up on or in lungs or the pancreas, it can be difficult to find the primary disease site.

That's why my mom was misdiagnosed at the beginning. My mom had a very rare case, one seemingly with no primary site. Without knowing where her cancer cells were originating, doctors couldn't effectively get rid of them. She had multiple tumors that were subdued with several double-dose cycles of chemo—she received the treatments for both lung and pancreatic neuroendocrine cancers—but in the end that medication damaged her body beyond repair too.

If you ever have to deal with cancer, and I certainly hope that you don't, I want you to know that her team of doctors at Northwestern University in Chicago and MD Anderson in Houston were able to extend her life from just a few months to three more years, long enough for me to meet and fall in love with Brian. You would do well to include both cancer centers in any conversation.

3: Signing On

So you need to keep in mind that at this point in the book, it's 2005. Back then, the Internet was still exploding, and while many people had mobile phones, text messaging hadn't become quite as ubiquitous as it is today. Another key point is that the websites I used—JDate, Match.com, and eHarmony—have all evolved since then. Their algorithms are different (though, I would argue, still very problematic), and so are the features on each of the websites. They don't necessarily sort or display by popularity now.

When signing on to JDate, I chose a username similar to Yozora, but I'm not writing it here. I decided on Yozora for the book because it's from a song that was popular while I was living in Japan, "Yozora no Mukou," by a group called SMAP. It means "beyond the night sky," and it's a hopeful ballad about a man longing for a woman.

In this chapter, I also introduce a number of venues and restaurants. I've changed these names too, to protect the identities of my various bad dates. Places I visited with Brian, which are explained starting in Chapter 12, all use the correct names.

This is the chapter where I first talk about George Michael. Since I reference his music a lot, I want to take a quick moment here to explain why I admire him so much.

I'm a classically trained musician. I started piano when I was four, clarinet when I was ten, saxophone at twelve, and flute when I was fourteen, and I toyed around with a cello the summer of my freshman year of high school. I very briefly considered becoming a studio musician, playing in the pit for Broadway musicals, so I attempted to master all of the woodwind instruments.

I was thrown into performance competitions very young, when I was still in elementary school. And though I started early, I had the great fortune to study with Melanie Mangas (piano) and Denise Chigas Kirkland (clarinet), who required a fairly intense curriculum of music theory, along with learning how to play the actual music itself.

I don't perform anymore (though I do play when no one's around to hear how terrible I now sound), but those many years of training fundamentally changed how I hear music. It's hard for me to be a passive listener. I involuntarily visualize what's happening inside a song, seeing chord progressions and instrumentation.

That brings me back to George Michael. It may be easy to brush off some of his work as silly pop tunes meant for big, commercial success. That's certainly true of his early stuff, like "Club Tropicana" and "Wham Rap!," which were both on Wham!'s *Fantastic* album. But alongside those tracks is a song called "Love Machine," which George mainly sings in falsetto. Forget about the cheesy grunts and disco homage—he has an impeccably controlled voice, creating delicate sub-melodies reminiscent of Stevie Wonder's best tunes. You won't find many pop stars today with the same talent, range, and control.

Years later, on *Listen Without Prejudice (Vol. 1)*, George covered Wonder's 1974 song "They Won't Go When I Go." The gospel arrangement, a chorus of soulful voices moving from bright to subdued tones, is mostly restrained until just the right time, when George pulls the trigger and explodes into emotion. He wrote, arranged, and produced "Heal the Pain," a deceptively simple ballad that actually weaves layers of instruments and voices into a gorgeous, tight tapestry of sound.

For me, his defining song is "Freedom 90." When it debuted in 1990, there was nothing else like it on the radio. He evoked "Funky Drummer" (James Brown) and "Think" (one of my favorite Aretha Franklin songs) with a great base line, driving percussion set, and clever use of a bright piano sound. And, of course, there's a fantastic gospel-inspired chorus right at the 5:34 mark. The lyrics were clever and biting, showing his cynicism about the music business. If you're my age-ish, you'll remember how popular the video was on MTV, and the fact that he'd refused to appear. Instead, all six minutes featured a trove of supermodels, and at the end he ignited the iconic Wurlitzer jukebox and leather USA jacket everyone knew from his first solo album.

I'm not a George Michael fan-girl because I grew up in the eighties. I'm a fan because I'm a former musician myself. I admire his voice, his choral arrangements, his intricate melodies, and, let's face it, his funk. He's spectacularly talented, and he makes music composition seem easy. That's the mark of a true master.

Finally, an interesting fact: The number of units it took me to complete the first draft of this book = 2,950. If you haven't read Nick Hornby, you should. He's a brilliant writer.

4: The Dates

As I mentioned, eight years passed between my breakup with Henry and when this book was first published. In that time, I certainly wasn't the only person to use a spreadsheet to track whom I was dating, or even to rate and rank those dates using different attributes.

In 2005, blogging was first reaching its zenith, since social networks hadn't really become mainstream. I had code and digital publishing skills, but my main objective in tracking data at that point was to prove to my family that I wasn't just being overly picky—that, in fact, there were no good men to date. I opted for a private group email list instead of a public (or even private) website. I wasn't trying to embarrass anyone or to gain notoriety as a blogger. I just wanted everyone to get off my back.

5: Bad Algorithms

In this chapter, I offer a detailed explanation of how online dating started. There are lots of facts and numbers to cite here.

I used the Centers for Disease Control's website to research divorce rates from 1960 to 2010. You can take a look yourself at http://www.cdc.gov. It's fascinating stuff.

I reference blood-typing as a means to determine personality, and this is something commonly done in Japan. Type ABs are cool, rational, and sociable but can be forgetful and are often criticized for having a split personality. Type Os (that's me) are supposedly optimistic and agreeable but can succumb to arrogance and jealousy. A few years ago, Japan's then prime minister, Taro Aso, listed his blood type (A—earnest, patient, stubborn) on his website. His chief rival for office at the time, Ichiro Ozawa (he was a B—wild, creative, and unpredictable), did the same. As strange as all this may sound to a Westerner, many Japanese believe in their blood types, and as a result, matchmaking agencies there use blood-type compatibility tests as part of their screening process.

Throughout this chapter, I reference the history of online dating. In order to tell that story well, I needed lots of original reporting from the 1960s. I found amazing details in the following sources:

- "Operation Match," by T. Jay Mathews, *Harvard Crimson,* November 3, 1965.

- "The Famous Founder of Operation Match," by David Leonhardt, *The New York Times,* March 28, 2006.

- "Vital Statistics of the United States 1961: Volume III—Marriage and Divorce," by the U.S. Department of Health, Education, and Welfare, 1965.

- Jeff Tarr, starring as a panelist on the U.S. television show *To Tell the Truth,* 1966.

- "New Dating Craze Sweeps the Campus. Boy . . . Girl . . . Computer," by Gene Shalit, *Look,* February 22, 1966.

- "Marriage and Divorce: Changes and Their Driving Forces," by Betsey Stevenson and Justin Wolfers, *Journal of Economic Perspectives*, Spring 2007.

- "The Originals: Matching Them Up," by Nell Porter Brown, *Harvard Magazine*, March–April 2003.

I also met and spoke with two dating-site insiders, one from Match.com and one from eHarmony.com, who explained how their sites launched and the basic premise for their algorithms and business models.

I pay homage to Steve Jobs just after I talk about divorce rates. Can you spot the phrase?

In this chapter, I talk in depth about what an algorithm is—and I know that some programmers will want to challenge me on my explanation. Yes, yes. I've oversimplified. I agree with you.

So I had a friend, Jeff Orkin, at the MIT Media Lab take a look at some of the earlier drafts of what I'd written. As of this book's first printing, Jeff is a PhD candidate in the Cognitive Machines Group and is focusing on collective artificial intelligence. He's built virtual worlds and presented professional papers all over the globe. In short, Jeff is an insanely smart badass programmer. He's someone who lives and breathes algorithms, and here's what he had to say:

> What you are calling algorithms, I would call equations or formulas. As you say in the surrounding text, an algorithm has a number of steps. That said, these formulas could be *used* in an algorithm, for example:

```
for each person in the database:
        match_probability := Compute_Match_Prob( person )
        if match_probability > max_prob:
                max_prob := match_probability
                best_match := person
        return best_match
```

> But the formulas on their own would not really be considered algorithms.

Jeff also took issue with my originally calling some of the formulas "match probability," with which I also agree:

> The formulas are labeled "match probability," but technically they are not probabilities. A probability always refers to a value between 0 and 1, but your formulas will not necessarily result in something between 0 and 1. I do see that you have weights for each component that sum to 1, which is good, but depending on the range

of the values that they are multiplied by, each component may be greater than 1, or the sum of the components may be greater than 1.

If you really cared to make your formulas truly work out correctly, you would have to normalize each component, by dividing by the maximum possible value for the component.

I also asked Michelle Sipics, a very close friend who's the director of news and strategic initiatives at Yale School of Engineering and Applied Science, to double-check my equations and explanations. She has a few degrees in computer engineering and an extensive background in mathematics. In the part where I'm first describing an algorithm, and how an old matchmaker brought people together, I originally had a few different possible equations. Michelle didn't like them. Not one bit. She said:

First, with the .45 and .55, it looks like you're trying to come up with something that could range between 0 and 1, with the stuff associated with the .55 being weighted slightly more heavily than the stuff associated with the .45.

As an example: say you rated the probability of you reading a book (somewhere on a 0–1 scale) based on how interested you were in its cover (that counts for 45% of your probability of reading it) and whether you like its author (that counts for 55% of your probability of reading it). Let's say it has an average cover, giving it a .5 there on the 0–1 scale, but you really like its author, giving it a .9 there on the 0–1 scale. So the overall probability of you reading it would be (according to this formula we've just made up):

$$p = .45[.5] + .55[.9] = 0.225 + 0.495 = .72 \text{ (on a scale of 0–1)}.$$

That make sense?

The other thing I would do is simplify it a bit. The squared/cubed/ etc. values—maybe it's just because I'm a math dork, but I'm interested to know "Why raised to the 5th? Why squared?" And it makes me curious enough to jar me out of the narrative, even if only for a minute or two. So maybe simplify that a bit. I'd also consider

breaking things up a bit more—you know, maybe in three segments
weighted by .25, .25 and .5 or something, instead of just two, only
because multiplying so many individual things together and then
weighting them as a group can muddy things up a bit.

I felt that it was important for me to explain the math and logic I used, but
as you can tell from the two brilliant minds above, it isn't easy to unravel everything into a nice, neat sentence or two. I also didn't want to destroy the main
narrative with extended definitions. So I simplified things in Chapter 5, but I
hope I've redeemed myself here.

If any of the programming or math stuff intrigued you in this chapter, that
makes me beyond happy. And so indulge me in a teensy, tiny public service announcement: Please support your local science, technology, engineering, and
mathematics programs—especially those that cater to girls. Skills learned in
STEM programs will last a lifetime—and hell, they may even lead you to true
love! There are lots of ways to get involved, from tutoring to donating supplies
or money to just promoting math and science among young people. Get yourself
to the Internet and see what's out there!

6: The List

The night I talked to Jay, I mentioned a Chinese shop way up in the north and
how the number eight was so important there. As you're probably already aware,
numbers in Asian languages can be written using characters rather than numer-
als. As a result, when reading those characters, they can often have double
meanings. For example, the number four in Japanese is considered to be very
unlucky. Like, way worse than our number thirteen in the West. The character
for four is 四, which has two pronunciations depending on the circumstance.
One of the ways to say that number is "shi," which is part of the word for
"death." Folks there take "shi" very seriously. They'll avoid holding important
events on the fourth of the month, and even dinnerware is sold in sets of five
instead of four.

In Chinese culture, the number eight is very auspicious. There are lots of
dialects and pronunciations, depending on where in the country you are, but in
all cases "eight" translates to prosperity, wealth, and happiness. You might have
heard something about this during the Beijing Olympics: the Opening Cere-
mony was held on 8/8/08 at precisely 8:08 P.M.

There are a handful of other tidbits in this chapter I wanted to elaborate on:

I mention that Jay was separated and that he couldn't select that as a choice on the various dating sites. Today, many of the online services allow users a bevy of choices, from "separated" or "friendship" to "long-term partnership."

My Three Peckered Billy Goat coffee mug is from the Raven's Brew Coffee company, which is based in southeast Alaska. They're a small, family-owned company, and their Three Peckered Billy Goat is really very good. I'm an unapologetic coffee snob, and shortly after Brian asked me to move in with him, he bought me a home coffee roaster. Since then, I've been importing and roasting my own beans, and I'm very particular about roasting points. So I can say with at least a little authority that the folks at Raven's Brew make a terrific dark roast.

You've probably seen (or at least heard of) *Curb Your Enthusiasm, Arrested Development,* and some of the other shows I mention in this chapter. Depending on your age, you may never have seen an episode of *Cheers.* Rectify that now! I watched *Cheers* when it was originally broadcast every week with my dad, and it's every bit as funny and poignant today as it was in 1984. The pilot is one of the best ever shot, and the season one final episode and season two opening episode are among the best television ever made.

I absolutely love Peter Sellers. You probably remember him from the original Pink Panther movies, but my favorite was *The Party,* a 1968 feature in which he played a hapless Bollywood extra named Hrundi V. Bakshi. There are maybe ten minutes of dialogue in the whole film—the rest is a study in body language and subtle facial expressions.

I should note that the list in this chapter is a replica of the original. It contains the same content, but my not-for-mass-publication handwriting is completely illegible. I sort of invented my own shorthand years ago that combines strange symbols, Japanese characters, and little squiggles. My smart team at Dutton asked me to re-create it so you could actually read what was on the paper, but rest assured, every detail from the original is there. Including some of the more embarrassing attributes I wanted in a man, and the amount of points I assigned to the "good in bed" criteria. I could have altered the list or changed the scores, but it would have been inauthentic, and that would have bugged me in perpetuity.

7: The Mirror of Truth

The R.E.M. concert I reference was in March 1989, and I'm still ticked at my parents for not letting me go.

I mention my MIT hoodie and the MIT Media Lab for the first time in this chapter. The Media Lab is pretty much the coolest place on earth. It's my version of Disney World. They're creating life-changing technologies that have social-good components, like prosthetic limbs with sensor technology to help people run naturally, and camera-equipped rings that communicate with an earpiece so people who are blind can comprehend the world around them. They're developing new, egalitarian forms of civic media to help people transform their societies and build democracies. I cannot say enough about the importance of what's being imagined and built at the Media Lab. I'm very happy where I ended up in life, but a part of me wishes that when I'd originally considered applying for one of the programs at MIT, I hadn't lost my confidence and thrown away the paperwork. There's hope yet: Our daughter's favorite T-shirt is pink and has the MIT letters across the front.

I also wanted to add a quick note on the matrix you see a few times in this chapter. I've found visualizing data to be a powerful tool, even on seemingly insignificant projects. Sketching out a grid and plotting where the men fell helped me to quickly assess them. I actually do the same thing today when making complex decisions for Webbmedia Group's clients, or when I'm trying to make sense of a multifaceted problem. Matrices are good.

8: Fuck You, Impostors!

Just a quick reminder—I changed all the usernames and most identifying details.

You'll probably think that in this chapter I'm asserting that JDate was full of shiksas, or non-Jewish women. You'd be right. In 2005, when I was using the site heavily, fewer than 20 percent of the women I encountered listed themselves as Reform, Conservative, or Orthodox Jew. Everyone else was either "willing to convert" or "culturally Jewish." While I was doing research for this book in the spring and summer of 2012, I logged on again as a man, so that I could note little site details and reenact the sign-up process. This time, it looks as though significantly more Baltimore and Philadelphia women on the site are listing themselves as some flavor of religious Jew.

Also, there are three great photo examples of women in this chapter, helping to counterpoint my original, terrible photos. Since I couldn't legally scrape and publish actual photos from any of the dating sites, I asked Brian's cousins, the lovely and talented web designer Esti Livingston, and the fun, smart ER nurse Diana Gerson, if we might borrow a few old pictures. They obliged, so that's what you see. (Don't get any ideas, fellas. They're both happily coupled in long-term relationships.)

9: Gaming the System

There's some math right at the beginning of this chapter. Remember factorials? You can use them for a bunch of things, from counting the product of consecutive numbers to figuring out a number of possible permutations. So, for instance, if you had five people and you wanted to figure out all of the different ways they could stand in a line, you'd use a factorial.

Again, math. It does a body good.

I say at the end of this chapter that my geeky friends would make fun of my using a word cloud. Sometime around 2002–2004, word clouds were cool among the digerati. Then, suddenly, a few websites launched that made it easy for anyone to create word-cloud art. There was massive backlash, and everyone I knew started mocking sites—especially newspaper websites—that relied on word clouds to show popular tags and topics. Even so, I still think they're useful. Haters gonna hate.

10: You're a 5-Apatow, 5-Seinfeld

This chapter could have easily been a hundred pages long, but I wanted to make all of it relevant to you, the reader. I learned a tremendous amount from my experiment. Some of the things I found were fascinating—the correlation between women who wore glasses and the number of times they referenced shopping or hanging out with friends, for example—but all that detail didn't drive the narrative forward. The key points—the ones that matter most to you—are in there. Many others are listed in the appendix.

11: The Super Profile

In this chapter, I describe the super profile I created. I need to be clear: this profile was only used on JDate, primarily because it was built specifically for the JDate audience. I didn't use the profile on Match.com or eHarmony.

12: Finding Bobo

This chapter opens with my running out of men to date in Philadelphia and realizing a way to fix my situation while out at a bar with Juliet and Ben. We were screening his latest movie that night. It's called *Cellar,* and it was a damn good film—especially given where Ben was in his career eight years ago.

For those of you unfamiliar with my part of the East Coast, this is the map I was looking at when considering how far to extend my dating radius:

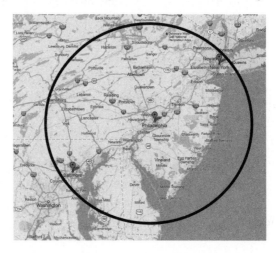

It may seem like Philadelphia's a long way from Baltimore, but Brian and I did that commute for eighteen months, before I finally moved down to be with him. It should be a two-hour drive along I-95, but since it's one of the busiest corridors in the country, it could sometimes take upward of four hours door to door. For those of you who've been on that stretch of highway, you'll have a good understanding of just how much we love each other.

This chapter includes a lot of instant messaging. You might be wondering why we didn't just use Facebook or text each other. That's in part because Facebook had just launched, and while I had early access, Brian didn't. In 2005, instant messaging was much more common than text messaging.

During one of our chat sessions, Brian mentioned gefilte fish. It's a Jewish dish of poached carp or other white fish, onions, vegetable oil or *schmaltz* (rendered chicken fat), salt, pepper, and eggs. And if you were in my family, matzo meal, which somehow made its way into just about every recipe. You eat it with horseradish usually on Passover and other holidays as part of a big meal.

Later, when Brian first met my parents and grandmother, gefilte fish came up in conversation. The fact that Brian had made his own (with *schmaltz*!) and that he could describe in detail how he'd done it made my mom and grandmother instantly fall in love with him.

Finally . . . the name Bobo. I outright refused to talk about Brian to anyone for the first three months, terrified that saying his name aloud would somehow ruin our budding relationship. My entire family called him Bobo during that time, and my uncle Todd would only call him Bobo the first year that we dated. Brian didn't mind at all, and in fact, he became very close with Todd. We talk a few times a week, and the *Seinfeld* "Helloooo" joke has never gotten old.

Well, maybe a little.

13: The Train Home

Even though I let Brian know about the list on date five, I continued scoring him during the first eighteen months of our relationship. I was absolutely head over heels in love with him, but I wanted to ensure that we were both on the right path. Each time, his score went up, until he reached 1,500. After that, I stopped counting.

Epilogue

I thought it was important to share the end of our story with you, but also to let Brian share his reaction to learning about my mom's cancer, the list I made, the scoring system, and my online dating experiment. My editor helped, of course, but what you see in the epilogue came straight from him. And from a PC, no less.

But I don't hold that against him.

Appendix

More Data.

I realize that some of you are currently in the middle of online dating yourselves and may now be wondering what to do next. How can you find your own Bobo?

If you and I were hanging out at Longshots and drinking coffee, here's what I'd tell you to do. First, make your own list. Now keep in mind, the night I made mine I was drunk and highly motivated after my date with the secretly married, *fercockta* Jay. If I were to have sat down at the same table with my notebook and pens at some other time, I probably wouldn't have filled three pages. To be perfectly honest with you, I was proud of what I'd accomplished—but embarrassed the next morning when I sobered up and read what I'd written. I mean, I'd basically listed everything except for what penis size I found acceptable.

I'd argue that the most difficult task in a true-love quest is the first step: being completely and totally honest about what you want. You might make your list in an hour, or it could take weeks. You could write thirty data points or three hundred. It's an amorphous process, one that you may find unpleasant. You'll know when your list is finished when the person you've described suddenly feels real and tangible. In my case, I could literally see Brian in my mind's eye before we'd even met. This isn't spiritual hoo-ha or some kind of "visualize your destiny and it will appear" bullshit. It's about digging deep and writing a really thorough character profile so that you can use it to find that person in real life.

Next, you need a framework. This is where you'll prioritize your list into one or two tiers and then assign a point value to each of your top attributes. For me, ten top-tier and fifteen second-tier attributes made sense. You might find that a different set of numbers works better for you. The goal with your scoring system is to push your emotional self out of the way so you can make good, logical judgments. I was so caught up in my whirlwind romance with Henry that I quickly dismissed how much a smoker's lifestyle was different from my own. If I'd have applied my scoring framework to Henry, I probably would never have spent that weekend with him in northern Japan. (In that case, the series of events that led me to meeting Brian would probably never have happened either, which makes me sick to my stomach to think about. But I digress.)

The experiment part, where I created those archetypes and logged in to JDate as a man . . . that you can skip—though you might sign on to whatever dating site you're using first as the opposite sex, just for some perspective. I always tell my gay friends that they have a mathematical leg up online, since they're able to see the entire dating pool in one spot.

So after you have your list, you should focus next on creating your own super profile. Really, this is an exercise in marketing. If you've determined that a five-foot-ten Catholic lawyer who is an avid tennis player and runner is what you want, then you need to reverse engineer your profile into what he's most likely hunting for online. Everyone approaches online dating in an aspirational way, so he'll want a woman who's sexy but whom he can still take to church on Sundays. If he's observant, then there are some keywords that will probably resonate with him. If he's an avid tennis player and a runner, he's probably going to click with profile photos of you in a short tennis skirt and somewhat revealing top or just before a race with your running number safety-pinned to your tank top.

Regardless of whether you're in the market for a Catholic lawyer or a Jew . . . ish eye doctor, some of the data and lessons I uncovered during my experiment are applicable to everyone.

Below is a bullet list of information by subject area. It's in raw form, without extensive narrative or additional explanations. You can use it explicitly or let it inform your own profile and behavior, but please keep this very important note in mind: I found Brian because I marketed myself specifically to him. Once you've figured out what you want, you need to do the same.

Vocabulary and Language

- Keep language aspirational, positive, and optimistic. Talk in generalities about your hopes, dreams, and passions, as long as those things are not controversial.

- I don't use the word *fun* to describe clothes or buildings. If you don't either, then don't use that word in your profile. But do find language you're comfortable with that connotes an easygoing spirit and friendly nature.

- Above, I used the word *aspirational*, and that's okay, since this is a book. I'm not suggesting that you dumb yourself down, but also don't try to sound writerly. Your online profile isn't the space to show off your near perfect SAT score. Keep your tone conversational and light. Read whatever you've written aloud. If it sounds like something you'd say to a friend during the course of normal conversation, great. If not, delete and try again.

- Don't talk about yourself in the third person. It's awkward and (I hope!) not something you'd do during conversation.

- Lead with your hobbies and activities, unless they require lots of description or explanation. Good = tennis. Bad = aikido. Really bad = I have a black belt in aikido. (I actually do, and I also had that on my profile at one point, which caused a whole bunch of other problems.)

- Don't mention your job. More on that below.

- If you're not Jewish, don't use the word *beshert*.

- As a rule, stay away from foreign words unless you have a good reason to use them.

Profile Length

- Keep your profile short but pithy. Aim for between ninety and one hundred words, which works out to about three sentences. It may seem like a much easier task to just whip out three sentences verses a few paragraphs of text about yourself, but crafting three amazing sentences that are optimized for your target audience is actually really hard to do. Choose your words carefully, and make each one meaningful. If you're not a good writer, figure out the keywords and points you need to make; then ask a friend to help you out.

- Use between three and five photos in your gallery. Galleries with more photos are more competitive, but after five they seem to pass a point of saturation and diminishing return.

- If you're using a dating service that offers lots of other options to list detailed information about yourself, be careful about what content you enter. If you're trying to cast the widest possible net to attract the largest selection of men or women, the last thing you should do is to start listing your income, political views, and the like.

Use of Humor

- I defined sense of humor using a framework that made sense to me. My Apatow-Seinfeld scale is probably not going to work for you. Can you define four or five categories that make sense within your own context?

- It's really, really hard to be funny in print. Especially if you're naturally sarcastic. During my experiment, I found that people who thought they were being funny in their profiles weren't. Not even close.

- If you want to use humor, write whatever you're planning to say down and show it to some friends or coworkers. Have them read it aloud. With your tone of voice and inflection, it may be hilarious—but out of your friend's mouth it may fall flat or even be offensive. Since whoever's looking at your profile can't hear your voice, they won't necessarily understand your intention.

- If you're worried about using humor, you can certainly talk about humor instead. Say that you like comedy clubs or that you're looking for someone who will make you laugh hard.

- Avoid mentioning specific comedians, shows, or movies unless those are top-tier attributes on your list. Turns out that Brian gets queasy and uncomfortable watching *Curb Your Enthusiasm*. Secretly, I think that's because he's a younger, balder, slightly nicer version of the Larry David we see on TV.

Accolades, Accomplishments, and Work

- Don't mention work, especially if your job is difficult to explain. You may have the most awesome and amazing career on the planet, but it might inadvertently intimidate someone looking at your profile.

- Listing what you do for a living can be tricky. Some of the dating sites offer a drop-down menu with code that hasn't been updated since 1997, so most of the job titles are out of date. On other sites, you can write in your own position. Brian's listing "Arctic Baby Seal Hunter" charmed the pants off me, but it really offended a whole bunch of other women on JDate. Brian has great stories about the hate mail he received from people who thought he was being serious. (That actually worked for him, since he was trying to weed out certain types of women.) So think hard about what to list.

- If you think there's something about what you've done in life that may be controversial or open for interpretation in a way that disadvantages you, then leave it off. I'm talking about political or activist work here, not things like jail time.

- Women: if you've won a Pulitzer or climbed Mount Everest or for some reason own a jet, this is wonderful news—just don't share it online. These are the types of details to work into a conversation on your first or second date. If you're this far into my book, you'll know that I'm driven by goals, hard work, and outsmarting whatever the situation is. I believe we're still enduring a fairly sexist corporate culture in North America, so the last thing I want is for women to play down their strengths. During our first date, I very happily revealed to Brian all that I've done and all that I plan to accomplish professionally, and that's a big part of the reason why he fell in love with me. So don't hide your accomplishments, but also don't lead with them in your profile or during your first emails and instant messages. Most people don't want to see a list of what you've done unless they're hiring you for a job.

Your Height, Weight, Hair, and Glasses

- Don't lie about your physical appearance. Doing so may land you a date, but think about how much that first impression counts. Not only will you not be the package your date is expecting, but you'll have absolutely ruined those critical first few moments together.

- I'm still not sure why women are doing this, but it seems like most are subtracting an inch or two from their height. I'd argue that there's really no difference between five foot five and five foot four, but if falling below some magical five-foot-five line makes you feel better, it's probably not a big deal to fudge that number.

- The sad truth is that bald men are going to have a rougher time online than men with full heads of hair, even if said hair is totally uncool. Don't try to cover things up by wearing a baseball cap. Eventually you'll show up on your date and he or she will feel lied to. Own your gorgeous bald heads! Some of us happen to think bald is sexy.

- The other sad truth is that women with curly hair are at a distinct disadvantage online and in the real world. I have no idea whether men prefer blondes, but I can say definitively that most men prefer women with healthy, long, straight hair. It can have body and bounce, but curls tend to be an obstacle. If you have curls and feel comfortable and look good straightening your hair, give that a try. If you're like me and like your curls the way they are, find a decent set of products and a good stylist who can defrizz you.

- Most people don't wear glasses in the U.S., and so we're not conditioned to finding men and women who wear glasses sexy. (John Slattery and Tina Fey aside, of course.) If you wear contacts some or most of the time, opt for contacts in your photos and on your first few dates. If you never wear contacts but need your glasses to see, find a good optometrist who can outfit you with a great frame, thin lenses, and a high-quality anti-reflective coating.

Photos

- Show some skin. This is more important for women than it is for men.

- Photos should focus on your waist up, unless you have amazing legs. Then it's okay to include one or two full-body shots in your gallery. The majority of your photos should be closer up, highlighting your face.

- Don't stage a smile. Instead, try to laugh just before the shot is taken. Flirty smiles that don't look cheesy also work.

- Make eye contact with the camera.

- Ensure that either you're the only person in the shot or that you are, absolutely and positively, the best-looking person in the frame.

- Don't use photos with your kids or pets. I explain why to leave off pets in Chapter 10. Why not kids? Because they're not the ones dating; you are. There are privacy issues you should consider, especially if your children are underage.

- Attempt good lighting. Sunset—also known as golden hour—provides the best natural light. Aim to take most of your photos outdoors.

- If you're a woman and you have any amount of cleavage, play it up. Wear a deep V-neck or a strapless dress and show off what you have.

- If you're a man and you have great arms, try to find a fitted shirt that will cling a bit. Avoid muscle shirts or tank tops.

- Look as healthy as possible. We're chemically attracted to others who appear fertile or virile. This doesn't mean you should pose next to a set of dumbbells. Try to appear as awake and vibrant as you can. Make your skin appear dewy and glowing.

Initial Contact

- Women: It's totally acceptable to make the first move. So do it!

- Make your initial contact short and sweet. Five sentences or less, or under 150 words.

- Don't ask someone out as part of your initial contact. Doing so will seem creepy.

- Avoid the types of abbreviations—*ur, u, luv*—you'd use in a text message.

- Continue to avoid being too specific. At this stage, you're just trying to pique someone's interest.

- If someone instant messages you while you're online, go ahead and IM them back if you want. Otherwise, wait twenty-two to twenty-three hours between email contacts for the first few messages.

- Don't send messages while most people are sleeping, even if you're wide-awake. Shoot for business hours or just after dinnertime.

How to Flirt

- Flirting in real life is difficult when you're trying. It's the same online. It should happen organically.

- A lot of people try to use sarcasm to flirt, and it tends not to read well.

- Most people who are successful at flirting do so via instant message instead of email.

- Try not to force things. If you're chatting about the last great book you read, don't offer up the *Kama Sutra*, which is going to seem manufactured and heavy-handed.

- The best way to flirt is to care deeply about whatever your date is saying and to focus all of your attention on him or her. We're flattered when people throw attention our way. So ask thoughtful questions. Take a keen interest in the conversation. Be enthusiastic.

Heavy Subjects

We all have problems. I struggle with anxiety and had to cope with the loss of my mother. I'm sure that you have troubles of your own. Wait until date three or four before bringing up whatever you're dealing with, unless that information might critically impact the person you've met. My anxiety is manageable, and while I miss my mother terribly, I know that death is an inevitable part of life. Hiding children you might have, or omitting the fact that you're going through a divorce—stuff like that—you need to own up to at the very beginning.

Don't Rush Things

The most important lesson I learned was the importance of pacing myself. That obviously applied to the frequency and timing of my messages, but it also carried over into how I was thinking about Brian and when I was divulging information about him to my friends and family. Because I was deliberate in my scoring of him, and because I outright refused to speak about him or to let myself daydream for several weeks, I didn't regress into my usual pattern of falling head over heels too soon. The slow burn that I'd cultivated forced Brian and me to get to know each other over a period of months rather than days or weeks. It ensured that I didn't accidently smother him or scare him off, and it forced me to stay true to my list and scoring system.

There you have it. I'm not a relationship coach or an expert on love. I'm just a woman who was tired of dating the wrong men and was desperate to find the perfect husband. I decided that the system was broken and, more importantly, that I was smart enough to fix it. Rather than complaining, giving up, or giving in, I used math and ingenuity to get what I wanted.

Make a list. Score your dates. Market yourself wisely.

Find your needle.

THE MOST IMPORTANT CHART

	1	2	3	4	5	6	7	8	9	10
Sam Freedman	♥	♥		♥	♥					
Suzanne Gluck	♥	♥			♥	♥				
Erin Malone	♥	♥	♥		♥	♥				
Jill Schwartzman	♥	♥	♥	♥						
Hilary Webb	♥	♥	♥		♥	♥	♥	♥		
Don Webb	♥	♥	♥		♥	♥				
Barbara & Howard Woolf	♥		♥	♥		♥	♥	♥	♥	
Cheryl Cooney				♥		♥				
Michelle Sipics										♥
Jeff Orkin										♥
Emily Caufield				♥						♥
Juliet Fletcher & Ben Hickernell	♥		♥		♥	♥		♥		
Bill McBain	♥									♥
Ericka Walman	♥				♥					
Greer & Sam Marks	♥	♥			♥					
Bonnie Shaw	♥			♥		♥				
Amanda Walker			♥			♥				
Carrie Swetonic			♥			♥				
Stephanie Hitchcock			♥							
Brian Tart		♥				♥				
Ben Sevier		♥				♥				
Christine Ball		♥				♥				
Eve Attermann			♥							
Maggie Shapiro			♥							
Donna's Cross Keys			♥							
JDate			♥					♥		
George Michael				♥						
Brian Woolf	♥	♥	♥	♥	♥	♥	♥		♥	♥

Acknowledgments

My most important influencers have always been teachers, and I'd like to start by thanking the teacher who's had the most profound impact on me. Sam Freedman was my narrative nonfiction book-writing professor at the Columbia University Graduate School of Journalism, and he drove me harder than anyone else has in my entire life. While studying with him, I slept fewer than four hours a night—and for the first time, I couldn't blame insomnia. He taught me how to dig deep, to uncover minute details that in aggregate told a much bolder, richer story. He led me through edit after brutal edit to make sure that every sentence drove my narrative forward. One Sunday morning, our paths crossed in Central Park. He was running and asked me to keep up with him as he dictated—from memory, citing page numbers and everything—some necessary changes to an essay I'd just given him. Sam is a best-selling author with a lengthy list of published titles. But he's a nationally recognized, award-winning, world-class teacher because he devotes every ounce of his being into surfacing his students' maximum potential. Without Sam, I'd have a great love story but no book. I'm now and will forever be in his debt.

It was Suzanne Gluck and Erin Malone, two exceptionally smart, savvy literary agents at William Morris Endeavor, who took a chance on me and gracefully taught me how the literary world works. They coached me on refining my proposal, advised me on content, and ultimately landed me a number of meetings with various big publishers. More than securing a book deal, they provided significant guidance, advice, and moral support. If Suzanne told me to jump off the Brooklyn Bridge, I wouldn't question her reasoning. The many times I relied on Erin to help me think through options or navigate the literary scene, her answers were always exactly right. I'm so honored that Suzanne, Erin, and their team at WME (in particular, Eve Attermann and Maggie Shapiro) took me under their collective wing; this whole process was better with their hands-on approach.

Of course, the real work happened over email, in person, and on the phone with my exceedingly patient editor, Jill Schwartzman. Yes, I spent 2,950 units writing this damn thing, but Jill must have contributed at least that many units editing. And probably even more units in myriad publisher, designer, marketing, and publicity meetings. I've always thought editors got a raw deal, not seeing their names on the covers next to the author's byline. Jill and her editorial assistant, Stephanie Hitchcock, have been a tremendously positive force in creating this book. Jill has a beautiful, logical mind and a good sense for how content should flow. Plus, she was willing to experiment with some new technology to map out my outlines and charts!

From the outside, it may seem like publishing a book is a solitary activity between a writer and an editor. In reality, there are legions of silent partners who are integral to the process. I'm so thankful to my wildly supportive, hardworking team at Penguin and Dutton. Amanda Walker is, hands down, one of the best publicists in the book business. Carrie Swetonic is incredibly progressive and thoughtful when it comes to marketing. What impresses me most about Amanda and Carrie is how open-minded they've been to my radically different approach to digital marketing and publicity.

Dutton's executive team, which includes Brian Tart (president and publisher), Christine Ball (vice president, director of marketing and publicity), and Ben Sevier (editor in chief), continues to impress me with its editorial and industry vision. In an era marked by so much change affecting book publishing, this powerful triumvirate is embracing innovation. It's been an absolute delight to work with them!

I'd like to thank Michelle Sipics, Jeff Orkin, Bill McBain, Ericka Walman, Juliet Fletcher, Ben Hickernell, and Greer and Sam Marks, who all read versions of the manuscript and offered fantastic advice. My dear friend Bonnie Shaw helped me brainstorm an experimental digital outreach plan, and she provided ongoing creative jolts when I needed them. Emma Carew Grovum helped implement our social outreach and build a community to support women like me. I admire each of these wonderful people, and I know how fortunate I am to have received their input.

Two of my coworkers were instrumental in my finishing this book on time. Emily Caufield, Webbmedia Group's graphic designer, created the acknowledgments chart and helped in our cover art discussions. (See http://www.emilycaufield.com for more of her amazing creations.) My assistant, Cheryl Cooney, who's a damn good children's fiction writer and poet, kept me on schedule and held Webbmedia Group together as I took on the additional full-time job of writing.

Also in the logistics category is Donna's Cross Keys, a restaurant near my house. On many Sunday mornings, well in advance of the brunch crowd, Donna's let Brian and me inside to sip coffee and review chapters before I sent them in to Jill. We got to commandeer a quiet table in the very back of the restaurant, sometimes a full two hours before they officially opened. We've been regulars there for years, and at the risk of ruining what's already a popular dining spot in Baltimore,

I'll say this: Donna's has the best tomato soup on the planet. And I'm someone who eats (occasionally) at Per Se.

I have an incredibly supportive, understanding family. My in-laws, Barbara and Howard Woolf, graciously agreed to watch our daughter as I worked, which I know destroyed their weekend plans more than once. We're very, very grateful for all of their help.

My father, Don Webb, helped me go back to re-create many of the scenes that involved my mom. This was an often painful and difficult exercise for us both. My dad's biggest gift to me was a childhood spent surrounded by books. He's a gifted storyteller and performer and read to me every night for many years, starting from when I was an infant. When I was old enough to read myself, he was a willing (and very patient) audience. When I made my list, many of the data points were modeled directly from my dad.

Hilary was kind enough to relive all of the moments of this book for the purposes of my reporting. We talked through every scene, re-created our original dialogue, and at times looked through old, terrible photographs of me. It should be obvious to you now that Hilary and I are very close. Hilary is an extremely talented opera singer, the consummate social butterfly, and a loyal friend. She's a constant companion and one of the only people I know who will give me an unfiltered, honest opinion when I ask for one. And often when I don't ask, too.

Finally, I want to thank Brian, my inspiration, my motivation, my 1,500-point man. This book is just one of many journeys you've agreed to go on with me, and I know that the path hasn't always been easy. I love you for always believing in and supporting my latest projects, whatever they may be and wherever they may take us. But I love you more for providing me counsel, teaching me what I need to learn, and allowing me the space and freedom to finish. Thank you for making the drive up to Philadelphia that warm fall day. It changed everything.